PRAISE FO

"The Greek gods are alive and still call to many us from the depths of our unremembered dreams or our genetic memories. I, for one, welcome Tony Mierzwicki's marvelous work, *Hellenismos*. In a single volume, it not only fills a vacuum in my education, it clearly and concisely provides fascinating insights into a world to which we are all indebted—a world of gods, and heroes, and spirits, and magick, and all that is great, judicious, and distinct in the western soul."

—Lon Milo DuQuette, author of
Homemade Magick and *Low Magick*

"Communion with the gods is grounded in everyday practice. *Hellenismos* provides the reader with the necessary tools to quickly enter into Pagan Greek religion. The book combines an accurate historical understanding with practices updated for today's needs. Tony Mierzwicki is a knowledgeable and ethical guide in the tradition of the great Pagan teachers. For those of us called to the path of the ancient Greek gods this is the book we have needed."

—Brandy Williams, author of
For the Love of the Gods and *The Woman Magician*

"Mierzwicki has succeeded in combining fine scholarship with deep vision to provide the reader with a comprehensive overview of Grecian polytheistic theory and practice. His offering brings to life an ancient tradition made relevant for modern times. Whatever your interest in Greek polytheism, this tome will be a valuable asset to your collection. A classic in the making."

—Kristoffer Hughes, author of *The Book of Celtic Magic*,
From the Cauldron Born, and *The Journey Into Spirit*

"*Hellenismos* is an excellent guide to practicing ancient Greek polytheism. Advancing from daily, personal practices, to the sacred lunar month, and finally to the annual festival cycle, Tony gently draws the reader deeper into Hellenic polytheism. More than a ritual handbook, this rich but readable book provides a wealth of information exploring the cultural context and mindset of the ancient religion, so modern Hellenic Pagans can make informed choices about their practice. A perfect introduction for those new to Hellenismos, but also a valuable resource for those who have worshipped the Greek gods for many years."

—John Opsopaus, author of
The Oracles of Apollo and *The Pythagorean Tarot*

"*Hellenismos* makes an open and shut case for the need to modify the ancient Greek religion to suit the modern world, rather than recreating it faithfully. Ancient Greece was a product of its time, an authoritarian society where a small, privileged male class enjoyed a life of leisure as menial tasks were performed by slaves. Most women were chattel. Foreigners had little hope of bettering their status. Animals were publicly slaughtered. Just as contemporary society has evolved towards egalitarianism, so too must the Greek religion. The author provides a wonderful guide to crafting your own personal path of venerating the ancient Greek gods and goddesses while remaining true to the spirit of the time."

—Karen Tate, author of *Walking An Ancient Path:*
Rebirthing Goddess on Planet Earth

"In *Hellenismos* author Tony Mierzwicki provides an invaluable resource for both novice and experienced practitioners of ancient Greek religion. The book illustrates the differences between public and private worship in the Hellenic world and explains how to develop a connection with the gods and goddesses of Olympus. Tony briefly examines the history and development of Greek society and guides serious students to primary sources that will further their understanding of the Greek gods. With instructions for holding daily, monthly, and annual observances, this book is nothing less than a toolkit for building your personal Hellenic path."

—Alaric Albertsson, author of *A Handbook of Saxon Sorcery and Magic* and *To Walk a Pagan Path*

HELLENISMOS

© JANET NEWNES

About the Author

Tony Mierzwicki is the author of *Graeco-Egyptian Magick: Everyday Empowerment* and has contributed to various anthologies and magazines. This book grew out of his research into the ancient Greek religion, which is one of the primary constituents of Graeco-Egyptian Magick.

Tony has been continuously running workshops and rituals recreating ancient magickal practices in the United States and on the east coast of Australia since 2001, drawing on his practice of ceremonial magick which he began in 1990.

Tony has completed three degrees at the University of Sydney: MA, BE, and BSc.

Born and raised in Sydney, Australia, he currently lives in Huntington Beach, California.

HELLENISMOS

PRACTICING GREEK POLYTHEISM TODAY

TONY MIERZWICKI

Llewellyn Publications
Woodbury, Minnesota

First Edition
Third Printing, 2021

Cover design by Kevin R. Brown
Interior map by the Llewellyn Art Department

Llewellyn is a registered trademark of Llewellyn Worldwide Ltd.

Library of Congress Cataloging-in-Publication Data
  Mierzwicki, Tony.
   Hellenismos : practicing Greek polytheism today /
  Tony Mierzwicki — First edition.
     pages   cm
  Includes bibliographical references and index.
  ISBN 978-0-7387-2493-5
  1. Greece—Religion. 2. Mythology, Greek. I. Title.
  BL783.M54   2014
  292.08—dc23
                                        2014030364

Llewellyn Worldwide Ltd. does not participate in, endorse, or have any authority or responsibility concerning private business transactions between our authors and the public.

All mail addressed to the author is forwarded but the publisher cannot, unless specifically instructed by the author, give out an address or phone number.

Any Internet references contained in this work are current at publication time, but the publisher cannot guarantee that a specific location will continue to be maintained. Please refer to the publisher's website for links to authors' websites and other sources.

Llewellyn Publications
A Division of Llewellyn Worldwide Ltd.
2143 Wooddale Drive
Woodbury, MN 55125-2989
www.llewellyn.com

Printed in the United States of America

ALSO BY TONY MIERZWICKI

Graeco-Egyptian Magick
Megalithica Books, 2006

ACKNOWLEDGMENTS

Has any book ever been written in a vacuum? To a lesser or greater extent every book has multiple inputs and this book is no different.

The most important person I have to thank is Elysia Gallo of Llewellyn, who identified a need for this book and suggested that I should write it. I was receptive to the idea and embarked on a long journey of exploring what the ancient Greek religion was, how it is currently being practiced, and how beginners could immerse themselves in it while remaining true to its original spirit. Without Elysia this book would never have been written.

I would like to express my appreciation to Llewellyn for their faith in this book, Elysia Gallo for her encouragement and editing, Connie Hill for her copy editing, Donna Burch-Brown for her interior design and layout, and Kevin Brown for his cover art and design.

While writing this book I joined as many publicly accessible Hellenismos internet groups as I could find in order to develop a feel for what practitioners were doing—what challenges they faced in their practice, the questions they had that were either answered inaccurately or were left unanswered, so I could try to address the majority of those issues in this book. I have learned something from everyone who has posted and those people with whom I discussed this book were very encouraging, while some made helpful suggestions. I am completely independent and not a member of any Hellenismos organization. As much as I would like to name those who have rendered the most assistance, I refrain from doing so as I am concerned about giving an impression of bias toward their respective organizations.

CONTENTS

FOREWORD

Tony Mierzwicki has already produced an excellent book on Graeco-Egyptian magic, so it comes as no surprise that he has now produced an excellent book on ancient Greek religion. Let me just qualify that statement: Tony's book is on the modern practice of ancient Greek religion, or even more precisely the worship of the ancient Greek gods. If your first reaction is "Why would anyone want to worship the ancient Greek gods and goddesses?" then pause for a moment and reflect. The Greeks and Romans were the basis of European culture. The Romans created a system of law, a network of roads, and some very beautiful architecture. But the Greeks were the foundation upon which the Romans built, and the Romans sent their children to Athens to learn philosophy, logic, rhetoric, and culture in the broadest sense. Even more to the point, the Greeks invented the only science that still survives today unchanged for 2500 years: Euclidean geometry. Neither physics, chemistry, nor botany can claim this although they too sprang from the work of a Greek, Aristotle.

For the Greeks the gods were also very important. These gods pre-date Christianity, Islam, Taoism, and Buddhism. Many people just think of the Greek gods as confined to the relatively small country of Greece, but since Alexander the Great's conquest of most of the "known world" beginning in 335 BCE, and for many centuries afterwards, the Hellenic culture he brought with him extended its influence and its language from the Mediterranean to the edge of India, including Egypt, Persia, Afganistan, Palestine, Turkey, and Syria, whilst there were significant Greek colonies in Italy and North Africa. It was not till the seventh century that Islam swept most of this influence away.

Of course, if you are a hardened atheist this book may not be for you, but the sheer beauty of their rites, their poetry, the temples they worshipped in, their statuary, much of which has never been equalled, and their sense of devotion, give us many reasons to enjoy and explore the ancient Greek gods. Many of the tales about these gods will of course be familiar from our childhood, although few schools now teach the classics. The study of the classics, of Greek and Latin, was very much a part of the school syllabus right up to the mid 1950s.

But the wonder of the child, or the aesthetic appreciation of the art and poetry these gods inspired, is only a beginning. Because of their deep roots in our culture, in our egregore (as some might say), they still exert an emotional pull. I remember one time in the early 1970s visiting Pompeii. Typically, I soon got tired of the platitudes of the guide, and set off to discover the city for myself. Turning into a narrow defile I heard the faint sound of chanting. Following the sound, I came across a hidden enclosure with a square horned altar off to one side. Leaning over it was a very serious looking bearded man with a sheep skin draped around his shoulders. I watched quietly from the shadows while he poured libations and performed other acts which I later realised were an invocation to one of the ancient gods. It was no play-acting, but for him deadly serious. It was only then that I realised that the ancient gods had not all died, or gone away, and that there were still a few people who desired their presence. Later on my way back to Naples I saw him again. He gave me a smile of recognition, but said nothing.

I thought my experience in Pompeii was a one-off, a rare glimpse into a living performance of a long dead rite. But I was wrong. Discovering that many people felt the same way, and had set about recon-structing those rites in this modern world came as a very pleasant surprise. This practice has come to be known as Hellenismos, just as the ancient Greeks thought of themselves as "Hellenes," and their culture as Hellenic culture.

Of course, the immediate reaction might be: is this just dressing up and play-acting? I do not believe it is where the rites are recreated fully from surviving classical texts (of which there are many), and where the devotees feel what they are doing with their whole heart. Such recre-ations often have more life in them than the staid repetition of the all too familiar Sunday morning church service conducted by vicars who no longer really believe in the mystery of their own religion.

So, if you have followed me this far, you might want to know where to find accurate information about this practice that now involves many thousands of people both in Greece and around the world.

Well, a very good place to start is with this book, as Tony not only has a good grasp of the magic and religion of ancient Greek, but is also an experienced ritualist and knows what it is like to produce a rite which carries conviction and feeling way beyond the limitations of play-acting. Helpful sections on the pronunciation of ancient Greek, the distinction between public and private religious rituals, and a compendium of the Greek gods with their characteristics round out the book.

—Dr. Stephen Skinner
Singapore 2018

INTRODUCTION

If you could time-travel anywhere in the ancient world, where would you go? Would you visit any of the Seven Wonders of the Ancient World? Or would you see one of the Oracles, or perhaps witness one of the epic battles? Would you be happy to merely visit like a tourist, or would you want to really experience the places you visited?

While we don't yet have the technology to travel back in time, there is a way to experience the mindset of the ancients, and that is through practicing their religion. The ancient Greeks were very influential in shaping present-day society, and it is through experiencing their religion that we can move from understanding them with our heads to understanding them with our hearts. The aim of this book is to equip readers with sufficient knowledge to quickly, easily, and inexpensively recreate the practice of ancient Greek religion, and only then take the first tentative practical steps. This is also a more affordable method than shelling out a huge amount of money at one time, as small amounts of money are spent over a period of time.

It is important to note that religious activity in ancient Greece was regulated by its lunar calendar. There were observances to be performed on a daily, monthly, and yearly basis. In recognition of this, readers will be encouraged to undergo a one-month trial. Those who enjoy the month will then have the option of experiencing a full year. Once readers are going through the motions of immersing themselves in ancient Greek religion, they can deepen their experience through additional study. Learning by doing is far superior to spending months, if not years, learning everything that is known about the practice of ancient Greek religion and only then taking the first tentative, practical steps.

In years gone by, the central focal point of the living room was the fireplace, or hearth, but without a doubt it is now the television. Typically households will have more than one television, which is testimony to the importance of this medium. While televisions can be used to play video games, their primary function is still the enjoyment of movies. One genre that has remained popular since the very first days that movies were produced is that of mythology. Dozens of ancient Greek–themed movies, such as *Clash of the Titans*, 2010; *Immortals*, 2011; *Wrath of the Titans*, 2012; and *The Legend of Hercules*, 2014; and TV series, such as *Hercules: The Legendary Journeys* and *Xena: Warrior Princess*, have been produced. These feature adaptations of various legends such as the Homeric writing—the *Iliad* with the battle over Helen of Troy and the *Odyssey*, Jason and the Argonauts, Hercules or Herakles, the Amazons, Orpheus, the Olympians, and the writings of the playwrights Aeschylus, Sophocles, Euripides, and Aristophanes.

The reason why familiarity with Greek mythology is very much part and parcel of our society and pop culture is because for hundreds of years classical education, which involves the study of ancient Greek and Latin texts, was standard throughout much of the Western world until at least the nineteenth-century. Ancient Greek writings are of considerable literary and intellectual merit,and have stood the test of time. Many of the core values of Western civilization can be attributed to the Greeks, including democracy and the right of individuals to have freedom of speech. As a byproduct of the widespread awareness of Greek mythology, more and more people are curious as to how the Greeks venerated their deities.

The second half of the twentieth century saw ancient Greek and Latin studies phased out of many school curricula. In response to the demands of the global economic climate, the focus of education shifted to science, technology, and business studies. While this led to a reduction of familiarity with classical texts among students, society itself began to embrace non-mainstream spiritual modalities such as Witchcraft, Wicca, Paganism, Magick, and the New Age. It would seem that as one door closed, another opened. Please note that in this book the spelling "magick" will be used so as to distinguish this spiritual modality from "magic," which refers to sleight-of-hand performing arts.

Many contemporary spiritual modalities incorporate the names of ancient deities, taken from one or more pantheons, along with various sundry technical terms within fairly modern frameworks. Here, the ancient deities are often seen as archetypal energies, being forces rather than spiritual entities in their own right. As a rebellion against this, Pagan circles have seen ever-increasing numbers of "reconstructionists," who base their practices on the ancient religion of their choice, using only what is genuinely known or plausibly inferred. Reconstructionists rely heavily on primary source texts, which are translations of ancient writings, and secondary source texts, which are contemporary academic discussions, as well as archaeological and anthropological discoveries in their quest for authenticity. The problem faced by reconstructionists working with ancient cultures is the absence of complete "how-to" manuals, which necessitates interpolations.

Since the 1990s, there has been a revival of ancient Greek religious practices. The reconstructionists involved would like to see the ancient Greek deities restored to their former grandeur. While much of this revival has occurred in Greece, it is rapidly emerging throughout the rest of the world. Reconstructionism is never straightforward, and there are four important issues that need to be addressed.

First, there was no word in the ancient Greek language for religion, probably due to it being seamlessly integrated into everyday life. As a result there is no general consensus as to what the current revival should be called. Greek reconstructionists, for want of a more appropriate term, refer to their tradition as Hellenismos, Hellenism, the Hellenic tradition, the Hellenic religion, or Hellenic polytheism. Others, focusing on the twelve deities from Mount Olympus, refer to their tradition as either Dodekatheism or Olympianism. For reasons that will be explained later, I have chosen to use the term Hellenismos in this book for reconstructed ancient Greek religion.

Second, should the practice of Hellenismos be limited to people of Greek descent? A number of groups in Greece tie in the practice of Hellenismos, or an equivalent term, with nationalism. Certainly being Greek makes the practice of Hellenismos easier—being familiar with the Greek language and having the same blood coursing through your veins as the ancient Greeks are obvious advantages. There are, however, historical precedents for non-Greeks practicing Greek religion, for example in an annual festival to honor Athene Polias called the Panathenaia (discussed in the "Greek Religion—Public, Household, Countryside" chapter), and hence, Hellenismos should be available to all who feel the call of the Greek deities and wish to venerate them. It is, however, important to remain respectful and mindful of the ethics of cultural appropriation.

Third, just which ancient Greek religious practices should be revived? The Greek religion was characterized by appeals to ancient tradition and was simple in practice. There was, however, no one religion that was practiced by all Greeks, but rather there were variations in different regions, and even these variations were subject to change over time. There was also a significant difference between religious practices in public rituals and those in the home. It has already been stated that some reconstructionists limit themselves to the twelve Olympian deities, which are arguably the central aspect of the ancient Greek religion. Such a limitation ignores the non-Olympian deities, daimones (or spirits), heroes, and ancestors. The simple answer is that just as there were numerous ways of practicing ancient Greek religion, so too there are numerous ways of practicing Hellenismos—each equally valid, with individual practitioners freely developing their own personalized versions.

Fourth, are all practices suitable for contemporary practitioners? Much within ancient Greek religion was noble, but it was part of a cultural milieu, or social environment, that entailed animal sacrifice, occasional human sacrifice, slavery, the subordination of women, the practice of magick, and copious drug use. Greek religion was a product of its time, and as such was paralleled by numerous other religions. Times have changed, and there is a clear need for adaptation. Thus, Hellenismos should not be a reconstruction of ancient Greek religion as it was, but rather a reconstruction of what Greek religion plausibly would be had it survived. It is known that the religion changed in ancient times in response to changing needs as time passed, and so it would have kept changing had it survived until today. At the risk of stating the obvious, no laws should be broken by the practice of Hellenismos, and there can be numerous equally valid ways of practicing the faith.

The ancient Greeks were able to practice their religion publicly with their community and in their homes with their families. Religion was the glue that held the fabric of society together. The reality is that the practitioner of Hellenismos will most probably be practicing on a solitary basis, but, if lucky, may have one or more members of the household joining in. On occasion, the practitioner of Hellenismos may have like-minded individuals to worship with. While these individuals may live in close geographical proximity, more than likely they will not, necessitating contact in cyberspace, perhaps as part of one of the numerous online Hellenistic reconstructionist communities. I look forward to the day when temples to the old gods spring up like mushrooms after the rain, affording the joy of public veneration to all those who want to avail themselves of it! Until these temples return, most rituals will be engaged in at home.

For those wishing to either follow pure Hellenismos as an exclusive spiritual path or to incorporate aspects of it into an eclectic path such as Wicca, there is a clear need to be well acquainted with what exactly constituted Greek religion. In turn, the religion needs to be understood within the context of a uniquely Greek mindset encompassing ethics and piety. Only by being well informed can appropriate decisions be made regarding the personal and group practice of Hellenismos. Fortunately, much data is now being revealed that had been swept under the carpet by previous generations of academics who apparently didn't want their rose-tinted view of the ancient Greeks being contradicted. I pray that the Muses inspire us sufficiently to succeed in our endeavor of experiencing the deities and practices of the ancient Greeks and incorporating them into our lives. We will begin with daily observances, then move to monthly practices, and finish by working through the entire year.

So, why is the revival of the ancient Greek religion being called Hellenismos in this book? The ancient Greek religion endured political upheavals over the centuries, but the death knell was finally sounded when the Emperor Constantine converted to Christianity in 312 CE. Under a succession of Christian emperors, the Roman Empire was progressively Christianized and all pagan religions were gradually suppressed. The only exception was Julian, who became emperor of the Roman Empire in 361 CE. During his short two-year reign ending in 363 CE, Emperor Julian attempted to replace Christianity with officially revived traditional Roman religious practices, central to which was the practice of what he termed "Hellenismos"—the legacy of Greek philosophy, religion, and culture. It is as my token of homage to Emperor Julian that the term Hellenismos is being used.

NOTE FROM THE AUTHOR

I wrote this book with the aim of inspiring others to rediscover the world of the ancient Greeks. I hope that readers will acquire an understanding of the mindset of the ancients while remaining relevant to a contemporary paradigm in order to bridge a connection to the Greek deities.

We will start by familiarizing ourselves with an overview of the ancient Greek religion and the cultural mindset of the everyday people of that time. We will then begin a brief study of the deities, daimones, and heroes.

Then we will take a break from theory and expand on our knowledge by beginning our own personal practice with the simple daily observances that the Greeks used, enjoying the richness of this ancient Greek religion. Our aim will be to make contact with deities and then deepen that connection to the extent that we can forge a personal relationship with them. In the process we will set up a personal altar and chronicle our achievements and experiences in a journal.

We will then resume our studies and learn the differences between public, household, and countryside practices, as well as how the mystery schools fit in. We will look at the history of the Greeks and familiarize ourselves with where further information can be found.

Delving even deeper into Greek practices, we will work through a typical month, but in keeping with the time, we will follow a lunar calendar. As we create ever-deepening connections with the deities, we will discover which ones we are most called to, and may want to pay more attention to, while making notations in our personal journals.

Next, we will take a long hard look at some of the more undesirable aspects of Greek culture—they were not saints, and just like other religions of the time they sacrificed animals, subjugated women, kept slaves, used drugs, and practiced human sacrifice at times—much like the Old Testament Hebrews. This is why we cannot slavishly recreate ancient Greek society or their practices. It's important to know the good along with the bad so as to make informed decisions and not repeat the mistakes and atrocities of history. We will not be sacrificing any animals, but rather using traditional bloodless sacrifices. Then we will look at how widely practiced magick was in Greece. Each of us will make a decision as to whether we want to include it in our personal practice of Hellenismos or not.

Finally, we will start following the annual Athenian calendar, which means adding more festivals to the ones we are already doing each month, for a total of 120 festivals. While we do not have to practice them all, it is certainly something worth trying for a while, or working up to. Perhaps only some will be meaningful, and we can select the ones that feel right. Then we will discuss where to go from here, how to connect with others, and so forth.

The point is not about doing everything perfectly, but rather to just get started on nurturing relationships with the deities.

By the way, we'll use Anglicized spellings of the Greek names or deities, but wherever possible, the original Greek spelling will follow in brackets like this: Demeter [Dêmêtêr].

In the appendices I have provided a pronunciation guide, which obviously includes the Greek letters; an overview of some of the many occult systems that have borrowed from the Greeks; and a list of the foods available to the Greeks, along with a couple of recipe suggestions so we can recreate some of their dishes. I have also provided a glossary for any possibly unfamiliar words.

So, shall we begin?

1: GREEK RELIGION—AN OVERVIEW

The ancient Greeks had no primary text outlining religious practices or a centrally organized church or priesthood. The Greek religion started at some unknown point in the unchronicled past, and had no prophet or lawgiver to set a doctrine in stone. What we know about Greek religion comes about from piecing together poetry, philosophy, plays, speeches, histories, inscriptions on various artifacts, votive offerings, and archaeological remains.[1] Even the least amount of study of Greek mythology will show that the ancient Greeks were polytheistic and viewed their gods and goddesses as being fully capable of, and even inclined to, take an interest in human affairs. Thus, ancient Greeks sought to create beneficial relationships with the deities, just as other cultures did at the time.

While the primary deities of the ancient Greeks were the twelve Olympians, there were numerous lesser deities, daimones, and heroes also enjoying patronage. The polytheistic and animistic world of the ancient Greeks pulsed with life. The deities were mostly anthropomorphic (having human form), and present everywhere, being able to influence

---

1. Robert Garland, *Religion and the Greeks* (London, Bristol Classical Press, 1998) ix.

   C. M. Bowra, *The Greek Experience* (New York, A Mentor Book, 1964) 54.

all activities and undertakings. However, they were neither omnipotent (having all power), nor omniscient (being all seeing), but rather were subject to natural law. While the deities would sometimes have their favorites for whom they cared, they appeared to be largely indifferent to the welfare of humanity as a whole, and would sometimes be hostile and vindictive.[2] It was thus important to secure the goodwill of the deities through a reciprocal relationship by providing them with gifts in exchange for blessings, whereby life could be improved.[3]

Public veneration of deities in order to secure their goodwill took place at numerous sanctuaries, which were presided over by priests or priestesses. Male deities were normally served by priests, while female deities were normally served by priestesses, and most scholars believe that there was no formal training or ordination. Many priests and priestesses only worked part-time and were given annual appointments. Priests and priestesses could not have any disabilities, blemishes, or deformities, and had to be of good character. Some of the older cults were served by priests or priestesses from a particular kin group [*genos*] who were related by blood or marriage. The role of the priests and priestesses was to look after the sacred objects stored within a sanctuary, and then supervise the rituals and sacrifices in a way that was pleasing to the gods, in order that blessings would be bestowed upon worshippers. While the priests and priestesses were not responsible for the slaughter and dismemberment of animals, as this was done by sacrificers, they nevertheless received portions of those animals—normally the skins, which were then sold.[4] There will be more information on sacrifices later (see the "Public Religion section of the Greek Religion—Public, Household, Countryside" chapter).

---

2. Garland, *Religion and the Greeks*, 2, 5–6.

3. Ibid., 131–2.

4. Robert Garland, *Daily Life of the Ancient Greeks* (Westport, CN, Greenwood Press, 1998) 141. Dr. Simon Price, in *Religions of the Ancient Greeks* (New York, Cambridge University Press, 2004) disputes the widespread belief that priests and priestesses had no training, as they were absolutely essential for the smooth functioning of the religious system.

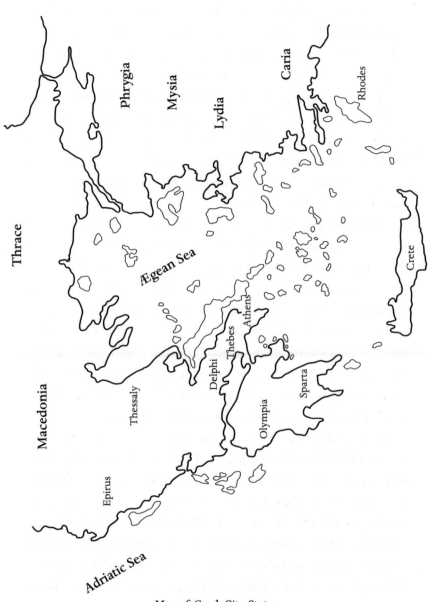

Map of Greek City-States

Careful interpretation of the Linear B Texts from Pylos (see A Thumbnail Sketch of Greek History, chapter 7) reveals that in Mycenaean times (1600–1100 BCE) there was an elaborate organization of a divine cult involving various cult personnel, including priests and priestesses. These cult personnel were not separated from the rest of society, and had many of the same rights and obligations.[5] This apparent part-time nature of their occupation suggests a continuity of priestly functions in broad terms from Mycenaean times to the Classical period (roughly 500–336 BCE). The Greeks customarily continued ancestral traditions, and this seems to be true even back to Mycenaean times.

The Greeks lived in several hundred small city-states which were all independent and differed from each other in many respects, including religious beliefs and practices. A second-century travel guide by Pausanias (see Further Study chapter) shows just how many different myths and cult practices there were in the various city-states. Further complicating matters, religious practices changed over the centuries. There is more known about Athens than any other city-state [*polis*], and so this is where most religious studies tend to place their primary focus. The most prolific writings pertaining to religion were those of philosophers and other intellectuals, but they were not necessarily representative of popular belief.[6]

Those readers who immerse themselves in secondary source texts will soon realize that there appears to be a tendency among some academics, especially in older texts, to project their own beliefs and prejudices onto ancient cultures, rather than seeking to impartially investigate the truth. One study was able to identify atheism among the professional philosophers, but only after narrowing the definition of the phenomenon to a mere denial of the ancient gods, and then conceded that they had very little influence on the greater masses of the popula-

5. James Hooker. "Cult-Personnel in the Linear B Texts from Pylos." (In *Pagan Priests*. Ed. by Mary Beard and John North, London, Duckworth) 159–174.

6. Jon D. Mikalson, *Athenian Popular Religion* (Chapel Hill, NC, North Carolina University Press, 1983) 4–10.

tion.[7] Thus the philosophers did not actually disbelieve in the gods, but rather disbelieved the popular accounts of them, which is a far cry from atheism as understood today.

Other academics claim to identify a monotheistic worldview in Book Lambda of Aristotle's *Metaphysics*.[8] It is claimed that Aristotle appears to be arguing that the gods are allegories of primary substances and that there is a principle of universal movement external to the universe, and that this separate unmoved mover is the supreme deity. Such a conclusion, however, is contradicted by Aristotle's numerous references to a multiplicity of gods, which indicate that Aristotle was a practicing polytheist.[9] Despite the fervent wishes of many academics to the contrary, the Greeks were devout polytheists.[10]

I believe that any serious examination of Greek religion, and philosophy for that matter, should begin with an examination of popular religious beliefs and practices. These beliefs and practices form a baseline from which other investigations can spring. As an example, popular

---

7. A. B. Drachmann, *Atheism in Pagan Antiquity* (Chicago, Aries Publishers Inc.) 1–4, 146–152. Professor Drachmann explored the possibility of atheism in the ancient world. For the purpose of his study, he narrowed his definition of atheism to a denial of the ancient gods. He conceded that, even using his narrowed definition, this phenomenon could only be identified among the intellectual elite, the professional philosophers, and that they had very little influence on the great mass of the population.

8. Richard Hope (trans.), *Aristotle—Metaphysics* (New York, Ann Arbor Paperbacks, 1990) 248–269.

9. Richard Bodeus, *Aristotle and the Theology of the Living Immortals* (Albany, NY, State University of New York Press, 2000) 1–13. Professor Bodeus goes against the dominant (monotheistic) interpretation to sensibly conclude that Aristotle was a polytheist who engaged in traditional forms of worship, just like all of his contemporaries.

10. H. D. F. Kitto, *The Greeks* (New York, Penguin, 1991) 194–5. Kitto developed the idea of Greeks searching for unity and order in the universe, which indicated to him that the Greeks should be monotheists. In exasperation he stated that instead the Greeks professed a "most luxuriant polytheism."

religious beliefs and practices permeate Greek drama.[11] After all, the best way to convey information is by starting with a baseline with which the audience is totally familiar.

The Greek deities had epithets ascribed to them. Some were derived from a fusion with originally independent deities, some were taken from the names of sanctuaries, while others were taken from spheres of influence, such as battle or fertility. Theoretically, epithets could be seen as designating aspects of a god, but in practice they were treated like different gods with distinct functions and cult centers.[12]

As an example, drinking symposiums began by drinking a toast of a few drops of unmixed wine in honor of Agathos Daimon (Good Spirit). Participants would bow three times and pour three libations—to Zeus Olympios and the other Olympians, to the heroes, and to Zeus Soter (Savior). Hymns would be sung to Apollon and Hygieia (goddess of Health).[13] Here, Zeus Olympios and Zeus Soter were treated like separate deities.

Attica was a territory of Greece that contained the Athens city-state. The area around Athens was divided into 139 or 140 constitutional structure units, each of which was called a deme [*dêmos*]. Demes ranged in size from small hamlets to large centers of population. Each deme was a political unit with its own local assembly which kept a record of all citizens over the age of eighteen. Importantly, there were variations in religious practice within each deme leading to thousands of apparently distinct deities and cult centers. For example, in the only complete surviving sacred calendar, which was for the deme of Erchia, there were forty-three deities and heroes, including six epithets each for Zeus and Apollon. Zeus had dozens of epithets throughout Greece, but the ones at Erchia are listed as follows.

---

11. Jon D. Mikalson, *Honor Thy Gods* (Chapel Hill, NC, University of North Carolina Press, 1991). Professor Mikalson has shown that popular religious beliefs and practices permeate Greek drama.

12. Walter Burkert, *Greek Religion* (Oxford, Blackwell Pub. Ltd, 2000) 184; Mikalson, *Athenian Popular Religion*, 68–73.

13. Garland, *Daily Life of the Ancient Greeks*, 141.

- Zeus Epakrios (on the Heights) who possibly functioned as a rain provider

- Zeus Epoptes (the Overseer) of unknown function

- Zeus Horios (of the Boundaries) who preserved boundary stones

- Zeus Teleios (of the Rite) was associated with Hera Teleia (of the Rite) and together they were overseers of marriage

- Zeus Polieus (of the City) concerned with the good of the city-state [*polis*][14]

- Zeus Meilichios (the Kindly) a chthonic (subterranean) deity regarded as a source of wealth who was portrayed as either a figure with a cornucopia and seated on a throne, or as a snake.[15] The snake form of Zeus Meilichios is an example of one of the few non-anthropomorphic Greek deities.

There were also many Greeks living in isolated rural areas. They lived off the land and may well have been considered backward in comparison to the dwellers in city-states, venerating deities most useful to their circumstances. These peasants led modes of life largely unchanged since pre-Classical times.[16]

While the Greeks had no word for religion, they had the word *thambos*, which literally meant astonishment or amazement.[17] The sense of the word was of a sudden realization of being in the presence of divinity, triggered by seeing something that is a part of nature—either a landscape, an animal, a soft wind, a thunderstorm, crashing waves, trees, an unusually

---

14. Ibid., 44–5; Garland, *Religion and the Greeks*, 31–2; Mikalson, *Athenian Popular Religion*, 68–70; Louise Brut Zaidman and Pauline Schmitt Pantel, *Religion in the Ancient Greek City* (New York, Cambridge University Press, 1994) 81–4.

15. Burkert, *Greek Religion*, 201; Jane Ellen Harrison, *Prolegomena to the Study of Greek Religion*, (Edmonds, Alexandrian Press) 13–28; Martin P. Nilsson, *Greek Folk Religion*, (New York, Harper Torchbooks, 1961) 69–70.

16. Nilsson, *Greek Folk Religion*, 5.

17. H. G. Liddell and Robert Scott, *An Intermediate Greek–English Lexicon* (Oxford, Oxford University Press, 2000) 358.

shaped mineral, or any other beautiful manifestation of nature. The feeling of *thambos* happened frequently and powerfully, and provided the principal and permanent element in Greek religion. This was the very essence of polytheism—experiencing divinities literally everywhere.[18] Further to this, Xenophon (a Greek historian, soldier, mercenary, and student of Socrates, who lived from c. 430–354 BCE) stated that the gods knew all things and at their discretion would give signs by means of "sacrifices, omens, voices, and dreams."[19] The Greeks sought intimate union with their deities and cultivated personal relationships with them. Rituals would be empty make-believe unless participants fervently desired to enter into personal contact with the divine.[20] Rituals had to be experiential in order to be meaningful, indicating that a reciprocal relationship solely to secure the goodwill of deities through the provision of gifts could not be sustained indefinitely. This meant that going through the motions without feeling the presence of the divine was an essentially worthless pursuit.

Worship typically took place in sanctuaries which normally had a water source, a tree or grove, a stone to indicate the location as being special, and an altar. A temple was not always built, and so the altar was the most important fixture.[21] The temple served as the house of a deity and the repository of the property of the deity. Worshippers would gather around the altar, which was outside in the open. The temple was normally oriented toward the east, and often roughly where the sun rose on the day of the main festival of the deity housed there.[22]

While Aristotle's *The Athenian Constitution*, written in 350 BCE, is an important text in its totality, a small portion of it (in 55.2) foreshadows a

---

18. Francois Chamoux, *The Civilization of Greece* (New York, Simon & Schuster, 1965) 210–211.

19. Mikalson, *Athenian Popular Religion*, 39.

20. Andre-Jean Festugiere, *Personal Religion Among the Greeks* (Berkeley and Los Angeles, CA, 1960) 1, 9, 19.

21. Jan N. Bremmer, *Greek Religion* (New York, Cambridge University, 1999) 27.

22. Simon Price and Emily Kearns (ed.), *The Oxford Dictionary of Classical Myth & Religion* (New York, Oxford University Press, 2003) 538.

number of issues which will be discussed in detail later (in the Ancient Greek Mindset and Controversial Issues in Greek Society chapters, as well as the Household Religion section). When Athenians stood for public office they were examined with a series of questions, which Aristotle outlines:

> *When they are examined, they are asked, first, 'Who is your father, and of what deme? Who is your father's father? Who is your mother? Who is your mother's father, and of what deme?' Then the candidate is asked whether he possesses an ancestral Apollon [Apollon Patroos] and a household Zeus [Zeus Herkeios], and where their sanctuaries are; next if he possesses a family tomb, and where; then if he treats his parents well, and pays his taxes, and has served on the required military expeditions.* [23]

The examiner sought to determine whether the candidate was a citizen of Athens, whether he was genuinely pious toward the gods in his household, as well as at public sacrifices, whether he fulfilled his obligations toward his ancestors and parents, and lastly whether he was a law-abiding citizen who paid his taxes and performed military service. Here we have a neat summation of what it meant to be an exemplary Athenian —each of the issues raised were equally important.

---

23. Sir Frederic G. Kenyon (trans.), *Aristotle: The Athenian Constitution* (www.fordham.edu/halsall/ancient/aristotle-athcon.txt).

2: THE ANCIENT GREEK MINDSET

Academics studying Greek religion often compare it to what enlightened Westerners recognize as religion in this day and age. Trying to understand the ancient Greeks from a Christian standpoint is unavoidably doomed to failure, as it is imperative to adopt the mindset of the Greeks.

The classical Greeks, or Hellenes, considered themselves different from the surrounding peoples. They referred to non-Greeks as "barbarians" [*barbaroi*], which literally meant foreigners—people who could not speak Greek. It was not just a matter of language; it was a matter of a different lifestyle and a different way of thinking. The Greeks thought of themselves as free, as they lived in a democracy where they were part of the decision-making process. Foreigners were thought of as virtually slaves, living under the rule of monarchs. In a sometimes mistranslated verse, the poet Pindar (518–c. 446 BCE) in *Nemean* (6.1–6) stated that gods and men were of one race and had one mother. Yet, in terms of power, men were nothing while the abode of the gods in the heavens endured forever. This was effectively the tragedy of man—dignified, yet weak.[1]

---

1. Kitto, *The Greeks*, 7–10.

PIETY

The Greeks were expected to demonstrate piety [*eusebeia*], which meant doing the right thing with respect to the gods, their parents, their city, and the deceased. Regarding the gods, it was important to observe all the public festivals as well as those in the home.[2]

The statesman and orator Demosthenes (384–322 BCE) in *Epistula* (1) stated that prior to beginning any undertaking it was proper to begin first with the gods.[3] Before the Athenians engaged in any sort of activity there would be either a prayer to, or a statement about, the deities. It was unthinkable to not give them priority in thoughts and actions.[4]

The Athenians were concerned with ensuring that the deities felt goodwill toward them, giving them opportunities for improvement in times of adversity, safety, as well as providing them with the necessities of life. This goodwill was maintained by performing the prescribed sacrifices, upholding oaths, and avoiding pollution [*miasma*]. Procedural uncertainties were resolved by consulting the deities through oracles.[5] I will be discussing pollution and oracles later in this chapter.

Success in agriculture was dependent upon rainfall from Zeus. Divine favor was assured through adhering to traditional festivals and sacrifices, including first fruit offerings, such as the *eiresione*, an olive branch to which were attached cakes, bread, figs, and other seasonal fruits. This was placed at the door and left there for a full year, whereupon it was replaced by another.[6] This would have smelled briefly, after which it would have been dry and odorless.

The acquisition of wealth and property could also be attributed to the deities.[7] As an example, Xenophon, in *Anabasis* (Book VII. VIII. 1–6),

---

2. Garland, *Religion and the Greeks*, 23–27.

3. Valerie M. Warrior, *Greek Religion: A Sourcebook* (Newburyport, Focus Pub.) 55.

4. Mikalson, *Athenian Popular Religion*, 13–17.

5. Ibid., 18, 53, 58.

6. Ibid., 21.

7. Ibid., 24.

heeded the advice of a soothsayer that his poverty was the result of neglecting Zeus Meilichios (the gentle one). Following his family tradition, Xenophon offered a holocaust (burned whole; none is eaten) of swine and then his circumstances changed for the better.[8]

While success in war was attributed to the deities, failure was blamed on a daimon, or the goddess Fortune or Tyche [Tuchê].[9]

Similarly, death was never ascribed to deities, but rather was blamed on Fortune, a daimon, or destiny. The circumstance of homicide brought in matters of pollution and avenging spirits.[10]

All in all, opportunities came from deities and it was up to humans to make the best of them. Success was attributed to the deities, who would then be praised and thanked. Misfortunes, failure, and death were blamed on a personal shortcoming in the human themselves, a daimon, or Fortune.[11]

It was the duty of the nearest relatives or friends of a free murdered man to carry on a blood feud against the murderer. Should the murder not be avenged, it was believed, even in the fourth and fifth centuries BCE, that the murdered man's spirit would become an avenging spirit raging against those who had failed him. Those who had no recourse to any earthly avengers would call on the Erinyes (the three underworld goddesses of retribution known as the Furies).[12]

Deities would become directly involved in legal cases involving perjury and impious acts such as violations of oaths, murder, and treason. Other crimes, so long as there was no impiety involved, were of no concern to the deities.[13] When swearing promissory oaths (to deities that a

---

8. H. G. Dakyns, *Xenophon: Anabasis*, c. 1895. http://www.gutenberg.org/files/1170/1170.txt

9. Mikalson, *Athenian Popular Religion*, 19.

10. Ibid., 501.

11. Ibid., 62, 65.

12. Erwin Rohde, *Psyche: The Cult of Souls & Belief in Immortality Among the Greeks* (New York, Harper Torchbooks, 1966) 174–82.

13. Mikalson, *Athenian Popular Religion*, 28, 30.

promise will be fulfilled), a number of deities would be called on as witnesses, so that the oath taker would risk divine punishment as well as prosecution.[14]

The Athenians believed that piety had a direct influence on national and personal property. Piety was involved in the legal system, tradition, and consensual opinion.

Charges of impiety were brought against individuals in the fifth and fourth centuries BCE for introducing new deities; shameless religious revelry; illegal religious assemblies; revealing or mocking the Eleusinian Mysteries; mutilation of Herms (sculpture with a head, possibly a torso, above a plain square pillar, with carved male genitals); robbing sanctuaries and chopping down sacred olive trees (which belonged to Athene). Sacrilegious acts were equivalent to robbing a deity.

While perhaps only vaguely related to impiety, excessive pride in abilities and good fortune [*hubris*] was an offense against the deities.

Fourth-century-BCE Athenians were so conservative that they would not change anything that had been handed down by the ancestors, especially regarding sacrifice, rites of the dead, and the family.

There was general agreement about the maintenance of oaths, as perjury would be punished by the deities; respecting asylum and hospitality; care of parents while they were alive, and then providing traditional rites upon their deaths.

All male citizens were required to swear an oath that they would maintain or improve their homeland, obey officials and laws, and not desert their comrades in battle. Cowards, murderers, and adulteresses were excluded from religious activities by law.[15]

It would appear that within a contemporary setting, demonstrating piety would involve living life honorably with respect to the community, and venerating the deities by observing all the public festivals. Observing the public festivals would have been a simple matter of attending festivals

---

14. Ibid., 31–34.

15. Ibid., 88, 91-2, 94, 95, 96, 98, 103, 104; Garland, *Religion and the Greeks*, 26.

which were already being celebrated in accordance with ancestral traditions. Contemporary practitioners may craft their own rituals complete with votive or first fruits offerings; recite preexisting hymns or write their own; spend time in research or contemplation; or dedicate an activity to the glory of a deity, such as a craft project to Athene or Hephaistos, music to Apollon, or an athletic endeavor to Hermes.

CONSERVATISM OF GREEK RELIGION

I assume that because it was believed that in ancient times humanity had direct contact with the divine, ancient rites must have been done in accordance with the wishes of the divine and so had to be diligently copied by future generations. Any sort of modifications to these rites had to receive divine approval through oracular consultation.

The orator and rhetorician Isocrates (436–338 BCE) in Areopagiticus (29–30) wrote about the conservatism of Greek religion. The collective ancestors of the Greeks did not have lavish sacrifices but carefully maintained traditional cults, not changing any rites that had been handed down to them.[16] This meant that the temptation to embellish should be resisted, and sacrifices should be simple and traditional.

The Neoplatonic philosopher Porphyry (c. 234–c. 305 CE) quoted an "eternal sacred law" of Draco to the inhabitants of Attica:

> ... that the Gods, and indigenous Heroes, be worshipped publicly, conformably to the laws of the country, delivered by our ancestors; and also, that they be worshipped privately, according to the ability of each individual, in conjunction with auspicious words, the firstlings of fruits, and annual cakes. So that this law ordains, that divinity should be venerated by the first offerings of fruits which are used by men, and cakes made of the fine flour of wheat.[17]

---

16. Warrior, *Greek Religion*, 249.
17. Thomas Taylor, *On Abstinence from Animal Food* in *The Select Works of Porphyry* (London, 1823).

Xenophon in *Memorabilia* stated that when the Pythia, Apollon's mouthpiece in Delphi, was asked about appropriate behavior during a sacrifice or the worship of ancestors, she replied: *"Act according to the law and custom of your state, and you will act piously."*[18]

Again, the theme is reinforced that it was important to obey laws and adhere to traditions.

Contemporary practitioners should opt for simple rather than lavish observances, based where possible on ancient procedures. This may not always be possible as either information is missing or a large number of people are required.

POLLUTION

The Greeks believed in avoiding pollution [*miasma*] whenever possible, which was caused, in increasing order of severity, by having sex, giving birth, coming into contact with the dead, and murder. While there were specialists available to advise on purification techniques, these normally involved bathing, salt water, fire, sulphur, and blood sacrifice.[19]

The most commonly used method of purification involved water. Fire was thought of as being able to purify everything. Fumigation with sulphur worked as a disinfectant and would banish noxious odors. As an added precaution against pollution, hands would be washed in pure water [*chernips*] prior to libation and sacrifice. There were vessels containing water at sanctuary entrances. The water would normally be from a spring, a fountain, or the sea. Wood taken from the altar fires would be dipped in water, whereupon the sanctuary, altar, and participants would be sprinkled. This would effectively join the purifying powers of water and fire together. It should be noted that before individual initiations and initiations into mystery schools it was important to bathe and dress in clean robes.[20] Before entering a sanctuary, those who were polluted from sexual intercourse needed to bathe.[21]

---

18. Dakyns, *Xenophon: Anabasis*, 1.3.1.

19. Garland, *Religion and the Greeks*, 37.

20. Burkert, *Greek Religion*, 76–79.

21. Mikalson, *Ancient Greek Religion*, 8.

The guidelines for pollution appear to be geared toward public worship. Presumably household religious practices would have been far more discretionary.

Contemporary practitioners will have to decide for themselves just what sources of pollution should be regarded as valid in an absolute sense and which are cultural. We have the advantage of showers which are quick and convenient. I would suggest that prior to a group ritual a shower is a matter of politeness, and should there be any sources of pollution to deal with, then it's a matter of being additionally thorough. I don't think that bathing prior to every meal-based offering is required (as this would be reminiscent of the diligence of Egyptian priests), but bathing prior to festivals would be appropriate. I note that sexual intercourse is the least serious of the sources of pollution listed, and probably should not be particularly worried about. I am, however, in agreement with the ancients that mortuary workers and others who come into contact with the dead should diligently observe hygiene because of the possibility of numerous health risks. Sulphur may be purchased inexpensively online and can be sprinkled on a smouldering charcoal block, in the same manner as incense.

GIFT OFFERINGS AND LIBATIONS

The nature of the relationship between the Greeks and their deities was one of reciprocal favor [*charis*]. Gifts were given in the hope of gratitude.[22]

Gift offerings were either first fruit offerings or votive offerings.

First fruits offerings, obtained either from agricultural practices or from hunting and gathering, were set down in a sacred place after which they were taken by the poor or animals, dropped into bodies of water, or burned. Technically, once burned, the offerings should be referred to as sacrifices.

Votive offerings were gifts presented in anticipation of or as a result of divine favor.[23] A vow would be made in front of witnesses promising a gift in return for a desired outcome. The gift could be first fruit offerings,

---

22. Burkert, *Greek Religion*, 189.

23. Garland, *Religion and the Greeks*, 16.

an animal sacrifice, a promise to found a new sanctuary, bestowing goods or slaves unto an existing sanctuary, war booty (primarily weapons), or even offering locks of hair.[24]

Other examples of votive offerings include flowers, branches, shells, gold implements, and clay images of offerings. The most widespread offering was a simple granule of frankincense strewn in the flames.[25]

Gratitude could be shown to deities by leaving lasting visible votive offerings of durable materials such as marble, bronze, silver, gold, and clay, as well as less durable materials such as ivory and wood.[26]

A libation [*spondê*] would be poured to the deities so as to request their protection. Libations would normally be one or more of the following: wine, honey, olive oil, milk, and water. There was also a libation to the dead or the chthonic deities [*choê*] (normally not wine).[27]

The Afterlife

The average Athenian believed in an afterlife, and for most it meant living in the underworld house of Persephone, although some believed in an ascension to the sky. There did not appear to be any expectation of reward or punishment, but the afterlife was expected to be bleak. Living life well in this world appeared to be more important than preparing for any uncertain afterlife.[28]

The mystery schools operated on the idea that there should be secret types of spiritual experience, known to a select few, in addition to the more general forms of honoring the divine. Most of the Greek states offered such services, and the priests were appointed by the state. Divulging anything about the experience to the uninitiated would result in public punishment for impiety. Some mysteries were selective in

---

24. Burkert, *Greek Religion*, 66–70.

25. Ibid., 62.

26. Simon Price, *Religions of the Ancient Greeks* (New York, Cambridge University Press, 2004) 58–63.

27. Garland, *Religion and the Greeks*, 17.

28. Mikalson, *Athenian Popular Religion*, 75, 77, 82.

admission. The Thesmophoria (see Experiencing the Annual Cycle—Athenian Festival Calendar chapter) admitted women of Athenian descent, of unblemished reputation, living in lawful marriages with Athenian citizens. Other mysteries were far less restrictive, so long as certain requirements were met.[29]

The best-known mystery school was the Eleusinian Mysteries, which focused on the worship of Demeter and her daughter, Persephone. The Eleusinian Mysteries were practiced for a thousand years, and were available to anyone who could pay the fees, including women, noncitizens, and slaves. Only murderers and those unable to speak Greek were excluded, which meant that they were very inclusive. Athens imposed the death penalty on those who divulged the Eleusinian Mysteries, and so very little is known about them. Those who were initiated, however, were assured of a blessed afterlife.[30] It has been suggested that "all important rites of Demeter in Attica seem to have been linked (at least loosely) to stages of the agricultural year."[31] This would tie in the Eleusinian Mysteries and the other major festivals with the sacred cycle of grain production.

REVIEW

We should demonstrate piety, which means doing the right thing and observing all festivals with simple ceremonies, using first fruit offerings or votive offerings and libations. We should be aware of pollution and purify as necessary.

29. Oskar Seyffert, *Dictionary of Classical Antiquities* (New York, Meridian Books, 1960) 409–10.

30. Garland, *Religion and the Greeks*, 83–87.

31. Helene P. Foley, *The Homeric Hymn to Demeter* (Princeton, NJ, Princeton University Press, 1999) 71.

3: OLYMPIC DEITIES

GENESIS OF THE DEITIES

The deities of the ancient Greeks cannot be fully understood without knowledge of their origins. The Greek poet Hesiod (active between 750 and 650 BCE) wrote *Theogony,* which was accepted as the standard account of the earliest history.[1] As a full account of all the deities is beyond the scope of this book, I am selecting only that which is relevant.

Hesiod's account begins with Chaos ("chasm" or "gaping void," not "disorder" or "confusion," as would be expected from later usage), who is treated as a female deity. She is followed by the independent coming into existence of "broad-chested Gaia" or Ge [Gaia or Gê] (Earth), Tartaros (a recess in the earth), and Eros ("love," "desire," the principle of sexual reproduction). From this point on, almost all entities would have a mother and a father.

Chaos and Gaia then generated further progeny through parthenogenesis, or reproduction not requiring a male partner, which would prepare the foundation of the three great dynasties. Chaos produced a son

---

1. Robin Hard, *The Routledge Handbook of Greek Mythology: Based on H. J. Rose's Handbook of Greek Mythology* (New York, Routledge, 2004) 21.

and daughter, Erebus [Erebos] (Nether Darkness) and black Nyx [Nux] (Night), who in turn produced a son and daughter, bright Aither [Aithêr] (Upper Air) and Hemera [Hêmera] (Day). Gaia brought forth Uranus [Ouranos] (Sky), who was her equal, Ourea (Mountains) and Pontus [Pontos] (Sea). While Chaos would subsequently bring forth various negative and harmful forces (through Nyx), Gaia brought forth that which was positive.

Gaia and Ouranos united to become the first couple, which became the first great dynasty, which eventually gave rise to the greatest deities. Gaia also united with Pontos to give rise to sea-deities, nymphs, and various monsters.[2]

Gaia and Ouranos produced three sets of progeny[3]: the Titans [Titanes], who consisted of six sons and six daughters, including Kronos and Rhea[4]; the one-eyed Kyklopes [Kyklôpes] (possibly better known as Cyclopes), three gigantic sons who resembled the gods but had a single eye in their forehead[5]; and the giants with one hundred arms and fifty heads, who came to be known as the Hekatoncheires (Hundred-Handers).[6]

Ouranos was terrified by the hideousness of his progeny and prevented them from emerging into the light, keeping them in the hollow of the earth. Gaia groaned in pain and hatched a plan which, of all her children, only Kronos had the courage to fulfill. Gaia produced a new metal, gray adamant, from which she fashioned a great jagged-toothed sickle. That night, when Ouranos lay on Gaia to have intercourse with her, Kronos reached out from his hiding place and hacked off his father's genitals. Kronos then hurled the genitals into the sea, where *aphros* (foam) gathered around them and in turn brought forth Aphrodite [Aphroditê].[7]

2. Ibid., 22–4; Fritz Graf, *Greek Mythology: An Introduction* (Baltimore, MD, Johns Hopkins University Press, 1996) 80.

3. Hard, *Handbook of Greek Mythology*, 32.

4. Seyffert, *Dictionary of Classical Antiquities*, 639.

5. R. M. Frazer, *The Poems of Hesiod* (Norman, OK, University of Oklahoma Press) 33; Seyffert, *Dictionary of Classical Antiquities*, 169.

6. Frazer, *Poems of Hesiod*, 34. Seyffert, *Dictionary of Classical Antiquities*, 271–2.

7. Frazer, *Poems of Hesiod*, 34–7; Hard, *The Routledge Handbook of Greek Mythology*, 32.

With the mutilation of Ouranos, Kronos became the supreme god, heading the second great dynasty with Rhea. Their progeny were Hestia, Demeter [Dêmêtêr], Hera [Hêrê], Hades [Haidês, Hadês], the loud-crashing Earthshaker Poseidon [Poseidôn], and Zeus. Ouranos and Gaia warned Kronos that he would meet with defeat at the hands of his son, and so he swallowed each of his progeny at birth.[8]

The Olympians were so named because of their residence on Mount Olympos in central Greece. The Olympians were the last of a series of dynasties, each of which came to power by usurping the previous one—thus Zeus usurped Kronos, and his fellow Titans, who in turn had usurped Ouranos. The Olympians consisted of their leader Zeus and eleven other deities, each of whom were either siblings or offspring of Zeus. While the composition of the Olympians changed over time, with Dionysos replacing Hestia, their number remained constant at twelve.[9] It has been suggested that originally Zeus and his siblings personified natural forces, while his offspring represented human attributes.

The earliest source of information about the deities is Homer (see "Comprehensive Study" chapter), and translation of the Linear B texts has provided further evidence for the historicity of his accounts, as some Homeric names appear, although some scholars dispute this. Many of the Olympic deities are mentioned: Zeus and Hera who were already paired, Poseidon, Hermes, Athene, and Artemis. An early form of *Paian*, which is a title of Apollon, as well as *Enualios*, a title of Ares, have been found. It also appears that a reference to Dionysos has been found. There does not appear to be any mention of Aphrodite and no definite mention of Demeter.[10]

While each of the deities have epithets, I will be limiting myself to those that appear in the Athenian Festival Calendar. These have been

---

8. Hard, *Handbook of Greek Mythology*, 67–8.

9. W. K .C Guthrie, *The Greeks and their Gods* (Boston, Beacon Press, 1961) 110–12.

10. Burkert, *Greek Religion*, 43–6, 120

extracted from the "Experiencing the Annual Cycle—Athenian Festival Calendar" chapter.

OLYMPIC DEITIES

The core pantheon of the ancient Greeks was that of the Olympians.

Zeus [Zeus]: described by Homer as the father of gods and men; the god of justice and the sky.

Zeus is the Sky Father, a rain and storm god. He is of clear Indo-European origin, with his name being similar to the Indic sky god *Dyaus pitar* and the Roman *Diespiter/Juppiter*, as well as having connections to the weather gods of Asia Minor. The Homeric epithets of Zeus were the cloud gatherer, the dark clouded, the thunderer on high, and the hurler of thunderbolts. He is the strongest of the deities and other deities are fearful of his thunderbolts, which destroy whatever they strike. Even in Mycenaean times he was considered to be one of the most important, if not the most important of the deities.[11]

Olympus, the dwelling place of Zeus, is on mountains where the clouds gather. This was eventually narrowed down to the highest mountain in Thessaly.[12]

According to Hesiod's *Theogony*, prior to Zeus' reign, the world was ruled by Zeus' father, Kronos, and his fellow Titans. Worried about being usurped by his son, Kronos swallowed all his children as they were born. Zeus' mother, Rhea, saved him by giving Kronos a stone wrapped in swaddling clothes to swallow.[13]

A Cretan *Theogony*, written after Hesiod, stated that the infant Zeus was raised in a cave on Mount Dicte in Crete by two nymphs. Outside the cave were youthful warriors known as the Kouretes beating their spears against their shields to prevent Kronos from hearing Zeus.[14]:

---

11. Burkert, *Greek Religion*, 125–6.
12. Ibid., 126
13. Frazer, *Poems of Hesiod*, 56–9.
14. Robin Hard, *Apollodorus: The Library of Greek Mythology*, 28.

Once he reached maturity, Zeus, armed with his thunderbolts, led the gods to victory in battle against the Titans.[15] As a result, Zeus was typically called upon to give victory on the battlefield.[16]

Zeus with his lightning, Poseidon with his trident, and Hades with his head turned back to front were the three powerful sons of Kronos who drew lots for the division of the cosmos after defeating the Titans.[17]

Zeus was very well known for his sexual exploits, sharing his bed with a slew of goddesses and mortal women, with late mythographers counting 115. He did not, however, limit himself to women, as he abducted the Trojan youth Ganymede. Zeus would often shapeshift into a number of animals, birds, and even golden rain, as part of his seductive technique. He was the only god to father powerful gods and goddesses, namely Apollon, Artemis, Hermes, Persephone, Dionysos, Athene, and Ares. Zeus was referred to as father by all humans and deities, whether or not he had actually sired them.[18]

In art, Zeus was represented as either a warrior hurling a thunderbolt with his right hand, or as a king seated on a throne holding a scepter. He was associated with the eagle and with bull sacrifices.[19]

His usual symbols included a thunderbolt, royal scepter, eagle, oak tree, and pair of scales.[20]

The epithets of Zeus specific to the Athenian calendar were:

- Zeus Eleutherios (the liberator) prayed to for victory
- Zeus Phratrios (the tribal brotherhoods)
- Zeus Soter (Savior)
- Zeus Polieus (of the City)
- Zeus Epopetes (the Overseer) of unknown function

---

15. Frazer, *Poems of Hesiod*, 60–1, 68–73.
16. Burkert, *Greek Religion*, 128.
17. C. Kerenyi, *The Gods of the Greeks* (London, Thames & Hudson, 1979) 231.
18. Burkert, *Greek Religion*, 128–9.
19. Ibid., 127.
20. Grant and Hazel, *Who's Who in Classical Mythology*, 345–9.

- Zeus Meilichios (kindly or open to propitiation or gentle)
- Zeus Teleios (of the Rite) associated with Hera Teleia (of the Rite) and together they were overseers of marriage
- Zeus Horios (of the Boundaries)
- Zeus Epakrios (on the Heights)
- Zeus Olympios (Olympian Zeus)
- Zeus Herkeios (household Zeus) protector of property boundaries
- Zeus Ktesios (Zeus of the house, or of property), protector of the storehouse and guardian against thieves

Hera [Hêra]: the youngest daughter of Kronos and Rhea, the wife and eldest sister of Zeus; the Queen of Olympos, who presided over marriage and married women. Her marriage to Zeus, called *hieros gamos* (holy marriage), was connected to rituals in her honor in a number of places. She was known in Mycenaean times and already associated with Zeus (on one tablet).[21]

Zeus' numerous infidelities led to her portrait as a wronged and vindictive wife who had frequent disputes with Zeus, and often tried to take revenge on his mistresses and their children.[22] Some ancient writers saw her as the personification of the atmosphere, others as the queen of heaven, or the goddess of the stars, or even as the goddess of the moon.[23] Hera was usually portrayed as a mature noblewoman, wearing a crown or a diadem (sometimes with accompanying veil) symbolizing her status as the bride of Zeus, or wearing a wreath and carrying a scepter.[24] Her symbols include the diadem, veil, scepter, peacock, pomegranate, cuckoo, lion, and cow.[25]

---

21. Price and Kearns, *Oxford Dictionary of Classical Myth & Religion*, 249–50.
22. Hard, *Routledge Handbook of Greek Mythology*, 138–9.
23. W. C. Guthrie, *The Greeks and Their Gods* (Boston, Beacon Press, 1961) 66–73; Graf, *Greek Mythology*, 195–6.
24. Hard, *Routledge Handbook of Greek Mythology*, 134–5
25. Burkert, *Greek Religion*, 131–5.

Her Homeric epithet was cow-eyed [*boopis*].[26]

The epithets of Hera specific to the Athenian calendar were:

- Hera Thelkhinia (uncertain meaning) and Hera Teleia (of the Rite) were associated with Zeus Teleios (of the Rite), and together they were overseers of marriage

Poseidon [Poseidôn]: the middle son of Kronos and Rhea and brother of Zeus and Hades; was the god of the Mediterranean sea, and was described as causing storms, but also calming the waters to grant safe passage.[27] The name Poseidon appears to mean 'lord (or husband) of Earth'.[28] He was attended by sea-nymphs and the beasts and monsters of the deep, and in later times by dolphins. Poseidon was described as the god of horses as well as of earthquakes, and called Earthshaker. He kept his bronze-hooved horses and chariot—with which he traveled over the waves—at his palace in the depths of the sea near Aigai, off the island of Samothrace. He was regarded as the creator of the horse, and chariot races would be held in his honor, while horses were sacrificed to him and kept in his sanctuaries. In Greek folklore, horses were often credited with the creation of springs. Horses were also one of the most powerful forces of nature that could be dominated. The symbol of Poseidon's power was the long-handled, three-pronged trident harpoon, which he used to shatter rocks and to stir up the sea and calm it down again. He was represented as a tall, mature, stately figure, distinguished from Zeus by his trident.[29]

The sacrifices offered to Poseidon were black and white bulls, wild boars, and rams. His symbols include the dolphin, the horse, the bull, and the trident.[30]

The Linear B Texts from Pylos indicate that, in Mycenaean times, Poseidon was the primary deity venerated, and most of the offerings to

---

26. Ibid., 131.
27. Price and Kearns, *Oxford Dictionary of Classical Myth & Religion*, 444–5.
28. Grant and Hazel, *Who's Who in Classical Mythology*, 280
29. Hard, *Routledge Handbook of Greek Mythology*, 98–102.
30. Burkert, *Greek Religion*, 136–9.

him were wheat, although there was a reference to wine, cheese, and an ox, in addition to wheat. It is not clear whether these offerings were to Poseidon himself or for the upkeep of his temple. The legendary island of Atlantis, known from two of Plato's dialogues, Timaeus and Critias, was the domain of Poseidon.[31]

There were no epithets of Poseidon listed in the Athenian calendar.

Demeter [Dêmêtêr]: the middle daughter of Kronos and Rhea, the sister of Zeus. Her name means 'Mother Earth'.[32] She was considered the mother of corn, or of all crops and vegetation, and consequently of agriculture and growth. Demeter also presided over fertility, nature, and the seasons. By her brother, Zeus, she was the mother of Persephone and Dionysus. Her most important myth concerns the rape of her daughter Persephone by her uncle, Hades, lord of the Underworld.[33] Zeus, without the knowledge of Demeter, had promised Persephone to Hades, and while she was gathering flowers, the earth suddenly opened and she was carried off by Hades Aidoneus (the personification of the underworld). Her cries were heard only by Hekate and Helios. Demeter searched ceaselessly for Persephone, during which time the earth was infertile and famine-stricken. As all life on earth was threatened with extinction, Zeus sent Hermes to the underworld to fetch Persephone. Hades released her, but gave her a pomegranate, which bound her to him for one third of the year when she ate the seeds. Persephone's time in the underworld corresponded with the unfruitful times of the year, and her return with springtime. This myth became the basis of the Eleusinian Mysteries.[34] The sacrifices offered to Demeter consisted of pigs, bulls, cows, honey-cakes, and fruits. She was represented either sitting, walking, or in a chariot drawn by horses or dragons, but always fully dressed. She wore a garland

---

31. Hooker. "Cult-Personnel" in *Pagan Priests*, ed. Beard and North, 159–174; Zeyl, "Timaeus" in *Plato*, ed. Cooper & Hutchinson, 1224–1291; Clay, "Critias" in *Plato*, ed. Cooper & Hutchinson, 1292–1306.

32. Grant and Hazel, *Who's Who in Classical Mythology*, 106.

33. Price and Kearns, *Oxford Dictionary of Classical Myth & Religion*, 159–60.

34. Hard, *Routledge Handbook of Greek Mythology*, 125–8.

of corn ears or a simple ribband, and held a scepter, corn ears or a poppy, sometimes also a torch and the mystic basket.

Her symbols included the poppy, wheat, torch, and pig.

Her Homeric epithets were *Agaue* (venerable) and *Epaine* (awesome),[35] but there were none in the Athenian calendar.

Hades [Haidês]: the brother of Zeus; lord of the dead; king of the underworld, where he ruled over the dead with his wife, Persephone [Persephonê], the daughter of Demeter.[36] His name in origin is probably an epithet meaning 'the Unseen'.[37] He was one of the three powerful sons of Kronos who, with his brothers Zeus and Poseidon, drew lots for the division of the cosmos after defeating the Titans.

Hades was dark-bearded, and was depicted as either Aidoneus (the personified underworld), holding a scepter or key while enthroned in the underworld, or as Plouton (Wealthy or Wealth-giver—as wealth comes from the ground as crops and minerals), holding abundance in a cornucopia.[38]

Hades had no epithets in the Athenian calendar.

Hestia [Hestia]: sister of Zeus; the goddess of the hearth—of Olympos, the city, and the family home. In the Mycenaean age, the king's throne room was in the center of the palace, while in the center of that room was a low hearth. In some cities, hearth fires were kept continuously burning. Mother cities would send fire from their own hearths to newly founded colonies as a token of continuity. Babies, brides, and slaves were inducted into families by rituals centered around the hearth. To begin from Hestia became a proverb and a custom, and so even at sacrifices of other deities she received a preliminary offering, and in prayers and oaths she was usually named first.[39]

---

35. Burkert, *Greek Religion*, 159–61.
36. Price and Kearns, *Oxford Dictionary of Classical Myth & Religion*, 238–9.
37. Grant and Hazel, *Who's Who in Classical Mythology*, 148.
38. Hard, *Routledge Handbook of Greek Mythology*, 107–9.
39. Price and Kearns, *Oxford Dictionary of Classical Myth & Religion*, 261.

Hestia was the first-born and last-born child of Kronos and Rhea, as she was the first to be swallowed at birth and last to be disgorged. At sacrifices she would receive the first offering or preliminary libation, while at feasts the first and last libations would be dedicated to her.

Hestia was the goddess of the sacrificial flame and fire was a pure (and purifying) element. When the gods Apollon and Poseidon sought her hand in marriage, she refused and Zeus allowed her to remain eternally a virgin and take her place at the royal hearth.[40]

According to the Greek historian Diodorus Siculus (first century BCE), Hestia invented the establishment of houses, and as a result was installed in almost every house, receiving worship and sacrifices.[41] "Hestia was depicted in some Athenian vase paintings and in classical sculptures as a modestly veiled woman. In one vase painting executed about the turn of the sixth and fifth centuries BCE, she was portrayed with a flower and a branch.[42] It has been suggested that the branch is possibly of a chaste tree [*Vitex agnus-castus*], which in ancient times was believed to be an anaphrodisiac, hence its name (see Pliny, in his *Historia Naturalis*).

Hestia had no epithets in the Athenian calendar.

Ares [Arês]: the son of Zeus and Hera, was the Olympian god of the destructive forces of war, battle-frenzy, and slaughter. This is in contrast to Athene, who represents intelligent and orderly war.[43] The other deities (apart from Aphrodite) didn't really like him because of his propensity to violence and bloodshed.[44] He was depicted as either a mature, bearded warrior dressed in armor, or a nude, beardless youth with helm and spear.[45]

Ares had no epithets in the Athenian calendar.

---

40. Hard, *Routledge Handbook of Greek Mythology,* 139–40.

41. Rice and Stambaugh. *Sources for the Study of Greek Religion*, (Atlanta, GA, The Society of Biblical Literature, 1979) 143.

42. Harrison, *Prolegomena to the Study of Greek Religion.* (Princeton: Princeton University Press, 1991) 366.

43. Price and Kearns, *Oxford Dictionary of Classical Myth & Religion,* 48–9.

44. Hard, *Routledge Handbook of Greek Mythology,* 168–70.

45. Seyffert, *Dictionary of Classical Antiquities,* 80–1.

Aphrodite [Aphroditê]: according to Homer, was the daughter of Zeus and the goddess Dione (but according to Hesiod sprang from the white foam that emanated from the castrated genitals of Ouranos when they were thrown into the sea); the goddess of love and beauty, and the embodiment of sexual pleasure (desire), seductive charm, and a capacity for deception. The Greeks thought of her as coming from the east and she was often given the name Kypris, the Lady of Cyprus.[46] As stated previously, Hesiod's tale is based on the supposed derivation of her name from *aphros* 'foam'.[47] She was also given the name Kytheria as on Cythera, off the Peloponnese, she had a shrine containing an armed wooden idol of Phoenician origin. It is likely she was an adaptation of the great Semitic love goddess known as the Phoenician Astarte or the Babylonian Ishtar. Aphrodite was the goddess of love, beauty, and fertility. She was depicted as a beautiful woman normally accompanied by the winged Eros (Love). She was often depicted nude.[48]

Her symbols included a dove, bird, apple, bee, swan, myrtle, rose, scallop shell, and mirror.[49]

Aphrodite had no epithets in the Athenian calendar.

Apollo/Apollon [Apollôn]: commonly referred to as Phoibos Apollon (Phoibos meant shining or radiant, and referred to his function as a god of light or the sun), was the son of Zeus and the goddess Leto; the twin brother of Artemis; and the god of the sun, presiding over prophecy and oracles; music and poetry; archery, healing, plague, purification, and the protection of young boys. He was comfortable with both his silver bow and his lyre.[50] His epithets were normally understood as meaning striking from afar—he could bring sudden death and disease to men and boys. Thus, *Hekatebolos* (strikes from afar, with his bow), *Hekebolos* (the afar, the distant one) and *Hekatos* (kills many, with plague). He was described as

---

46. Price and Kearns, *Oxford Dictionary of Classical Myth & Religion*, 36.

47. Grant and Hazel, *Who's Who in Classical Mythology*, 36.

48. Hard, *Routledge Handbook of Greek Mythology*, 194–8.

49. Burkert, *Greek Religion*, 152–6.

50. Price and Kearns, *Oxford Dictionary of Classical Myth & Religion*, 38–40.

the most Greek of the gods. He was depicted as a handsome, beardless youth with long hair, but a youth elevated to its ideal, which was manifest in the divine. His symbols included: the sun, a wreath and branch of laurel, bow and quiver, raven, lyre, dolphin, wolf, swan, and mouse.[51]

The epithets of Apollon specific to the Athenian calendar were:

- Apollon Patroos (ancestral Apollon) divine ancestor of the Athenians
- Apollon Lykeios (wolf god)
- Apollon Metageitnios (from the month Metageitnion)
- Apollon Pythios—Pythian Apollon (slayer of the python)
- Apollon Delphinios—Delphian Apollon (protector of the shrine at Delphi)
- Apollon Apotropaios (averter of evil)
- Apollon Nymphegetes (leader of the nymphs)
- Apollon Epikourios (the helper)

Artemis [Artemis]: the daughter of Zeus and Leto and the twin sister of Phoibos Apollon; the goddess of the moon, presiding over childbirth and the protectress of girls up to the age of marriage, as well as hunting and protecting young wild animals, and the wilderness they live in. Although not all scholars agree, it seems that she was known in Mycenaean times.[52] Artemis was portrayed as a tall young maiden wearing a short, knee-length chiton (tunic), carrying a bow and quiver, and accompanied by a stag or doe. She was often in the company of nymphs, hunting boars and swift deer, as well as dancing. She could bring sudden death and disease to women and girls. She was eternally virginal and her Homeric epithet was Mistress of Wild Animals.[53] Her symbols in-

51. Burkert, *Greek Religion*, 143–9.
52. Price and Kearns, *Oxford Dictionary of Classical Myth & Religion*, 59–60.
53. Hard, *Routledge Handbook of Greek Mythology*, 186–8.

cluded the moon, deer, hound, she-bear, snake, cypress tree,and bow and arrow.[54]

The epithets of Artemis specific to the Athenian calendar were:

- Artemis Hekate (the two became identified at a fairly early point, and sometimes even formed a triad with Selene)
- Artemis Agrotera (the Huntress)
- Artemis Elaphebolios (Shooter of the Deer)
- Artemis Lygodesma (willow)
- Artemis Caryatis (chestnut)
- Artemis Cedreatis (cedar)
- Artemis of Munichia (hilltop Artemis temple where victory of the Greek fleet over the Persians at Salamis was commemorated)

Hermes [Hermês]: the son of Zeus and Maia (Maia was the eldest of the seven Pleiades, who were mountain nymphs); the god of communication (messenger of the gods), and hence roads and travel; commerce, thievery, animal husbandry, hospitality, heralds, diplomacy, language, writing, persuasion, quick wit and cunning wiles, athletic contests, gymnasiums, astronomy, and astrology. He was the personal agent and herald of Zeus, as well as a psychopomp (guide bringing the dead to the underworld). He married Dryope, the daughter of Dryops, and his son was Pan, the god of nature. He was once thought to have been associated with the practice of creating a cairn of stones [*herma*] as a form of boundary, which developed into the ever-present quadrangular pillar with a bearded head and erect phallus called a herm. He was already known in Mycenaean times.[55] Hermes was depicted as either a handsome and athletic beardless youth, or in earlier art as a mature bearded man. He would normally have winged sandals or a winged hat.[56] His symbols included the herald's wand

54. Burkert, *Greek Religion*, 149–52.
55. Price and Kearns, *Oxford Dictionary of Classical Myth & Religion*, 254–6.
56. Hard, *Routledge Handbook of Greek Mythology*, 158–61.

[*kerykeion*] (Latin *caduceus*—a staff entwined with two snakes), winged boots or sandals, sometimes a winged traveler's cap and chlamys cloak, stork and tortoise (whose shell he used to invent the lyre).[57]

Hermes had no epithets in the Athenian calendar.

Athene [Athênê]: commonly referred to as Pallas Athene. (Depending on the tradition, Pallas was either a relative or companion, or a nymph, whom Athene accidentally killed as they practiced combat skills. A mournful Athene then took the name Pallas for herself.)[58] Her name may also have been taken from the appellation of a Mycenean warrior-goddess who was her predecessor.[59] She was the daughter of Zeus and the Titan Metis; the goddess of wisdom, women's handicrafts including weaving and spinning, courage, heroic endeavor, strategic warfare, and protectress of cities.[60]

Athene's father, Zeus, swallowed her mother, Metis (Titan goddess of wisdom, skill, or craft), while she was pregnant. Athene sprang from Zeus' head fully armed. She was a virgin with shining eyes, normally portrayed armed, crowned with a crested helmet, armed with shield and long spear, and wearing a goat-skin cloak [*aigis*] adorned with the monstrous head of the Gorgon.[61] Her symbols include the owl and the olive tree.[62]

The epithets of Athene specific to the Athenian calendar were:

- Athene Soter (savior or deliverer)

- Athene Polias (of the city)

- Athene Hygieia (Health)

- Athene Skiras (The festival of the Skira or Skirophoria was held at a sanctuary dedicated to Athene, under a ceremonial canopy called the skiron, in a place called Skiron, near Eleusis)

---

57. Burkert, *Greek Religion*, 156–9.
58. Hard, *Routledge Handbook of Greek Mythology*, 182–3.
59. Grant and Hazel, *Who's Who in Classical Mythology*, 57
60. Price and Kearns, *Oxford Dictionary of Classical Myth & Religion*, 68–70.
61. Hard, *Routledge Handbook of Greek Mythology*, 180–2.
62. Grant and Hazel, *Who's Who in Classical Mythology*, 55–57.

- Athene Phratria (*phratry* means "brotherhood" or "kinfolk," which was a social division of the Greek tribe)
- Athene Ergane (Labor)
- Athene Tritogeneia (possibly from her birthplace, Lake Tritonis in Libya, or the place where she was worshipped, the stream Triton in Boeotia, or from *tritô* (head) to signify she was born out of the head of her father)

Hephaistos [Hêphaistos]: the son of Hera, being born by parthenogenesis (without intercourse); the god of fire and the forge, presiding over blacksmiths and artisans. Despite being crippled and lacking bodily perfection, he was married to Aphrodite, who cuckolded him with Ares.[63] He was of foreign and probably Asiatic origin and was extensively worshipped in Attica by the craftsmen whose trades depended on using fire. Despite his great skills in fashioning objects from metal, his clumsy activities were laughed at by the other deities.[64] He seems to have originally been a volcanic deity with his cult spreading from the Aegean island of Lemnos to other volcanic regions.[65]

He was usually depicted as a bearded man holding a hammer and tongs—the tools of a smith.[66]

Hephaistos had no epithets in the Athenian calendar.

Dionysos [Dionusos]: the son of Zeus and the mortal Theban princess Semele; the god of wine and intoxication, vegetation, fertility, theater, festivity, epiphanies, and ritual madness or frenzied ecstasy. His dark side involved cults, blood sacrificing, and murderous frenzies. He was already known in Mycenaean times.[67] It used to be believed that he was a deity of foreign origin who arrived at a relatively late period. In earlier representations he was portrayed as a mature bearded man in long

---

63. Price and Kearns, *Oxford Dictionary of Classical Myth & Religion*, 248–9.

64. Hard, *Routledge Handbook of Greek Mythology*, 164–6.

65. Grant and Hazel, *Who's Who in Classical Mythology*, 157.

66. Seyffert, *Dictionary of Classical Antiquities*, 277–8.

67. Price and Kearns, *Oxford Dictionary of Classical Myth & Religion*, 169–74.

robes or wearing a panther skin or deerskin, wreathed in ivy or vine, holding a cup or drinking horn. Later representations show him as a youthful, effeminate, beardless figure, either lightly dressed or naked. His special emblem was the *thyrsos* (a staff tipped with a pine-cone or similar looking ornament, often entwined with ivy or vine).[68]

He was usually accompanied by a troop of satyrs and Mainades (Maenads—female devotees or nymphs). His symbols include the *thyrsos,* drinking cup, fruiting vine, ivy, tiger, panther, leopard, dolphin, and goat.[69]

The epithet of Dionysos specific to the Athenian calendar was:

- Dionysos Leneus (of the Wine-Trough)

---

68. Hard, *Routledge Handbook of Greek Mythology,* 170–80.
69. Burkert, *Greek Religion,* 161–7.

4: OTHER DEITIES, DAIMONES, AND HEROES

While the primary deities of the ancient Greeks were the twelve Olympians, there were numerous lesser deities, daimones (spirits), and heroes also enjoying patronage. The polytheistic and animistic world of the ancient Greeks pulsed with life. In one memorable scene in Homer's *Iliad*, Zeus summoned the gods to Mount Olympus. Apart from the twelve Olympians, all the nymphs and rivers came.[1]

The Greeks venerated an incredible number of non-Olympic deities, spirits [*daimones*], and heroes [*heros*].

The daimones lived in deserts, mountains, forests, rocks, and bodies of water. They brought positive and negative energies and experiences to mankind. Daimones occurred throughout nature and included the Centaurs.[2]

The daimones were intermediate beings, occupying a middle ground between deities and humanity. They communicated messages, prayers,

---

1. E. V. Rieu (trans.), *Homer: The Iliad* (Baltimore, MD, Penguin Books, 1961) 366.
2. Price and Kearns, *Oxford Dictionary of Classical Myth & Religion*, 257–8.

sacrifices and gifts from humanity to the divine, and subsequently commands and recompenses from the divine to humanity.[3]

The heroes included virtually all the Homeric characters as well as other humans who still exerted influence from their graves. Hero cults tended to be limited to a small locality, whereas deity cults were far more universal. Hero cults were unknown to the Mycenaeans and only became widespread in the eighth century BCE. Hero cults could be similar to worship paid to a deity at one end of the scale, and similar to the offerings paid to a dead relative at the other end.[4]

The Greek equivalent of ancestor worship involved caring for the graves of the ancestors. After burial, with its attendant sacrifices and banquet, the sacrifice and banquet were repeated on the third and ninth days. On the ninth day, food was brought to the grave. On the thirtieth day, which marked the end of the mourning period, a communal feast was held. After this, the dead were honored on the same day that the entire city honored its dead, the *genesia*.[5]

Let us look at a very small sample of deities, daimones, and heroes.

Hekate [Hekatê]: the daughter of Perses (Titan god of destruction) and Asteria (Titan goddess of divination), and cousin of Apollon and Artemis. She first appeared in Hesiod where she was portrayed as harmless, was not mentioned in Homer, and emerged in the fifth century as being associated with magick and witchcraft, lunar lore, creatures of the night, dog sacrifices, and illuminated cakes (sacrificial cakes with lit miniature torches), as well as doorways and crossroads. She was venerated in liminal places such as forks in the road. Her favorite offerings included red mullet (a scavenging fish tabooed in other cults), illuminated cakes (which could also be offered at the full moon), and puppies. Suppers of Hekate (offerings at the crossroads on the new moon) consisted of breadstuffs, eggs, cheese, and dog meat.[6]

---

3. Burkert, *Greek Religion*, 331–2.

4. Price and Kearns, *Oxford Dictionary of Classical Myth & Religion*, 257–8.

5. Burkert, *Greek Religion*, 194.

6. Price and Kearns, *Oxford Dictionary of Classical Myth & Religion*, 242–4.

Hekate was equated with Artemis from the fifth century BCE onward. She was portrayed as a virgin carrying torches (although these were sometimes also carried by Artemis) and accompanied by dogs. She was known as the goddess of the crossroads, which were actually meeting places of three pathways. Her triple-form character arose from the practice of hanging three masks at crossroads. Like Artemis, Hekate was a goddess of the moon (aspected to the dark of the moon), and as such, was much invoked by Thessalian witches.[7] Hekate may have originally come from Caria [*Karia*] in Asia Minor. According to Hesiod her name means 'she who has power far-off' and Zeus honored her more than any other deity, giving her power over land, sea and sky.[8]

Hekate had no epithets in the Athenian calendar.

Pan [Pan]: a god for whom there were fourteen versions of his parentage, but mostly his father as Hermes, while his mother was usually a nymph. He was portrayed as a man with goat feet and horns, and usually ithyphallic, or having a constant erection. He was a shepherd god and protector of shepherds, to whom were sacrificed kids, goats, or sheep, or alternatively presentations were made of votive offerings of herdsmen statuettes. He was also a hunting god presiding over small animals and birds, with Artemis was concerned with larger game.[9] Pan's name means 'shepherd' or literally 'feeder' [early Greek *Paon*]. He could sometimes be frightening as suggested by the derivation of *panic* from his name.[10]

He was venerated in caves and symbolized procreation. He invented the panpipe (seven-reed syrinx) and was capable of causing panic in individuals, animals, and armies. He was the god of nature, and lord of the satyrs.[11]

Pan had no epithets in the Athenian calendar.

---

7. Burkert, *Greek Religion*, 171.
8. Grant and Hazel, *Who's Who in Classical Mythology*, 151.
9. Price and Kearns, *Oxford Dictionary of Classical Myth & Religion*, 401–3.
10. Grant and Hazel, *Who's Who in Classical Mythology*, 254–5.
11. Burkert, *Greek Religion*, 172.

Nymphs [Numphai]: female nature spirits [*daimones*] living in mountains, trees, springs, and bodies of water. The name means 'young woman' or 'bride'.[12] See Greek Religion—Public, Household, Countryside chapter.

The Good Daimon / Agathos Daimon [Agathos Daimôn]: the only daimon to be venerated universally. He was represented as a snake and protected houses. The first libation in wine drinking was offered to him. (The Greeks normally diluted their wine with water.) He also received small libations of unmixed wine after meals.[13]

Hercules / Herakles [Hêraklês]: the son of Zeus and Alcmene [Alkmênê], and the greatest of Greek heroes. There were many legends of his epic feats. Herakles slayed or captured animals, and overcame fabulous monsters. He was closely guided by Athene throughout his adventures. He was adopted as a patron by many young men, especially those in military training or in gymnasiums.[14] His name literally means 'Hera's glory'.[15]

Asclepius / Asklepios [Asklêpios]: the son of Apollon and a mortal woman Coronis [Korônis], thus a hero. He was eventually elevated to the status of a healing god. In statues he was portrayed as a mature bearded man holding a staff with a snake coiled around it. In his healing sanctuaries, he was presented as a snake. Homer referred to him as a king of Thessaly who learned healing from the centaur Chiron.[16] The symbol of the Staff of Asklepios is still used in modern times to represent medicine and health care, but is often confused with the staff of the god Hermes, the caduceus [kerykeion].

---

12. Grant and Hazel, *Who's Who in Classical Mythology*, 233.
13. Price and Kearns, *Oxford Dictionary of Classical Myth & Religion*, 12.
14. Ibid., 251–3.
15. Grant and Hazel, *Who's Who in Classical Mythology*, 160.
16. Ibid., 62–4.

Nonspecific References to Deities

There were a number of references in literature to deities, without actually specifying which ones. When an Athenian wanted to consult the gods, invariably Zeus of Dodona and Apollon of Delphi were meant. The god sending rain meant Zeus. Jurors would swear by Zeus, Poseidon, and Demeter.[17] Thus, swearing to these gods would be the equivalent of today's "I swear to God."

---

17. Mikalson, *Athenian Popular Religion*, 66–7.

5: PERSONAL PRACTICE—
DAILY OBSERVANCES

Ancient Greek religion was characterized by appeals to ancient tradition and was simple in practice. The modern practice of Hellenismos must of necessity be different from that of the ancient Greek religion as society is very different now. No two people will practice Hellenismos exactly the same way unless they are following someone's instructions. My aim is to get people started as quickly, easily, and inexpensively as possible, whereupon they can find their own way. While elaborate regalia certainly has its place for some, it is unnecessary for beginners.

The Athenian religious calendar can be seen to consist of three cycles. First are the daily meal-based observances. Second is the monthly cycle, where certain days of the lunar month are devoted to particular deities. Last is the annual cycle which involves the major festivals. It would take a year of dedicated observance to experience them all. For those who have dedicated themselves to Hellenismos, this is a way of life and a blessing, and certainly not a burden.

I propose a one-month trial to experience an entire lunar cycle, which will be covered in the next chapter. One month is not an overly excessive period of time, but it is sufficiently long to experience the flavor of Hellenismos, with its deceptively simple yet deeply profound practices. But first, let's take a look at some preliminaries.

Purification of the Body

Regular bathing should take care of most everyday types of pollution, but anything more serious such as giving birth, coming into contact with the dead, and murder would require a combination of salt water, fire, and sulphur fumes. (Disinfectants should also have their place!) Just as the ancient Greeks were expected to be law-abiding citizens, practitioners of Hellenismos should be also. The unfortunate circumstance of murder is a matter for law enforcement authorities to deal with.

It is known that as an added precaution against pollution, prior to entering a sanctuary, hands were washed in pure water [chernips] poured from a jug. Given that rituals that were performed in sanctuaries will now be performed primarily in private homes, a small quantity of supermarket spring water can easily be used for this purpose, and can even be poured straight from the bottle. While not actually stipulated, a small quantity of this water can be poured on the hands prior to any worship, including daily meal-based rituals. Other practitioners may well be satisfied with the clean drinking water that flows through their plumbing, but I personally prefer spring water. Drinking water is treated with various chemicals which are then present in residual amounts. Spring water is derived from underground wells, but it may unfortunately also be tainted by chemicals seeping in through the soil, and so it's important to investigate its source.

It is not known whether there was some sort of ritual attached to bathing and/or washing the hands. I suggest visualizing all the pollution being washed away.

For major festivals, a more formal suggestion would be to pray to Hygeia, the goddess of health, during any bathing. A prayer can be improvised following the formula given in the chapter on Public Religion where to a certain extent you are praying from your heart. Alternatively, prayers can be preexisting, such as those taken from Homer's or Hesiod's writings, or even the Orphic and Homeric Hymns (these are written in a Homeric style, but postdate Homer's writings by several centuries).

The Orphic Hymns below were translated by the English Neoplatonist Thomas Taylor (1758–1835), and as such have a rather quaint sound.[1] The original Orphic Hymns were of course written in Greek and had Greek deity names in them. However, the fashion up until fairly recently was to refer to Greek deities by their corresponding Latin names. In keeping with this, Taylor's translation used Latin names. The hymns below have had the Greek names restored, which occasionally upsets their flow.

Orphic Hymn LXVII. To Hygeia [Health]

The Fumigation from Manna
O Much-desir'd, prolific, gen'ral queen, hear me,
life-bearing Hygeia, of beauteous mien,
Mother of all; by thee diseases dire,
of bliss destructive, from our life retire;
And ev'ry house is flourishing and fair,
if with rejoicing aspect thou art there:
Each dædal art, thy vig'rous force inspires,
and all the world thy helping hand desires;
Hades life's bane alone resists thy will,
and ever hates thy all-preserving skill.
O fertile queen,
from thee forever flows to mortal life from agony repose;
And men without thy all-sustaining ease,
find nothing useful, nothing form'd to please;
Without thy aid, not Aides' self can thrive,
nor man to much afflicted age arrive;
For thou alone of countenance serene,

---

1. Thomas Taylor, *The Hymns of Orpheus* (Los Angeles, The Philosophical Research Society, 1981).

dost govern all things, universal queen.

Assist thy mystics with propitious mind,

and far avert disease of ev'ry kind.

PURIFICATION OF SACRED OBJECTS AND VOTIVE OFFERINGS

The issue of pollution is specific to humans. It is pertinent, however, to ask whether sacred objects or votive offerings should be purified, and if so how this should be accomplished. For me it seems appropriate that anything placed in the service of deity should be as pure as possible.

There is very little pertinent information on this issue, but it is known that piglets were washed in the sea prior to being sacrificed for the Eleusinian Mysteries. Salt water was also one of the purification techniques used by humans, the others being bathing, fire, sulphur fumes, and of course, washing in pure water. Perhaps the same techniques can be used for sacred objects and votive offerings? Thus, each object or offering should be considered on a case by case basis and one of the techniques could be used. Sulphur fumes will work on most inanimate objects, as some objects will be ruined by water and others by fire. Regardless of the technique chosen, it is a good idea to visualize impurities being removed.

While the purification issue will not be mentioned again, it should be understood that everything used in the suggested rituals that follow is to undergo purification prior to use.

BRINGING HESTIA INTO THE HOME

The focal point of Greek religious practice was the hearth, which was used for cooking as well as heating, and was never extinguished. This was not an issue as it was constantly being used.

Right from the very beginning compromises and decisions have to be made, as in our society cooking and heating are normally separated. The closest equivalent to a hearth is the fireplace, but this is not normally used for cooking. Also, fireplaces are normally only used when there is a need for heat, meaning on cold winter days and cold nights. It seems somewhat extravagant to have a fire burning every day, even on the very hottest days. There is, however, nothing to stop a practitioner of Hellenismos from throwing small offerings of food into the fireplace, when it is lit. An obvious problem is that not every home has a fireplace.

Another option is to use some sort of grill or barbecue (barbeque) where food is cooked on a grate above hot charcoal. Offerings can then be made into the flames or onto the hot charcoal. A grill only produces heat when food is being cooked.

If a brazier and a charcoal block are being used to burn incense, then small food offerings can be made directly onto the glowing charcoal.

Each of these techniques would require a quick rededication to Hestia before each meal.

One way of discreetly simulating a hearth is to have a long-burning candle dedicated to Hestia. Once lit, it should burn until it almost extinguishes, whereupon it is used to light the next candle. As an example, there are inexpensive seven-day candles in tall glass containers which can be used, and a long matchstick can be used to transfer the flame to a new candle. Repeating this procedure would result in an inexpensive eternal flame to symbolize Hestia. Alternatively, an oil lamp could be used. Tiny offerings of food could be made by either holding them with tweezers or skewering them with a toothpick. Should the candle snuff out, it, or a new one, should be rededicated to Hestia. The problem is if you have small children or cats, such a candle or oil lamp could be tipped over, causing a fire hazard. If you wanted to try this technique, you would need a safe fireproof area, but this is not always possible in small apartments.

Another possible solution is to consider a modern stove as being roughly equivalent to the hearth, as it cooks food, but falls short in heating the home. In the case of gas stoves, the pilot light is always on, while in the case of electric stoves, the electricity is always present, except during a blackout of course. Those families who like to cook together may well see the stove as the heart of the home.

Practitioners need to intuit a way of having Hestia as part of their homes that resonates with them and feels right. Practitioners should never do anything that doesn't feel right, as the only way of making a true connection to the gods is through the heart. If the heart isn't resonating with a process then a true connection will remain elusive.

Again, a prayer can be improvised following the formula given in the chapter on Public Religion, or alternatively a preexisting prayer, such as an Orphic Hymn could be used.

Orphic Hymn LXXXIII. To Hestia

The Fumigation from Aromatics.
Daughter of Kronos, venerable dame,
the seat containing of unweary'd flame;
In sacred rites these ministers are thine,
Mystics much-blessed, holy and divine
In thee, the Gods have fix'd place,
strong, stable, basis of the mortal race:
Eternal, much-form'd ever-florid queen,
laughing and blessed, and of lovely mien;
Accept these rites, accord each just desire,
and gentle health, and needful good inspire.

CHOOSING DEITIES TO FOCUS ON

Given the large number of ancient Greek deities it is natural for practitioners of Hellenismos to focus on one to a greater extent than the others. There are historical precedents for this: cities would be dedicated to particular deities, as would various groups in society, as well as priests and priestesses. Individuals would feel called to serve particular deities. It is, however, important to not neglect other deities, and this is especially true for the twelve Olympians.

While practitioners of Hellenismos who dwell in the country could readily devote themselves to the rural deities outlined in the Countryside Religion chapter, the reality is that most practitioners live in cities and towns, and so the Athenian deities outlined in the Public Religion chapter would be most appropriate.

Choosing deities to work with is a matter of personal preference. We may feel drawn to particular deities, because of either familiarity, or because they correspond to an area of intense interest (thus, musicians may be drawn to Apollon, scholars to Hermes, tradesmen to Hephaistos). Alternatively, it may develop quite naturally—as we start working with the various deities in the Athenian Festival Calendar, we may find ourselves resonating with some of them more than others.

More is known about the intricacies of the Athenian calendar and of the religious practices of its people than anywhere else. Should such detail be ever made available for any other city-state, then that would be a very viable alternative for practitioners of Hellenismos.

Setting Up an Altar

Those who dedicate themselves to Hellenismos often have multiple altars to multiple deities, both inside and outside the home. But it is possible to get by with one if space is an issue, although one inside and one outside is much better. Traditionally, altars were small and made out of stone. This may not always be practical, and so the choice of the altar is really up to taste, perhaps being custom-made from wood or stone. A very practical inexpensive alternative is to use a night stand over which a piece of cloth is draped, or even setting aside a bookshelf. However, most bookshelf units only have twelve inches between shelves, and so it can be dangerous to light candles on them. Another alternative is to attach an inexpensive single shelf to a wall, which won't take up much space. Unless space is lacking, it is a good idea to set aside a permanent designated area for religious practices.

As an aside, one interesting nontraditional technique I have come across for being mindful of all twelve of the Olympians is to have twelve candles on a circular altar (tea lights work very well for this). The twelve candles can be arranged in a circle around a representation of Hestia (a long-burning candle or oil lamp), so as to symbolize the central position she occupied in Greek religion. Thus, regardless of the deity being venerated, all twelve Olympians will be borne in mind. A logical development of this is to assign a permanent position to each of the Olympians, marking the spot with a name, a picture, symbol, or statue. Of course, once this is done, the candles can either be left or dispensed with altogether. Should you choose to use this technique, I would suggest a second altar for non-Olympian deities would be required to ensure that they are not neglected.

The sun had a huge influence on the ancient rites and customs of all cultures. Funeral rites in particular reveal the universal belief that the east is the source of light, life, warmth, and happiness, while the west is the abode of darkness, death, cold, and sorrow. One author pointed out that "In acknowledgment of the divinity of the Sun, the Pagans turned to the east in prayer, and so constructed their temples that even the buildings themselves should pay homage to the rising sun."[2] The ancient Greeks were no exception, and I have previously pointed out that their temples faced the east.

It appears that the optimal direction to face when addressing deity is the east. My personal preference is to set up a home altar that enables me to face east.

Daily Meal-Based Offerings

The practitioner of Hellenismos can use every meal to reaffirm their bond to Hestia by offering her the first tiny morsel of food from every meal. This morsel should be offered in, or on, the chosen Hestia representation and allowed to burn completely. I would suggest a short prayer, or at least a thought, to Hestia while making the offering.

The beverage of choice for the Greeks was wine, which was drunk diluted with water. A few drops of unmixed wine were poured on the ground at the end of the meal as a libation to the Good Daimon or Aga-

2. William Tyler Olcott, *Sun Lore of All Ages: A Collection of Myths and Legends Concerning the Sun and Its Worship* (New York, G. P. Putnam's Sons, 1914) 265–273.

thos Daimon. In our society, not everyone drinks wine with every meal, and when wine is drunk, it is not diluted. A few drops of whatever beverage is being drunk should be saved as a libation for the Good Daimon at the end of the meal. Pouring a few drops of beverage onto the floor as was done in ancient Greece is obviously not advisable. It is possible to improvise by pouring the libation into a planter pot filled with dirt, which can then be periodically taken to a garden, following which the planter can be refilled with dirt. A nontraditional alternative is to have a large potted plant in the home, the watering of which can be supplemented with a few drops of libation—take care to not scald the plant should a hot beverage be used. A short prayer should be said while making the offering. Remember that without the prayer or dedication, a libation is nothing but spillage.

The offerings to Hestia and the Good Daimon effectively mark the beginning and end of the meal, and are relatively easy to incorporate into the daily routine. There are, however, other household deities to consider.

Apollon Patroos was the divine ancestor of the Athenians. Can practitioners of Hellenismos adopt him as a "spiritual" divine ancestor? By way of answer, it is important to remember that the whole household in ancient Athens venerated the household deities together. The household consisted of Athenians and non-Athenians—slaves and possibly metics (resident aliens without citizen rights in their Greek city-state [*polis*] of residence). I consider that having non-Athenians venerating Apollon Patroos sets a precedent. Practitioners of Hellenismos should persevere in building a relationship with Apollon Patroos to hopefully eventually avail themselves of the privilege of having him as a divine ancestor.

Zeus Herkeios, the protector of property boundaries, had his altar in the courtyard before the house. Strictly speaking, practitioners of Hellenismos should set up an outside altar, but this may not always be practical. Some practitioners live in apartments, in which case they could use their balcony or patio, while others simply wish to be discreet about their practices. Zeus Herkeios effectively protects the outside of the home, up to the perimeter of the property.

Apollon Agyieus protected the front door of the house from the outside in the form of a statue or even a small pillar. A small pillar by the front door would appear decorative and would effectively be a very discreet way of protecting the home from intruders. Herakles was also sometimes used in this role.

Zeus Ktesios (who actually had the form of a snake), the protector of the storehouse and guardian against thieves, had his altar inside the house. Strictly speaking, practitioners of Hellenismos should set up a separate altar with a representation of a snake on it, as well as a jar (traditionally two-handled, but plain glass will do) topped with a strip of white wool, filled with water, olive oil, and various seeds, grains, and fruits. The finished jar stood in the storeroom, and acted as a charm to increase household goods.[3] (See Appendix 3: Diet for a list of foods consumed).

So, how should these deities be venerated? The quickest and easiest way would be to make offerings to them immediately after the offering to Hestia, this way only one altar will be necessary.

Thus, practitioners of Hellenismos have two meal-based offerings, one short and one a little longer. Both should be preceded by washing the hands with pure water.

In the short version, one morsel of food is offered to Hestia, and the meal ends with a libation to the Good Daimon.

In the longer version, four morsels of food are offered. The first is to Hestia, goddess of the hearth. The second is to Apollon, our divine ancestor. The third is to Zeus, guardian of the outside of our home. The fourth is to Zeus, guardian of the inside of our home. At the end of the meal a libation is offered to the Good Daimon.

While one of these versions should be used at every meal in the home, how often the longer version is used is a personal choice as this information is not available. The short version strengthens the bonds

---

3. Jennifer Larson, *Ancient Greek Cults: A Guide* (New York, Routledge, 2007).

between the members of the household, while the longer version incorporates ancestral linkage and protection.

If time is an issue, wafting incense (frankincense being the incense of choice) enables the practitioner to venerate the household deities as well as deodorize the house.

COMMUNICATING WITH DEITIES

Rituals eventually lead to personal contact with the divine. This means a two-way flow of communication. Information that is received is normally personal, meaning that it is specific to our circumstances. It is not normally information that needs to be preached and shouted from the rooftops. This information can take the form of messages received in dreams, or even feelings intuited during the course of the day that have a quality of being distinct from our own thoughts.

A daily diary journal is the most important tool you can have in your own growth as a practitioner. Use it to keep track of your prayers, offerings, and experiences. Start with offerings that were traditional and experiment from there. Practitioners sometimes find that they obtain their best results with nontraditional offerings. Remember that the goal is to establish a personal relationship with the divine.

While a scientific understanding of the world around us has enabled amazing technological progress, I feel that it has contributed to our separation from the divine. A sense of childlike wonder, as encapsulated by the previously discussed word *thambos* (astonishment or amazement) is an important technique to reconnect with the divine. There is a world of difference between experiencing a storm front as a low pressure system as compared to a manifestation of the power of Zeus. Try to see the divine in everything around you. Food is a gift from Demeter. The love you feel in your heart is from Aphrodite and Eros. International travel, instant worldwide communication, and the information superhighway are all in the province of Hermes. The essence of polytheism is to experience divinities everywhere. In my experience, deities are quick to respond to those who earnestly seek them, but you need to open yourself up to them first. This is through opening your heart and not just your mind to the beauty and wonder of everything around you as well as each new day. This is done in the same manner that you open your heart to those you love.

The term used in various reconstructionist communities to describe such information is Unverified Personal Gnosis (UPG), and there is an element of controversy associated with it. Some reconstructionists dismiss it outright as heresy, saying that our sole focus should be on reconstructing ancient religion and practicing it. Others embrace it as a blessing but keep the details private. Still others embrace it and feel a calling to share it with anyone who is willing to listen. Practitioners will have to choose where they personally stand.

My attitude is that Hellenismos rituals have to be experiential to be meaningful. While I admire the dedication of those who devote themselves to performing rituals to the best of their ability in accordance with their understanding of how the ancients performed them while cultivating what they believe is the optimum mind-frame, I find them somewhat sad. Many people leave mainstream religions seeking something experiential. I could not in all conscience advocate a spiritual practice that is so inflexible that it yields no tangible results whatsoever. In a world where so many mainstream religions are offering boring and sterile rituals, why should Hellenismos be added to the list?

UPGs add vitality to personal practice as practitioners realize that the deities are real. Sharing notes with other practitioners about UPGs, and finding points of similarity is exciting. But trying to force UPGs as universal truth on others is generally not appropriate. As stated above, UPGs tend to be messages for individual use and/or growth.

REVIEW

Purify the body of miasma if necessary.

Wash hands in pure water.

Offer Hestia a tiny morsel of food at the beginning of every meal, while focusing mentally on her or using an Orphic Hymn.

Offer a few drops as a libation at the end of the meal to Agathos Daimon, while focusing mentally on him or using an Orphic Hymn.

By now, you should have purchased a notebook or journal and begun writing notations of your experiences and/or UPGs with the Greek deities. As you work with the deities, study the myths associated with them, in particular those having themes that tie in with your experiences. See the chapter on Comprehensive Study for a listing of references. This way the myths start to take on a life where you intuit what the writers were attempting to convey. This leads to a very personal understanding beyond anything attainable through study alone.

6: GREEK RELIGION— PUBLIC, HOUSEHOLD, COUNTRYSIDE

PUBLIC RELIGION

Public religion in ancient Greece consisted of a three-step process—procession, sacrifice, and prayer. Let's take a look at each.

Procession

Public rituals would typically begin with a procession [*pompê*]. Participants bathed, dressed in clean clothing, and wore twig garlands on their heads.[1]

The processions would vary, depending on the festival and the deity. Normally they would start from the city or town in question and end at the temple or sanctuary of the deity.

In one local festival to Artemis, described by Xenophon of Ephesus (probably second century CE), those present would carry sacred objects, torches, baskets, and incense; and would be followed by horses, dogs, hunting equipment, and seductively dressed young girls along with young men. This is just one example of a procession, and is not necessarily typical.

---

1. Burkert, *Greek Religion*, 56.

In the Panathenaia, which was the main annual festival to honor Athene Polias (of the city), the lavish procession was headed by sacrificers bearing sacrificial materials; a heifer, sow, and ewe to be sacrificed; two shawm [*aulos*] players (a shawm is a single- or double-reed pipe played in pairs); a lyre player; and worshippers carrying olive branches.[2] Numerous citizens were involved, including hoplite warriors and cavalrymen, old men, and young women who wove the embroidered, saffron-dyed robe [*peplos*] to be worn by the olive-wood cult statue of Athene. There were also resident aliens and foreigners, and possibly even slaves. The festival was very much a statement demonstrating the unity and grandeur of Athens.[3] It was also a statement that non-Athenians were welcome to participate.

The Panathenaia was celebrated during Hekatombaion, the birthday of Athene. Every fourth year it was celebrated more elaborately as the Greater Panathenaia. According to Aristotle's *The Athenian Constitution* (chapter 60) there would be a musical competition, athletic contests, and a horse race, with prizes being awarded to the winners.[4]

While not all festivals included competitions, when they did occur, they were always part of a religious festival.[5]

The point of the procession was to bring the whole community together and transport everything necessary for the sacrifice to take place in accordance with ancestral traditions.

Sacrifice

The central aspect of public religion was the slaughter and consumption of one or more animals as part of a festivity for the whole community. The most prestigious animal to sacrifice was the cow or ox, but sheep, goats, pigs, and cocks were far more common. Another consider-

---

2. Price, *Religions of the Ancient Greeks*, 29–33.
3. Zaidman and Pantel, *Religion in the Ancient Greek City*, 105–6.
4. Rice and Stambaugh, *Sources for the Study of Greek Religion*, 117–121.
5. Zaidman and Pantel, *Religion in the Ancient Greek City*, 107.

ation was that certain deities preferred various sacrifices, for instance Athene liked cows and Demeter liked pigs.[6]

Sacrificial victims were carefully examined, as they had to be pure and unblemished of body and spirit. The historian, Middle Platonist, and Delphic priest Plutarch (c. 50–120 CE) outlined a number of these tests in *Moralia* (437a–b). Homer's writings have numerous accounts of the blood sacrifice [*thusia*].[7]

The victims were led to the altar by the priest and sacrificers. The victims were wreathed, entwined with woolen ribbons, and their horns gilded. At the place of sacrifice, everyone gathered around the altar. The sacrificial basket containing the sacrificial knife underneath barley grains or cakes was carried on the head of a blameless maiden leading the procession. Someone else brought a vessel of water, there was normally an incense burner, and at least one flute player. The sacrificial basket and water vessel were carried around the outside of the assembled throng, effectively tracing out a circle separating the sacred from the profane.

Water was poured from a jug over the hands of each participant and on the head of the victim, causing it to nod its agreement to the sacrifice. Barley grains were thrown by each participant at the altar and the victim. The sacrificer then produced the knife and cut some hairs from the victim's forehead, and threw them on the fire.

To the accompaniment of a ritual scream from the women the victim was slaughtered. Smaller animals were held above the altar and had their throats slit. An ox would be stunned by an axe blow, after which its throat was slit, and blood would gush over the altar.

The victim would be skinned and roasted, and a small portion of thigh meat (the least edible part) rolled in fat was thrown into the fire for the deity. The rest of the meat was distributed among the participants.[8]

---

6. Garland, *Religion and the Greeks*, 12.
7. Warrior, *Greek Religion*, 57–62; Rice and Stambaugh, 107–8.
8. Garland, *Religion and the Greeks*, 12–14. Burkert, *Greek Religion*, 56–7.

The normal Greek diet was based on plant foods and dairy products. Meat was a luxury item that many could not afford.[9] The blood sacrifice was a form of social welfare that brought the community together and ensured that all received a fair portion, while demonstrating piety.

By way of contrast to the practice of blood sacrifice, the Neoplatonist philosopher Porphyry (c. 234–c. 305 CE) related the story of the most famous oracle in Greece, the Delphic oracle, singling out a poor man called Klearchos (Clearchus) as the most pious of his time. Klearchos

> ... diligently sacrificed to them [the Gods] at proper times in every month at the new moon, crowning and adorning the statues of Hermes and Hekate, and the other sacred images which were left to us by our ancestors, and that he also honored the Gods with frankincense, and sacred wafers and cakes. He ... performed public sacrifices annually, omitting no festive day and that in these festivals he worshipped the Gods, not by slaying oxen, nor by cutting victims into fragments, but that he sacrificed whatever he might casually meet with, sedulously offering the first-fruits to the Gods of all the vegetable productions of the seasons, and of all the fruits with which he was supplied. ... some of these he placed before the [statues of the] Gods, but that he burnt others on their altars; and that, being studious of frugality, he avoided the sacrificing of oxen.

Summarizing, all Klearchos' sacrifices were bloodless, consisting of incense, barley-cakes, wheat-cakes, and first fruits. He was careful to attend every single public festival and performed all his domestic observances.

Porphyry then related the story of certain tyrants offering Apollon magnificent sacrifices of hecatombs (100 beasts) after the Carthaginians were conquered. They afterward inquired of Apollon which of the offerings he was most pleased with, whereupon he indicated the cakes of

---

9. Price, *Religions of the Ancient Greeks*, 34.

Docimus. Docimus was a poor farmer from Delphi, who had sacrificed a few handfuls of meal from a bag that was fastened round him.

Porphyry then bolstered his argument by quoting the poet, Antiphanes:

In simple offerings most the Gods delight:
For though before them hecatombs are placed,
Yet frankincense is burnt the last of all.
An indication this that all the rest,
Preceding, was a vain expense, bestowed
Through ostentation, for the sake of men;
But a small offering gratifies the Gods.[10]

Porphyry stated that Triptolemus, the most ancient of the Athenian legislators, established laws for the Athenians, and that three of his laws still remain in Eleusis, which are:

"Honor your parents; Sacrifice to the Gods from the fruits of the earth; Injure not animals." [11]

Porphyry's *On Abstinence from Animal Food* is essential reading for anyone who mistakenly believes that blood sacrifice is the only sort of sacrifice that is pleasing to deities. Porphyry actually went so far as to claim that bloodless sacrifices were superior.

Returning to the acceptability of humble offerings, Socrates believed that his small sacrifices were not inferior to those from people wealthier than himself, making frequent and large sacrifices. He believed that the joy of the gods was "greater in proportion to the holiness of the giver," and was an admirer of Hesiod's statement:

"According to thine ability do sacrifice to the immortal gods." [12]

Socrates said that there was no better motto for a man than: *"Let a man do according to his ability."* [13]

---

10. Taylor, *On Abstinence*, 2.16–17.
11. Ibid., 4.22.
12. Hesiod. *Works and Days.* 336
13. Dakyns, *Xenophon: Anabasis*, 1.3.

While the blood sacrifice was the best-known aspect of public religion, there were certainly those who fulfilled their obligations toward deities with small humble sacrifices as well as bloodless offerings. Bloodless sacrifices are described as pure—*hagna thymata* (pure sacrifices).[14]

According to the playwright Aristophanes (c. 446—c. 386 BCE) and the commentary of an ancient scholiast, the wealthy would leave offerings of dinner, consisting of bread and other things, to Hekate on the thirtieth, while the poor would live off these offerings. The thirtieth was the new moon and the offerings would traditionally be left at a crossroads. This is a form of social welfare very similar to the public sacrifice detailed above.

My preference is for bloodless sacrifices. Those who choose to offer meat can set aside portions from store-bought meat. I do not think that animal sacrifice has any place in contemporary society. However, a couple of exceptions come to mind. Those who legally slaughter their own food, either by working on a farm or in a slaughterhouse, could offer the life of the animal to the deity they're venerating. Those who hunt could make offerings to Artemis for large game or Pan for small game, while those who fish could make offerings to Poseidon.

In ancient times, a procession was a group of people with pre-assigned roles taking an animal to a place of slaughter. If you're fortunate enough to have a group of practitioners you can also have a procession from a meeting point to a place of offering. Given that offerings were meal based, it would make sense to treat a procession like a formal picnic or potluck, with everyone having preassigned roles, and walking to a spot to share a meal. For the ancients, a festival was much more than sharing food, thereby building community. There were friendly competitions—athletic events, poetry recitals, and the playing of musical instruments—with prizes awarded to the winners.

---

14. Burkert, *Greek Religion*, 59.

Prayer

In *Euthyphro* (14c) Plato suggested that sacrificing was making a gift to the gods, while prayer was asking them for something. In *Politicus* (290c–d) he pointed out the priests were intermediaries who used sacrifices to give gifts on our behalf to the gods and then prayed on our behalf to acquire things.[15]

Prayers would typically commence with citing a number of the deity's titles and where the deity ruled. The deity would be reminded of what services the petitioner had performed in the past, and what they were prepared to perform in the future. A relationship of reciprocity was thus formed.[16]

An example of a formula that can be employed is borrowed from the very beginning of Homer's *Iliad*, which opens with a prayer for vengeance to his god by Chryses, the priest of Apollon.

> *"Hear me," he cried, "O god of the silver bow, that protectest Chryse and holy Cilla and rulest Tenedos with thy might, hear me oh thou of Sminthe. If I have ever decked your temple with garlands, or burned your thigh-bones in fat of bulls or goats, grant my prayer, and let your arrows avenge these my tears upon the Danaans."*

Its structure is very simple and can readily be adapted to use for any deity:

> "Hear me,
> < *insert epithets or titles of deity and description of role of deity* >,
> If ever I have …
> < *remind deity of sacrifices and offerings made in the past* >
> … bring this prayer to fulfillment:
> < *insert request to deity* >"

---

15. Warrior, *Greek Religion: A Sourcebook*, 55.
16. Garland, *Religion and the Greeks*, 11–12.

Obviously the request has to be in keeping with the nature of the deity being called. In this case, the priest asked Apollon to unleash his spears of pestilence. If insufficient sacrifices and prayers were made in the past to sway the deity being called, promises of future sacrifices and offerings can be made, or even the completion of a task.

When praying to the deities, Socrates used a simple formula:

Give me that which is best for me.

This was an expression of trust that the deities know best what good things are. Prayer was based on reciprocity—the worshipper would establish a relationship where deity remembered the gift or sacrifice and felt well disposed in the future. This did not imply indebtedness.[17]

As part of prayer, gestures were important. To invoke the heavenly deities, the hands are raised to the sky with upturned palms. To invoke sea deities, the hands are extended toward the sea. To invoke a cult image (statue or picture), the hands are stretched toward the image. To invoke the dead or the chthonic (underworld) deities, lay on the ground and pound the earth with the fists,[18] somewhat reminiscent of a child having a tantrum.

HOUSEHOLD RELIGION

Ancient Greek Homes

The earliest Greek country homes were free standing and typically consisted of a single large room, with a porch on one side and a hearth in its midst. They were surrounded by a courtyard, which in turn was surrounded by a wall or fence. In cities, a lack of space caused this design to be modified with houses adjoining, fences disappearing and courtyards shrinking.[19]

---

17. Dakyns, *Xenophon: Anabasi*, 1.3; Pulleyn, *Prayer in Greek Religion*, 12–13.
18. Burkert, *Greek Religion*, 75.
19. Nilsson, *Greek Folk Religion*, 65–66.

In cities, the houses of the poor consisted of one room, in which partitions would be used to make up different living spaces. The houses of the wealthy, however, would have a central courtyard flanked by rooms on all sides and with one entrance coming from the road. The women had their own separate quarters [*gynaikeion*].[20]

The hearth was the source of warmth and the place for cooking within the house. It was also the center of the house cult.

Household Worship

The main household deities were as follows.

Hestia (a small amount of food was offered to her before the meal); the focal point of the household was the hearth, and it was to the hearth that all members of the household were bound. At every meal the bond to Hestia was reaffirmed by giving her the first morsel of food.

The other household deities were:

Apollon Patroos, divine ancestor of the Athenians.

Apollon Agyieus (of the street), protected the door of the house from outside in the form of a statue or even a small pillar. Sometimes Herakles would take over this role.

Zeus Herkeios (of the fence), protector of property boundaries, whose altar stood in the courtyard before the house—his function was to protect the home against intruders.

Zeus Ktesios, protector of the storehouse and guardian against thieves, who actually had the form of a snake and whose altar was inside the house. He was represented by a two-handled jar, wreathed with a white

---

20. Garland, *Daily Life of the Ancient Greeks*, 83–85.

woolen fillet, and filled with water, olive oil, and various seeds, grains, and fruits.

The father of the household would acknowledge the contribution of these deities on a daily basis, either with a small offering to them, incense, or just a word.

The Good Daimon or Agathos Daimon, another snake form, for whom a few drops of unmixed wine were poured on the ground as a libation at the end of the meal.

Athenians standing for public office were asked if they had shrines to Apollon Patroos and Zeus Herkeios. There is no record of them being asked how they venerated these two deities, as that was probably up to their personal discretion.

Worship at the household shrines was organized by the head of the household, probably on a daily basis, and the entire household, including slaves, participated. This would ensure that the entire household was protected by the gods. The exact specifics of worship would have undoubtedly varied from house to house. There was no formal training for priests and priestesses, so obviously there would be no formal training for heads of households. It is likely that each family had their own practices handed down from generation to generation.

Inclusion into the Household

As mentioned, the center of the house cult was the hearth. Anyone who was to be included in the household had to be brought to the hearth.

In Athens, five-day-old babies would be brought into the household for the first time, probably from the women's quarters. The baby would be carried by a member of the household who ran around the hearth, thereby assuring the baby of Hestia's protection.

Who actually carried the baby is uncertain as it could have been the parents, the midwives, or the head of the household. New slaves and in-laws were admitted to the household in a shower of "dates, small cakes, sweetmeats, dried figs, and nuts." [21]

COUNTRYSIDE RELIGION

The Greeks tended to focus on the deities they had around them. Thus, the peasants living in the countryside focused their attention on nature deities.

Rain was of vital importance in agriculture, and so Zeus, the cloud-gatherer and thrower of the thunderbolt, whose home was on the highest mountain in the area, was prayed to. The flocks had to be looked after, and to this end Hermes, Apollon Lykeios, and Pan were prayed to. As a babe, Hermes had stolen the oxen of Apollon; Apollon's epithet Lykeios refers to protection against wolves. [22]

A prominent nature deity was the Arcadian god, Pan, who was partly human, but had the legs, horns, beard, and libido of a he-goat, played the syrinx, and would protect flocks but could also induce sudden panic. [23]

The worship of the earth goddess Gaia/Ge was very simple, having developed from the practice of pouring libations, and involved carrying water to an indentation in the ground. The winds were sacrificed to, often to affect harvest prospects. [24] The gods of the four winds were Boreas in the north, Zephyros in the west, Notos in the south, and Eurus in the east. [25]

It was believed that rivers were gods and the springs were nymphs. Their worship was limited to specific localities and each city would worship its own river or spring. The river gods were represented as bulls or bulls with human heads. A river would normally have a temple to receive

---

21. Mikalson, *Athenian Popular Religion*, 84.

22. Nilsson, *Greek Folk Religion*, 5–10.

23. H. J. Rose, *Gods & Heroes of the Greeks: A Handbook of Greek Mythology* (Peter Smith, Publisher, 1928), 24; Nilsson, *A History of Greek Religion*, 10.

24. Burkert, *Greek Religion*, 175.

25. Seyffert, *Dictionary of Classical Antiquities*, 98, 703.

offerings. Children reaching puberty would dedicate their hair, votive offerings were brought, and animals were sacrificed. These offerings demonstrate that the Greeks did not take their fresh water supply for granted.
The system was not perfect as in Lerna the large spring became polluted
by excessive sacrifice.[26] There was even a proper way to cross a river. Hesiod wrote that one should say a prayer and wash one's hands in its water.[27]

Nymphs were female nature spirits [*daimones*], who were normally
described as the daughters of Zeus, Gaia, or various river gods. While
the nymphs were primarily associated with springs, they could also be
associated with rivers and lakes. Wood nymphs inhabited the glades and
dells of the forest regions. Their cult places were associated with natural features such as rivers, springs, and caves.[28]

Nymphs are distinguished by epithets such as Naiads or spring-
nymphs (*naein* means "to flow"), Oreads or nymphs of the hills (*oros*
means hill or mountain), Potamiads of rivers (*potamoi* means river), as
well as Dryads (*dryades* from trees, especially oak), Hamadryads who
haunt trees and die when the tree dies.[29] Other trees that nymphs are associated with are the plane tree, black poplar, elm, and ash, as well as fruit
and nut trees. They can also be associated with grasses, flowers, and ferns.

Nymphs were capable of possessing susceptible individuals, in a
phenomenon referred to nympholepsy, leading to heightened awareness and improved verbal skills. A nympholept was a solitary male individual who was very devoted to the nymphs. There are accounts of
nympholepts dwelling in caves, sometimes carving out stairs and stat-

26. Burkert, *Greek Religion*, 174–5.
27. Hugh G. Evelyn-White, *Hesiod, Homeric Hymns, Epic Cycle, Homerica*,
    (Cambridge, MA, Harvard University Press, 2000), 57.
28. Jennifer Larson, *Greek Nymphs: Myth, Cult, Lore* (New York, Oxford
    University Press, 2001) 3–5; George Rawlinson, *The Religions of the Ancient
    World* (New York, John B. Alden, Publisher, 1885), 132.
29. Rose, *Gods & Heroes of the Greeks*, 25.

ues, and sometimes planting gardens. These caves would become cult sites with visitors leaving offerings.[30]

According to the historian Pausanias, frankincense with honey-kneaded wheaten cakes were burned on altars to the nymphs in Olympia, but no libations were poured.[31]

The leader of the nymphs was the goddess Artemis, who was the twin sister of Apollon and the most popular goddess of Greece. She was a huntress known as the "Lady of Wild Things" and was found in the mountains and meadows. She was closely associated with the tree cult, and had the epithets *Lygodesma* after the willow, *Caryatis* after the chestnut, and *Cedreatis*, after the cedar.[32]

The Greek geographer Strabo (63 or 64 BCE—c. 24 CE) wrote that near the mouth of the Alpheios River—in sacred precincts generally full of flowers because of the abundance of water—there are shrines of Artemis Alpheionia or Alpheiusa (the epithet is spelled both ways), Artemis Elaphia and Artemis Daphnia. The country is also full of temples of Aphrodite and the Nymphs, there are multiple shrines of Hermes along the roads, and temples of Poseidon on the capes.[33]

The nymphs were the best known of the nature spirits. Other nature spirits lived in deserts, mountains, forests, and rocks. They brought positive and negative energies and experiences to mankind, and hence neither construed to be good or evil, rather, neutral. The Sileni (forest men with horse ears and sometimes also horse tails and legs) were fountain spirits, which were also fertility spirits along with the satyrs (originally forest men with pointed ears, but later took on goat attributes).[34]

---

30. Larson, *Greek Nymphs,* 10–11, 13–20.

31. Zaidman and Pantel, *Religion in the Ancient Greek City,* 41; Peter Levi (trans). *Pausanias: Guide to Greece: Volume 2 Southern Greece* (New York, Penguin Books, 1985) 244.

32. Nilsson, *Greek Folk Religion,* 15–16.

33. Jones, *Straho,* 47–49.

34. Nilsson, *History of Greek Religion,* 106–111.

A particularly poignant anecdote regarding nature deities can be found in the *Phaedrus*, written around 370 BCE by the classical Greek philosopher Plato (c. 427 BCE–c. 347 BCE), who together with his teacher, Socrates, and his student, Aristotle, lay the philosophical foundations of Western culture. The *Phaedrus* features a dialogue between Socrates and his young friend Phaedrus, who appears in several of Plato's dialogues. They found themselves a resting-place by a cool stream on a shaded slope of fresh grass, where they enjoyed the chorus of cicadae and fragrances. It was noon, which was the time most likely to yield divine epiphanies. Socrates began to experience nympholepsy, resulting in poetic inspiration.[35] Seeing ornaments and images, they deduced that it was a spot sacred to Achelous and the nymphs. Achelous was the chief of all river deities as he was the patron deity of the largest river in Greece, the Achelous River. At the end of their dialogue, Socrates offered a prayer to the local deities:

> *Beloved Pan, and all ye other gods who haunt this place, give me beauty in the inward soul;*
> *and may the outward and inward man be at one.*
> *May I reckon the wise to be the wealthy,*
> *and may I have such a quantity of gold as a temperate man and he only can bear and carry.*
> *—Anything more? The prayer, I think, is enough for me.* [36]

It is a reasonable assumption that the ancient Greeks had a very respectful attitude toward all of nature, as there was no place where deities and spirits were not present. The large number of shrines mentioned suggests that at least an awareness of deities and spirits was shared by many people, while the nympholepts felt the presence of nature spirits in a very real and powerful way.

---

35. Festugiere, *Personal Religion Among the Greeks*, 9, 19.
36. Benjamin Jowett, *Phaedrus by Plato*, http://www.gutenberg.rg/etext/1636.

Review

Are you journaling your experiences and/or UPGs on a regular (preferably daily) basis?

Are you doing background reading to enhance your knowledge and relationship with deities?

Have you been making regular meal offerings?

Have you chosen specific deities to concentrate on more than others?

Do you have an altar set up yet?

Have you made room for the additional household deities: Apollon Patroos, Apollon Agyieus (or Herakles), Zeus Herkeios, and Zeus Ktesios?

Have you made an offering jar for Zeus Ktesios?

7: A THUMBNAIL SKETCH OF GREEK HISTORY

Greek religion did not develop within a vacuum, but rather within the context of historic events. Both the turmoil of war and trading in times of peace brought foreign influences into Greece. Having a basic understanding of Greek history aids in understanding the development of religion as an integral part of Greek culture.

MINOAN AND MYCENAEAN CIVILIZATIONS

Greek culture developed in the coastal areas around the Aegean Sea, and the islands within it, rather than on the land masses of the Greek mainland.[1]

The culture of the inhabitants of the island of Crete rose beyond the Neolithic level at the end of the fourth millennium BCE, when copper began to be used. It is thought that this technology was introduced from Syria or southern Asia Minor, and then enhanced through trade with Egypt and other Aegean islands. The culture that developed is now referred to as Minoan, taking its name from Minos, the legendary king

---

1. Morton Smith. *The Ancient Greeks* (Ithaca, Cornell University Press, 1960) 1.

of Crete. The Minoans traded beautiful works of art for which they were renowned.[2]

Until recently it was believed that the Minoans were a peaceful society with no need for fortifications. In May 2010 a team of archaeologists debunked this myth by announcing that they had found formidable defenses around the Minoan town of Gournia. The townspeople had engaged in making wine and working bronze and stone, and prudently opted to protect their livelihoods.[3]

Traders carried Minoan culture throughout the eastern Mediterranean, and eventually developed a culture along the eastern coast of Greece around 1600 BCE. This Greek culture is now referred to as Mycenaean, after the first site to be excavated—Mycenae, where the legendary Agamemnon had ruled.[4]

By about 1500 BCE the Mycenaeans began to challenge the Minoans by trading copies of their artworks. Sometime after 1400 BCE Crete was attacked, quite possibly by Mycenaean raiders, resulting in the end of the Minoan culture. The Mycenaeans traded with Egypt and Syria, as had the Minoans, as well as southern Italy and Sicily.[5] In June 2010, archaeologists announced finding evidence that the Mycenaeans had also traded with the pagans who lived in the area now known as Israel, in the form of intact 3,500-year-old cultic vessels. Some of these vessels had been imported from Mycenae.[6]

The famous Trojan War took place around 1200 BCE, and appeared to mark the beginning of the end of the Mycenaean civilization, which vanished by about 1100 BCE (or 1150 BCE depending on the source consulted). To this day, it is uncertain exactly why the civilization ended.

---

2. M. Smith, *Ancient Greeks*, 1–2.

3. Owen Jarus, "Crete Fortifications Debunk Myth of Peaceful Minoan Society," *The Independent*, May 5, 2010.

4. M. Smith, *The Ancient Greeks*, 2–3.

5. Ibid., 3.

6. Tzvi Ben Gedalyahu, "Rare Discovery of 3,500-Year-Old Objects," *Israel National News*, June 7, 2010.

It has been suggested that several civilizations, including the Mycenaean civilization, met their end in 1175 BCE (the eighth year of Ramesses III) as a result of attacks by "Sea Peoples," whose actual identity remains the subject of dispute among scholars. The Sea Peoples were finally defeated by the Egyptians after 1200 BCE. Even if the Mycenaeans survived the attacks, it is quite possible that trade routes were severely cut, which could have led to domestic revolution.[7] There is no agreed-upon consensus among academics as to the dates when the Mycenaean civilization met its end and when the Sea Peoples were defeated, which can lead to confusion when quoting from multiple sources.

Most academics believe that Greece at this point entered a Dark Age. Fortunately, Greece's glorious past was not forgotten, but enshrined in legends. The possibility of this belief being erroneous is discussed below.

Later Greeks believed in a non-Hellenic indigenous population called Pelasgian, remnants of whom survived into Classical times. Herodotus (discussed in the Comprehensive Study chapter) explained that the Greeks consisted of two main branches—the Ionians (who were Pelasgians by descent) and the Dorians (who were the Hellenics). Athenian legends insisted that the Athenians were Ionians and indigenous.[8]

During the Dark Age, in the three centuries after the Trojan War, Greek traditions detail a number of movements of the various tribes. In ancient times it was believed that the Dorians originated in the northerly mountainous regions and swept south displacing other tribes in the process, occupying southern and eastern Peloponnesus, Crete, Rhodes, and southwestern Asia Minor. The Achaeans, who had occupied Mycenae and southern Peloponnesus, moved to northern Peloponnesus and displaced the Ionians. The Ionians, assisted by kinsmen from Athens, took over the central islands of the Aegean and the central part of the west coast of

---

7. Gary Beckman, "Hittite Chronology," *Akkadica*, 119/120 (2000). Beckman is a professor at the University of Michigan.

8. Kitto, *The Greeks*, 15.

Asia Minor. The Aeolians from Thessaly moved to the island of Lesbos and the northern section of the coast.[9]

The Homeric Greek language, as spoken by the Dorians, is closely related to numerous other languages from Europe and Asia, including Vedic Sanskrit, Hittite, and related Anatolian languages, suggesting that there was a spoken proto-language called Indo-European. Just where the Indo-Europeans originally came from is subject to speculation, with suggestions being offered ranging from the Altai Mountains in Siberia to northern Germany.[10]

The Dark Ages saw a return to barbarism. Monumental building stopped. Technical expertise in the production of artwork and pottery declined. Writing stopped.

Eventually a cultural tradition reestablished itself. Greece began to prosper again in the eighth or ninth century BCE, and the Dark Age was finally over. The end of the Dark Age coincided with the writing of the poetry of Homer (discussed in the Further Study chapter).[11]

It used to be believed that the Mycenaean culture of the second millennium BCE was pre-Hellenic and ended in the twelfth century BCE, while the Archaic Greek period began with Homer in the eighth century BCE. Study of the pottery of these two periods gave rise to the idea of Mycenaean art (elegant with simple motifs and concentric circles) and Geometric art (straight lines and geometrical motifs), respectively. While it was believed that there was a complete break between the Mycenaean and Archaic Greek periods, continuities were detected between the art styles of these periods.[12]

In 1900, English scholar Sir Arthur Evans (1851–1941) found ancient scripts in Crete, which he called Minoan writing. He identified three phases. The earliest, which he termed hieroglyphic, consisted of recog-

---

9. Smith, *Ancient Greeks*, 6.

10. Burkert, *Greek Religion*, 15–16.

11. Smith, *Ancient Greeks*, 7.

12. Chamoux, *Civilization of Greece*, 37.

nizable symbols, similar to the early pictorial script of Egypt, and were dated to 2000–1650 BCE. He called the next stage Linear A, where the symbols had been reduced to outlines, and were dated to 1750–1450 BCE. Linear A is unique to Crete. He called the final stage Linear B, which was a modified script, and could be dated to 1400 BCE.[13]

Drawing heavily on the work of Professor Alice Kober (1906–1950),[14] architect Michael Ventris (1922–1956) succeeded in translating the Linear B script in 1952, proving that it was Greek. This indicated that there had been a Minoan-Mycenaean culture on Crete that was writing in Greek some 500 years earlier than had been previously thought. In deciphering the text and reconstructing the vocabulary and grammar, Ventris was assisted by John Chadwick (1920–1998), a Lecturer in Classics at Cambridge University. Linear B texts have also been found on the Greek mainland, suggesting that Linear B was the result of adapting Minoan script for the writing of Greek. The use of the Linear B tablets so far found has been limited to record keeping purposes for the palaces of Knossos, Pylos, and Mycenae, and contain inventories, lists, and statements of dues. Thus, the Linear B tablets provide an insight into everyday life of the Mycenaean and Minoans.[15]

The Mycenaeans were definitely Greek. Many of their personal names were obviously Greek. Curiously, all of the Linear B inscriptions are limited to tablets and inscribed jars. There is nothing on any buildings or gravestones. Literacy appeared to be limited to palace scribes. There is also evidence for the historicity of some of Homer's accounts.[16]

---

13. John Chadwick, *The Decipherment of Linear B* (New York, Modern Library Paperback, 1958) 12–13.
14. Laura A. Voight, "Professor Alice Kober: 1907–May 16, 1950," in *Breaking Ground: Pioneering Women Archaeologists*, ed. Getzel M. Cohen and Martha Sharp Joukowsky (Ann Arbor Michigan University of Michigan Press, 2006.
15. Chamoux, *Civilization of Greece*, 38–9.
16. Chadwick, *Decipherment of Linear B*, 101–33.

As an illustration of the lack of absolute certainty in any studies of ancient Greece, even the almost universally accepted concept of the Dark Age may be false. Many Mycenaean features reappeared with very little change in the new Greek society of the Geometric period, including jewelry making, ivory carving, weaving, carpet manufacture, similar painted pottery motifs, bronzes, and ceramic models. Also, the Greek alphabet of the eighth century BCE is commonly assumed to be derived from the Phoenician alphabet of the same period. Near Eastern experts, however, are increasingly drawn to the idea of the Greeks borrowing the Late Proto-Canaanite alphabet from 1200–1050 BCE, leading to the question of why there are no examples of the Greek alphabet before the eighth century BCE. From an analysis of many similar examples to these, as well as how Old World chronology was developed, a compelling case can be presented for the late Bronze Age in the Eastern Mediterranean ending around 950 BCE rather than 1200 BCE, effectively negating continuity problems.[17] Accepting this theory would entail modifying the chronology of the entire ancient world. There is always resistance to any sort of major change within the academic community.

GEOMETRIC PERIOD, THE HOMERIC AGE

It is almost universally accepted that the Hellenic world emerged in the ninth century BCE, after the Dark Ages. The pottery of the ninth and eighth centuries BCE is referred to as geometric pottery because of the character of the patterns on it. The oldest alphabetic inscriptions are from the second half of the eighth century BCE. The Greeks introduced the innovation of recording vowels when they adapted the Phoenician (or Late Proto-Canaanite as the case may be) alphabet. The first two literary works to be recorded are Homer's the *Iliad* and the *Odyssey*.[18]

---

17. Peter James, *Centuries of Darkness*, (London, Pimlico, 1992) 72–85, 311–320.
18. Chamoux, *Civilization of Greece*, 54–65.

ARCHAIC PERIOD (EIGHTH TO SIXTH CENTURY BCE)

The Greek alphabet made possible the recording of various events, including noting that the year 776 BCE marked what were supposed to be the first Olympic Games.[19] The Olympic Games were started in Olympia, on the peninsula of Peloponnesos, probably in mid-summer, but this estimate is disputed by some scholars. (I will subsequently be focusing on the Athenian calendar, and the Olympic Games will not be mentioned as they weren't held in Athens.) The English classical historian George Grote (1794–1871) in *History of Greece* (1846) wrote that the "real history" of Greece started with these first recorded Olympic Games.[20]

The Greeks lived in numerous individual city-states, each of which consisted of a hereditary ruler and the heads of the main families who owned the land. Competition for limited resources or rivalry gave rise to colonization far and wide. Expansion to the east was initially a profitable venture, but by the mid-sixth century BCE drew the attention of the Persian Empire.[21]

The king was originally vested with political and priestly authority. Following revolutions royalty lost its political power, reverting to a priesthood. In *Politics Book 3*, Aristotle stated that while kings originally had absolute power, some renounced it, while others had it taken away from them, leaving them in care of the sacrifices. Plutarch in *Roman Questions 63* gives a similar account. Herodotus provides an example from the city of Cyrene in the form of Battus, a descendent of the kings, who lost all the power of his fathers, but took care of worship.[22] This meant that political power lay in the hands of powerful aristocratic kin groups (*genos*, singular). Power was finally taken away from the aristocracy and given over to the citizenry by the politician Kleisthenes, the "father of democracy," in 507 BCE. Each citizen's political identity became

---

19. Chamoux, *Civilization of Greece*, 70.
20. Michael Grant, *The Ancient Mediterranean* (New York, Charles Scribner's Sons) xvi.
21. Chamoux, *Civilization of Greece*, 71–109.
22. Fustel de Coulanges, *The Ancient City*, 227–8.

a product of his father and the deme to which they belonged. The Athenian political system was then able to represent the interests of all citizens.[23] As a matter of interest, it has been argued by some academics that ancient Greek democracy actually emerged in the course of the sixth century, long before Kleisthenes' reforms, throughout Greece as well as in the colonies.[24]

THE CLASSICAL PERIOD (FROM THE PERSIAN WARS TO ALEXANDER THE GREAT)

From 492–479 BCE, the Persians launched attacks against Greece. The Persian attack of 480 BCE may have been the largest military operation ever seen, involving possibly a total of 300,000 attackers. Many, but not all Greek city-states came together to fight the Persians. The first attempt to stop the Persians was the famous suicidal attempt by King Leonidas and his Spartan warriors, who detained the entire Persian army for a week. A number of battles eventually defeated the Persians and their Phoenician subjects, the Carthaginians.[25]

From 460–450 BCE Pericles dominated Athenian politics. He set up an empire centered on Athens. He provided a livelihood for 20,000 citizens and had hundreds of workmen working on the Acropolis for more than twenty years. Athens was at the apex of her power. The Parthenon was built from 447–438 BCE. Also built were monuments and statues, including that of Athene Parthenos. Athens was engaged in war with Sparta and her allies from 431–404 BCE, whereupon Athens was captured.

After her defeat, Athens lost its democratic government and instead had a commission of thirty citizens. This failed within two years and democracy was reestablished.[26]

---

23. Garland, *Daily Life of the Ancient Greeks*, 9.
24. Eric W. Robinson, *The First Democracies* (Stuttgart: Franz Seiner Verlag, 1997).
25. Smith, *The Ancient Greeks*, 43–48.
26. Chamoux, *The Civilization of Greece*, 126–141.

From this time on, no Greek city-state was able to create a united empire. Phillip II, King of Macedon, with its semi-Greek population living in northern Greece, came to power in 359 BCE. He set about conquering many Greek city-states, organizing them in a league under Macedonian control until his assassination in 336 BCE.[27]

HELLENISTIC AGE

Upon Phillip's assassination, his son, Alexander, came to the throne at the age of twenty. Alexander reigned until his death in 323 BCE. He left an empire stretching from the Aegean to the Indus River, encompassing Greece, Asia Minor, Syria, Egypt, Mesopotamia, and Persia. After Alexander's death the empire was Hellenized by introducing a common language, and allowing trade and travel for intellectuals and artists. Religions were blended throughout the empire, but the most influential was the Greek religion.

The Hellenistic age is often defined as beginning with Alexander's conquest of the Persian Empire in 331 BCE until Octavian's defeat of Antony and Cleopatra at Actium in 31 BCE.[28]

It can be argued that the Hellenistic age ended earlier than this for Greece. Rome became the most powerful city in Italy in 295 BCE, whereupon it began expanding into Greek territories.[29] Greece was finally annexed by Rome, with the sacking of Corinth in 146 BCE.[30]

During the early period of the Roman Empire, the culture of the Hellenistic Empire continued and is often referred to as Hellenistic Roman.

---

27. Smith, *The Ancient Greeks*, 82–90.

28. Frederick C. Grant, *Hellenistic Religions* (Indianapolis, IN, Bobbs Merrill Co., 1953) xi–xiii.

29. Charles Freeman, *The Greek Achievement: The Foundation of the Western World* (New York, Penguin Books, 1999) 391–6.

30. John Boardman, et al. *The Oxford History of the Classical World* (New York, Oxford University Press) 349; Will Durant, *The Life of Greece*, (New York, Simon & Schuster, 1939) 666; Helmut Koester, *Introduction to the New Testament: Volume One, History, Culture and Religion of the Hellenistic Age* (Philadelphia Fotress Press, 1982) 19.

The Hellenistic and Hellenistic Roman periods were characterized by syncretic religions that blended the religions of all the countries in the known world. These competing religions and cults eventually were forced to give way to Christianity.[31]

Christianity became the state religion of the Roman Empire in 312 or 313 CE. Christian persecution began slowly, with only the short-lived Julian attempting to reverse the tide. The Delphic Oracle was closed in 385 and sacrifices were banned in 391. Temples were transformed into Christian churches, and shrines were raided for their riches. Plato's Academy was finally closed down in the sixth century. While some aspects of Greek religion crept into Christianity, such as marriage laws and slavery, its light was finally extinguished with very few survivals in rural areas.[32] When the Hellenistic Roman period actually came to an end is an academic question, as its influence began diminishing with the adoption of Christianity by the Roman Empire.

---

31. F. Grant, *Hellenistic Religions*, xiii–xv.

32. Freeman, *The Greek Achievement*, 428–30; Pierre Chuvin, *A Chronicle of the Last Pagan* (Cambridge, MA, Harvard University Press, 1990) 14.

8: COMPREHENSIVE STUDY

To grow in the practice of Hellenismos requires further study of primary and secondary source texts, and then putting into practice what is learned and resonates well with you.

ANCIENT AUTHORS

It is pertinent to consider the most influential texts known to the Greeks, relating to religious practices, which are referred to as primary source texts.

Homer

The two epic poems of Homer [Homēros], the *Iliad* (about the siege of Troy by the Greeks) and the *Odyssey* (the tale of Ulysses' long journey home after the siege of Troy) are among the greatest texts of Western culture. The question of who actually wrote the Homeric poems and when has been the subject of debate since ancient times, and will probably never be unequivocally answered.

Hellanicus [Hellanikos] was a chronicler born in Mytilene [Mutilêne] on the island of Lesbos about 480 BCE and lived to the age of eighty-five.[1] Hellanicus placed Homer in the twelfth century BCE, probably assuming that his vivid accounts of the siege of Troy were eyewitness accounts. Herodotus (page 101) wrote that Homer lived four hundred years before his own time, which would place him in the ninth century BCE.[2] It is currently generally agreed that the siege of Troy took place c. 1200 BCE, and Homer's epics were composed in the second half of the eighth century BCE, reaching their final form in the sixth century BCE.[3]

In ancient times, seven places laid claim to being Homer's birthplace. The Homeric poems most probably originated on the west coast of Asia Minor (now Turkey), which strongly suggests the truth of an old tradition that Homer was born in Aeolian Smyrna (now Izmir), and composed his poems on the Ionian island of Chios. One tradition stated that he was blind, although it is more probable that he lost his sight in his old age. The story of his blindness may have come about from assuming that Homer had modeled the blind poet/singer in the *Odyssey*, Demodocus [*Dêmodokos*], on himself. In ancient times there were some grammarians who believed that the *Odyssey* had been written by a later poet, as it appeared to bear witness to a more advanced conceptual style. Some modern scholars accept this view.[4] Other scholars believe that the Homeric poems are a patchwork of numerous poets of varying skill.[5]

The vast majority of people in ancient times had no doubt that the *Iliad* and the *Odyssey* were the work of one author.[6] This, however, is a view shared by only a small minority of contemporary scholars, and even then, there are often reservations. One concedes that Book 10 of the *Iliad* and a portion of Book 11 of the *Odyssey* (565–627) could be

---

1. Seyffert, *Dictionary of Classical Antiquities*, 275.
2. Kitto, *The Greeks*, 44.
3. Warrior, *Greek Religion*, 13.
4. Seyffert, *Dictionary of Classical Antiquities*, 301–5.
5. Rieu, *Homer: The Iliad*, xi.
6. Chamoux, *Civilization of Greece*, 65.

post-Homeric.[7] Another concedes that while a line here and there may be a later interpolation, the only long passage is in Book 20 of the *Odyssey* (67f.) where Penelope prays to Artemis, referring to her in the third person is post-Homeric.[8]

The first century CE saw the first systematic attempts to undermine the historicity of Homer's writings. These attacks persisted until the nineteenth century, when despite the scoffing of professional scholars, the German archaeologist Heinrich Schliemann (1822–1890 CE) demonstrated that Homer's Troy (also known as Ilion) could be identified with a hilltop site in Turkey (historically Anatolia) called Hisarlik tell. *Hisarlik* in Turkish means "Place of Fortresses," while a *tell* is an artificial hill, built up over centuries of inhabitation. Schliemann, following the lead of amateur archaeologists who excavated the site in the early to mid-nineteenth century, excavated Troy from 1871 to 1872 and found numerous artifacts. In 1873, he made headlines around the world when he found a cache of gold and silver precious objects.[9]

"Homeric archaeology" shows that while some of Homer's descriptions conform to Mycenaean realities, others have been modified to be better understood by his contemporaries.

Many details in Homer can be paralleled from excavated remains. Translation of the Linear B tablets has provided further evidence for the historicity of Homer's accounts, although some scholars dispute this. There are numerous examples. Homer and the tablets both imply a Mycenaean economy centered on the palace, and a high degree of specialization in trades. Chariot bodies and wheels were stored separately. Numerous personal names which occur in the tablets also occur in Homer. Warrior helmets with boars' tusks and suits of bronze armor as described by Homer have been found.[10]

---

7. J. V. Luce, *Homer and the Heroic Age* (London: Futura Publications Ltd, 1979) 17.
8. Rieu, *Homer: The Odyssey*, 9.
9. Luce, *Homer and the Heroic Age*, 21–25.
10. Ibid., 55, 86, 93–7, 116, 120.

There are, however, other details in Homer that are incorrect. Burial rites in Homer typically involve cremation on a pyre followed by the raising of a mound and a grave marker. In the Mycenaean period, inhumation (burial) was almost universal, with cremation being practiced comparatively infrequently. Homeric burial rites are attested (proved to be real) in excavations and vase paintings from 900 BCE onwards, and possibly as recently as the eighth century BCE, which is very close to Homer's time. It has been suggested that perhaps aristocratic Mycenaean families chose cremation over inhumation as it was more dramatic and impressive.

In the Mycenaean period, warriors would battle with a single thrusting spear. In the early Iron Age, warriors began using a pair of thrusting spears, while in the Geometric period they would use a pair of throwing spears. In the *Iliad* warriors are described as battling with two throwing spears. Chariots in the ancient world would break enemy lines by charging at them. Homer's chariots on the other hand are more like a taxi service, bringing warriors to the front lines, where they fought on foot, and then returning them to safety.[11]

The value of Homeric poetry comes about as it has absorbed the earliest surviving Greek legends. These legends concern the deeds of kings and warriors living in the late Bronze Age (between the fifteenth and seventh centuries BCE) and their war against Troy, as well as its aftermath. The legends within Homer were thought factual throughout the ancient world. Reconstructions of early Greek history by the Greek historian, Thucydides (c. 460 BCE–c. 395 BCE), and the Classical Greek philosopher, Plato (428/427 BCE–348/347 BCE), were based on Homeric poetry.

It is claimed by some that the Greeks did not have any sacred literature to parallel the Christian Bible.[12] Such a sweeping statement obviously hinges on exactly how the Bible is viewed.

---

11. Luce, *Homer and the Heroic Age*, 107–110, 121, 127–130.

12. Garland, *Religion and the Greeks*, ix.

There are, however, good reasons to consider Homer's the *Iliad* and the *Odyssey* to be the ancient Greek equivalent of the Bible. These epic poems were the basis of formal school education and permeated the culture. Fifth-century Athenian schoolboys would memorize the poems. Every question, whether it concerned morals or appropriate behavior, in the human realm, the realm of the divine, as well as the interaction between these realms, could be answered by quoting verses from Homer. Homer's writings were seen as a repository of all wisdom and knowledge, and provided inspiration for artists, poets, politicians, and philosophers, as well as providing guidance on duties toward the family and the deities. They also gave the Greeks a sense of unity despite the never-ending squabbling between the various city-states.[13]

As an illustration of the importance of Homer's writings, the *Symposium*, a Socratic dialogue by Xenophon, dramatizes a discussion of Socrates and company at a dinner where each participant describes the thing of which they are the most proud. Niceratus answered:

"My father, in his pains to make me a good man, compelled me to learn the whole of Homer's poems, and it so happens that even now I can repeat the *Iliad* and the *Odyssey* by heart."[14]

Homer's writings are characterized by repetitive epithets such as the "wine dark sea" and "swift-footed Achilles," and are composed in rhythmic form (dactylic hexameter). Rhythmic poems are much easier to memorize than prose passages, thus enabling the transmission of moral principles and cultural knowledge. Homer was the law, religion, and entertainment of Hellenic Greece.[15]

Because Homer incorporated a necromancy sequence in Book 11 of the *Odyssey* where Odysseus called up the ghost of the prophet Tiresias,

---

13. Kitto, *The Greeks*, 44–5; Garland, *Greek Way of Life*, 134; Flaceliere, *Daily Life in Greece at the Time of Pericles*, 97; Freeman, *The Greek Achievement*, 62.

14. Dakyns, *Xenophon: The Symposium*.

15. Daniel R. Fredrick, *The Voice Inside the Pen: What Rhetoric and Composition Can Learn from Orality and Literary Studies*, 2007. http://www.speakingwritingconnection.com/swc.fredrick_voice.pdf.

he came to be regarded as an authority on Graeco-Egyptian necromancy and magick in general.[16] Some later authors saw Homer as a necromancer. As pointed out in the Magick in Ancient Greece chapter, Homeric verses were used as incantations between the first and fourth centuries CE for protection, healing, overcoming misfortune, and cursing enemies.[17] By way of comparison, verses from the Bible have also been used in the practice of magick (the practice of Conjure is a good example).

Homer's writings are among the greatest writings that the Western world has ever seen and were the best known writings of the ancient world. They are arguably the supreme cultural achievement of the ancient Greeks. For nearly three millennia they have exerted a profound influence on Western thought and continue to do so. There is a rawness to Homer's writings that is at loggerheads with contemporary political correctness. While the settings are very different, the issues faced—the challenges, triumphs and tragedies of morality, politics, love and death—are not far removed from our own experiences. Immersion in the Homeric epics broadens perspectives and improves analytical skills, as we compare our own responses to those of the ancients.

Homer's writings are, in my opinion, the most important primary source texts to study for the practice of Hellenismos. They provide important lessons on the mindset of the ancient Greeks and just how to interact with deities. They give insights into the mythology of deities and on the practice of magick. Homer's writings can also be seen as the foundation of all the philosophizing which followed. The lack of political correctness in Homer's writings means that they have to be understood in the context of the time in which they were written, rather than thoughtlessly applied to contemporary situations.

---

16. Daniel Ogden, *Greek and Roman Necromancy*, (Princeton, NJ: Princeton University Press, 2001) xxiii-xxiv, 259.
17. Derek Collins, *Magic in the Ancient Greek World* (Malden, MA: Blackwell Publishing, 2008) xiii, 104–5.

Hesiod

Hesiod [*Hesiodos*] and Homer authored the oldest surviving Greek writings. The ancients were unsure as to exactly when Hesiod lived, with some (such as Herodotus) thinking that he was a contemporary of Homer. Hesiod was born in Boeotia in central Greece.[18]

Hesiod was familiar with the writings of Homer and sometimes imitated them, indicating that he lived after Homer. His writing was harsher and lacked the aestheticism of Homer.[19] Hesiod was probably writing around 700 BCE.[20]

Two poems survive which most scholars believe can be attributed to Hesiod: the *Theogony* and the *Works and Days*. Both poems claim inspiration by the Muses. Nevertheless, some scholars doubt that the same person composed both poems. There are, in addition, a number of fragments that may possibly have been authored by him, while the *Shield of Herakles*, which was attributed to him in antiquity, cannot have been written by him, as it is influenced by art from the sixth century BCE.[21]

The *Theogony* is a compilation of numerous local Greek traditions concerning the gods, organized as a narrative that tells about the origin of the cosmos and the gods from chaos to the triumph of Zeus and the Olympians. The *Works and Days* is a didactic (having moral instruction as an ulterior motive) poem on the necessity and inevitability of work, and contains an outline of the five ages of the world.[22]

Hesiod's Muses seem to have been very familiar with Near Eastern literature, specifically that of the Babylonians, Hittites, and Phoenicians. This influence is clearly seen in the Succession Myth of the *Theogony*. There are numerous examples, but only a few will be cited.

---

18. Seyffert, *Dictionary of Classical Antiquities*, 291.

19. Chamoux, *Civilization of Greece*, 69.

20. Warrior, *Greek Religion*, 14.

21. Frazer, *The Poems of Hesiod*, 3–4.

22. Evelyn-White, *Hesiod, Homeric Hymns, Epic Cycle, Homeric*.

Enuma Elish, the Babylonian epic of creation,was composed around 1100 BCE, and has Apsu and Tiamat giving rise to five generations, the last three of which were ruled over by Anu, Ea, and Marduk, who correspond to Ouranos, Kronos, and Zeus, respectively. Marduk comes to power by defeating Tiamat, which corresponds to Zeus defeating Typhoeus.

In the fourteenth and thirteenth centuries BCE, the Hittites produced mythological texts heavily influenced by the Hurrians, whom they had conquered. The Kingship of Heaven text describes four generations each ruled over by Alalu, Anu, Kumarbi, and the storm god, the last three of which correspond to Ouranos, Kronos, and Zeus, respectively. Kumarbi defeats Anu by biting off his genitals, which corresponds to Zeus' defeat of Kronos. The *Song of Ullikummi* text describes Ullikummi, the stone monster, being defeated by the storm god, which corresponds to Typhoeus being defeated by Zeus.

The mythology of the Phoenicians (otherwise known as the Canaanites) known to us from fourteenth-century-BCE texts is very similar to that of the Hittites. Again there are four gods—a highest god, a sky god, El, and Baal, the storm god, the last three of which correspond to Ouranos, Kronos, and Zeus, respectively. El castrates the sky god, and Baal defeats a monster of chaos called Yamm, which corresponds to Zeus defeating Typhoeus.[23]

While Greek traditions have a flavor all their own, a study of Near Eastern literature shows that they did not develop in a vacuum, but to a large extent in response to external influences.

I consider the writings of Hesiod to be almost as important as those of Homer. They provide information pertaining to the understanding and worship of deities not adequately covered by Homer. They also stress the importance of a work ethic.

---

23. Frazer, *Poems of Hesiod*, 8–9; Walter Burkert, *The Orientalizing Revolution: Near Eastern Influence on Greek Culture in the Early Archaic Age* (Cambridge, MA: Harvard University Press, 1992) 88–127; Bremmer, *Greek Religion*, 7.

Herodotus

Herodotus [*Hērodotos*], called the Father of History, was born between 490 and 480 BCE at Halicarnassus [*Halikarnassos*] in Asia Minor (present-day Bodrum in Turkey).[24]

While Herodotus took it upon himself to focus on the clashes between the Greeks and the "barbarians" (peoples of Asia Minor) culminating in the battles of his childhood, he also reported on the travels he embarked on during which he saw much of the known world. His writings combined his own observations with oral and written sources.

Herodotus' histories were the first surviving writings to be produced in prose, rather than in verse, in order for reported events to be conveyed in plain language.[25]

Since ancient times, Herodotus' writings have been hailed by some, but criticized by others who questioned their veracity. Modern discoveries have vindicated a number of Herodotus' statements. The statements which remain doubtful concern folklore and myths, and it appears that Herodotus was rather uncritical in accepting certain statements from his informants. Nevertheless, Herodotus' writings are invaluable in providing a glimpse into what a well-traveled and well-educated Greek in the fifth century BCE would have believed about his world.

Regarding Homer and Hesiod, Herodotus stated:

Whence the gods severally sprang, whether or no they had all existed from eternity, what forms they bore—these are questions of which the Greeks knew nothing until the other day, so to speak. For Homer and Hesiod were the first to compose Theogonies, and give the gods their epithets, to allot them their several offices and occupations, and describe their forms; and they lived but four hundred years before my time, as I believe. As for the poets who are thought by some to be earlier than these, they are, in my judgment, decidedly later writers. In these matters I have the authority

---

24. Seyffert, *Dictionary of Classical Antiquities*, 289–90.

25. M. Smith, *The Ancient Greeks*, 70.

of the priestesses of Dodona for the former portion of my statements;
what I have said of Homer and Hesiod is my own opinion."2.53 [26]

Herodotus was not saying that Homer and Hesiod invented the
gods but rather were the first to reveal their forms, functions, and relationships.

Almost all the names of the gods came into Greece from Egypt. My
inquiries prove that they were all derived from a foreign source, and
my opinion is that Egypt furnished the greater number. For with the
exception of Poseidon and the Dioscuri, whom I mentioned above,
and Hera, Hestia, Themis, the Graces, and the Nereids, the other gods
have been known from time immemorial in Egypt. This I assert on the
authority of the Egyptians themselves. The gods, with whose names
they profess themselves unacquainted, the Greeks received, I believe,
from the Pelasgi, except Poseidon. Of him they got their knowledge
from the Libyans, by whom he has been always honored, and who were
anciently the only people that had a god of the name. The Egyptians
differ from the Greeks also in paying no divine honors to heroes. 2.50 [27]

Herodotus was not referring to actual names, as he constantly pointed
out the equivalence between various deities—for example, Zeus and
Amon. The name of a deity involved its personality, and thus the Greek
deities were defined, along with their attributes, by Egypt.[28] To put it
plainly, Herodotus believed that many of the Greek deities had Egyptian
origins.[29]

---

26. A. J. Grant, *Herodotus: The Text of Canon Rawlinson's Translation, with the
    notes abridged* (New York, Charles Scribner's Sons, 1897) 164–5.

27. Ibid., 163.

28. W. W. How and J. Wells. *A Commentary on Herodotus: Volume I* (London:
    Clarendon Press, 1964) 191.

29. David Grene, *Herodotus: The History* (Chicago: University of Chicago
    Press, 1988) 153.

Besides these which have been here mentioned, there are many other practices whereof I shall speak hereafter, which the Greeks have borrowed from Egypt. The peculiarity, however, which they observe in their statues of Hermes they did not derive from the Egyptians, but from the Pelasgi; from them the Athenians first adopted it, and afterwards it passed from the Athenians to the other Greeks. 2.51

Herodotus here outlined an exception, in the way of the Hermes statues with the phallus erect, otherwise known as the ithyphallic Hermes, a god of fruitfulness, as coming from the Pelasgians, rather than the Egyptians.[30]

The Egyptians were also the first to introduce solemn assemblies, processions, and litanies to the gods; of all which the Greeks were taught the use by them. It seems to me a sufficient proof of this that in Egypt these practices have been established from remote antiquity, while in Greece they are only recently known. 2.58 [31]

Herodotus stated that there are many similarities between the religious festivals of Greece and Egypt.[32] Again, much of which is thought of as Greek had an Egyptian origin.

While a study of Herodotus is nowhere near as important to the study of Hellenismos as is that of Homer and Hesiod, Herodotus provides a well-rounded education, illuminating the origins of various practices which might otherwise remain an enigma. As stated previously, it's important to know as much as possible about what we are practicing as knowledge is power and we are not sheep. We can also gain a closer relationship to the gods with the additional knowledge we gain from reading source texts

---

30. David Grene, *Herodotus: The History* (Chicago: University of Chicago Press, 1988) 153; *Volume I*, 192.

31. A. J. Grant, *Herodotus*, 163-4.

32. How and Wells, *Commentary on Herodotus, Vol. I*, 195.

Pausanias

Pausanias was a doctor from Greek Asia Minor who spent ten or twenty years traveling through mainland Greece in the second century CE. He is remembered for his *Guide to Greece* in ten volumes, which describes ancient Greece from firsthand observations and inquiries from local residents.[33]

As with Homer, Pausanias was largely dismissed by nineteenth- and early twentieth-century classicists (scholars of ancient Greek and Latin). However, just as Schliemann discovered Troy by studying Homer, he similarly discovered six royal shaft tombs in Mycenae by digging within the circuit of walls, following information in Pausanias. Pausanias had stated that the graves were of Agamemnon and his companions. Unfortunately, Schliemann's interpretation of the chronology was faulty and while the graves were magnificent, they were not of Agamemnon and his companions.[34]

Despite a number of inaccuracies in his accounts, Pausanias is now considered a reliable guide for contemporary archaeologists.

While Pausanias wrote well after the end of the Classical period, he provided fascinating accounts of local mythology and cultic practices in the many regions of Greece which he visited. Many of these accounts are not to be found anywhere else.

PRIMARY SOURCE TEXTS

Orphic Hymns

During the Heroic Age, the musician, poet and magician singer Orpheus preached the immortality of the soul, abstaining from meat and living peacefully. The mystery cults offered a new religion by combining Orphic practices with the worship of Dionysus. The Orphic Hymns were composed for this religious group in western Asia Minor in the second or third century CE. Despite being composed at a time when Christianity was on the ascendancy, there are no Christian elements whatsoever in them—they are totally pagan. The hymns are devoted to

---

33. Seyffert, *Dictionary of Classical Antiquities*, 464; Levi, *Pausanias: Guide to Greece: Volume 1*; Levi, *Pausanias: Guide to Greece: Volume 2*.

34. Luce, *Homer and the Heroic Age*, 27–28.

various deities and to cosmic elements. Each hymn typically suggests an offering, and implores peace and health.[35] The offerings suggested are "fumigations" which means that incense or an aromatic substance is burned for its fragrant odor. I like to use frankincense as a default if no fumigation is listed or the fumigation is uncertain.

There are unfortunately only two translations of the Orphic Hymns.

The most widely available is Thomas Taylor's *The Hymns of Orpheus* (1792). In the fashion of the time, Taylor often used Latin deity names rather than Greek deity names, and also distorted his translation somewhat by forcing it to rhyme.

A much easier to read translation was produced by Professor Apostolos N. Athanassakis of the University of California, Santa Barbara (UCSB), titled *Orphic Hymns: Text, Translation, and Notes* (1977). While the first edition is out of print and prohibitively expensive, at the time of writing this book, it has now been reprinted.[36]

Homeric Hymns

For a long time the ancients believed that the so-called Homeric Hymns were composed by Homer. Once the Alexandrians dispelled this belief, the hymns were neglected both in ancient and modern times. The hymns, however, are quite old, with some of them coming from the eighth and seventh centuries, others from the sixth and fifth, and a few later, but probably predating the Hellenistic period. They are devotional songs sung in honor of numerous deities as part of religious festivals.[37]

At the time of writing this book, there are quite a number of translations available of the Homeric Hymns.

---

35. Jennifer Larson, *Greek Nymphs: Myth, Cult, Lore* (New York: Oxford University Press) 268–9; Apostolos N. (trans.) Athanassakis, *Orphic Hymns: Text. Translation, and Notes* (Baltimore, MD: Johns Hopkins University Press, 1976).

36. At the time of going to print, I learned of a soon to be published third translation by Associate Professor Patrick Dunn of Aurora University in Illinois, titled *The Orphic Hymns: A New Translation for the Occult Practitioner*.

37. Apostolos N. Athanassakis, *The Homeric Hymns: Translation, Introduction, and Notes* (Baltimore, MD: Johns Hopkins University Press, 1975) i–xiii.

Hugh Gerard Evelyn-White (1874–1924), the English archaeologist and Coptologist, produced *Hesiod, Homeric Hymns, Epic Cycle, Homerica* (1914).

Professor Athanassakis produced *The Homeric Hymns: Translation, Introduction, and Notes* (1976).

Greek Religion Sourcebooks

The beauty of sourcebooks is that someone has done all the hard work for you. Their advantage is that they are a quick way of accessing primary source text extracts dealing with Greek religion. Their disadvantage is that you never quite know what has been omitted unless you consult the primary source texts yourself.

David G. Rice and John E. Stambaugh produced *Sources for the Study of Greek Religion* (1979).

Valerie M. Warrior, a scholar of Greco-Roman history and religion, produced *Greek Religion: A Sourcebook* (2009).

While more of a mythological rather than a religious text, Dr. Robin Hard translated *Apollodorus: The Library of Greek Mythology* (1998). This is a unique sourcebook of myths compiled in the first/second century CE.

Greek Magick Sourcebooks

Professor Hans Dieter Betz, of the University of Chicago, edited a collection of spells from Egypt in late antiquity in *The Greek Magical Papyri in Translation* (1986). This is actually one of my all-time favorite books. Years of heavy usage ruined my original softcover to the extent that I had to obtain the hardcover.

Professor Georg Luck (born 1926), of the Johns Hopkins University, collected numerous literary references to Greek magick and witchcraft in *Arcana Mundi: Magic and the Occult in the Greek and Roman Worlds* (1987).

Professor John Gager (born 1937), of Princeton University, translated a selection of binding spells, a number of which are from ancient Greece, in *Curse Tablets and Binding Spells from the Ancient World* (1999).

Continuing the work of Professor Luck, Professor Daniel Ogden of the University of Exeter produced *Magic, Witchcraft, and Ghosts in the Greek and Roman Worlds: A Sourcebook* (2002).

SECONDARY SOURCE TEXTS

Secondary Source Texts on Greek Religion

While each of the newer scholarly texts on Greek religion has much to offer, there is one that stands out as being the absolutely essential reference text, and that is *Greek Religion* by Professor Walter Burkert (born 1931) of Switzerland's University of Zurich. This text was originally written in German in 1977 and translated into English in 1985 with very little change.

Professor Jan N. Bremmer (born 1944) wrote *Greek Religion* (1999) to essentially be a companion book to Burkert's text, by focusing on new developments since 1977.

Also very important are two texts by Professor Jon D. Mikalson (born 1943) of the University of Virginia. *Athenian Popular Religion* (1983) gives an account of the religious practices of the average Athenian citizen. *The Sacred and Civil Calendar of the Athenian Year* (1975) covers all the festivals in the Athenian (Attic) calendar.

Another unique contribution is from Professor Martin Persson Nilsson (1874–1967), of Sweden's University of Lund, who outlined the religious practices of ancient Greek peasants in *Greek Folk Religion* (1961).

An accessible introduction to Athenian religion can be found in *Religion in the Ancient Greek City* (1994), which was written by Professor Louise Bruit Zaidman and Professor Pauline Schmitt Pantel, both of the University of Paris, and translated by Professor Paul Cartledge (born 1947), of Cambridge University.

An important overview of Greek prayer can be found in *Prayer in Greek Religion* (1997) by Dr. Simon Pulleyn, of Merton College, Oxford.

An excellent comprehensive guide to Greek mythology was written by Dr. Robin Hard, titled *The Routledge Handbook of Greek Mythology: Based on H. J. Rose's Handbook of Greek Mythology* (2004).

Secondary Source Texts on Greek Magick

A comprehensive outline of the practice of ancient Greek necromancy can be found in Professor Daniel Ogden's *Greek and Roman Necromancy* (2001).

A wonderful overview of the prolific scholarly literature dealing with ancient Greek magick can be found in *Magic in the Ancient Greek World* (2008) by Professor Derek Collins of the University of Michigan.

ADDITIONAL REFERENCES

There are of course numerous other texts, but those above are my favorite ones. See the Bibliography for additional references.

The study of Hellenismos is certainly not a static pursuit. New scholarly texts and journal articles are being published constantly. It is also a good idea to stay abreast of archaeological discoveries as every few weeks something of relevance pops up—the Internet makes this a very simple task.

REVIEW

Remember the review at the end of the Greek Religion—Public, Household, Countryside chapter? All the references to journaling, making regular meal offerings, choosing specific deities, setting up an altar, and incorporating additional household deities are still to be adhered to.

By all means use the hymns in this book, or download them online. In the long term, I would recommend Professor Apostolos N. Athanassakis' *The Orphic Hymns* and *The Homeric Hymns*. These are accurate and very easy to read.

In addition to this, we need more background information, hence the chapters A Thumbnail Sketch of Greek History and Further Study. The writings of Homer and Hesiod are essential as a starting point. Remember, the more knowledge you gain through study, the deeper your relationship with the deities will become through your true devotion.

9: EXPERIENCING THE LUNAR CYCLE

PREAMBLE TO EXPERIENCING THE LUNAR CYCLE

There was no single standard calendar in ancient Greece. There were a number, but the best-known one was the Athenian state religious calendar. It consisted of lunar monthly festival days concentrated at the beginning of each month and annually recurring festivals. The monthly festivals were as follows:

Day 1: Noumenia

Day 2: Agathos Daimon

Day 3: Athene

Day 4: Herakles, Hermes, Aphrodite, and Eros

Day 6: Artemis

Day 7: Apollon

Day 8: Poseidon and Theseus[1] (Theseus was the legendary founder-king of Athens.)

---

1. Mikalson, *The Sacred and Civil Calendar of the Athenian Year*, 24, 201; Zaidman and Pantel, *Religion in the Ancient Greek City*, 102–4.

While not strictly part of the Athenian calendar, we know from the playwright Aristophanes (c. 446–c. 386 BCE) that sacrifices were made to Hekate on the 30th, the last day of the lunar month, and corresponding to the dark moon.[2]

Certain days of the lunar month were devoted to particular deities. It will be noted that certain Olympic deities appear to have been left out. Those working the annual cycle, as well as the lunar monthly cycle, will experience most of the Olympic deities and have a few bonuses!

In the Athenian calendar, the first day of the lunar month was called the Noumenia. In its broadest context, the Noumenia honored all the deities and symbolized new beginnings.

Plutarch in *Moralia* described the Noumenia as "the holiest of days."[3] Normally during the course of a year there were twelve Noumeniai and these were treated as sacred and independent by the Athenians. No annual religious festivals or organizational meetings were ever held on the Noumenia.[4]

Returning to Porphyry's narrative about Klearchos (see the chapter on Greek Religion), it was stated that in every month at the new moon (Noumenia), he would crown and adorn his statues of Hermes and Hekate, and the other sacred images which were used by his ancestors. Klearchos would then honor the dieties as always with bloodless offerings of incense and cakes.[5] It was also common to place frankincense on statues.[6]

The other monthly festivals do not appear to have been as important as the Noumenia. The same bloodless offerings as used by Klearchos are appropriate. (Additional ideas can be found in the chapters on Olympic Deities as well as Other Deities, Daimones, and Heroes.)

---

2. Rice and Stambaugh, *Sources for the Study of Greek Religion*, 133.
3. Fowler, *Plutarch: Moralia, Volume X*, 319.
4. Mikalson, *The Noumenia and Epimenia in Athens*.
5. Taylor, *On Abstinence from Animal Food*, 2.16.
6. Mikalson, *The Sacred and Civil Calendar of the Athenian Year*, 15.

Each month in the Athenian calendar was either 29 or 30 days long. The months that were 29 days long were referred to as "hollow," while those that were 30 days long were "full." In the case of hollow months, the 29th day was omitted so that each month would always end on the 30th day.[7] Thus, as stated above, Hekate would always be venerated on the 30th.

The ancient Greeks did not wear special robes at public rituals, but rather wore clean everyday clothing. Presumably they would have bathed first, thus removing miasma (pollution). They would then wash their hands with pure spring water prior to the ritual. This somewhat casual approach can be used as a guide for preparing for the rituals in the lunar cycle. As mentioned above, I would suggest praying to Hygeia while bathing and visualizing pollution being washed off. It's important to incorporate your practices into your daily schedule—it makes sense to perform rituals after bathing. For some this could be first thing in the morning, for others, it's before going to bed.

While meal-based offerings are normally used, I would recommend an addition to make the rituals feel a little more special. I particularly enjoy burning incense when working with deities. While there are various plant-based substances associated with many of the deities (listed as fumigations), frankincense was the most widely used offering, and so is very appropriate for a one-month trial. While a granule can be held over a fire dedicated to Hestia (fireplace, candle, or something similar) with beading tweezers (do not use eyebrow tweezers, as their small size could result in the granule dropping out, and fingers being burned), it is much more effective to use a brazier and a charcoal block.

As luck would have it, there are Orphic Hymns available for all the deities that will be venerated during our trial lunar month. So, we have a choice of either improvising a prayer following the formula given in the chapter on Public Religion or using an Orphic Hymn. For the purposes of our one month trial, I would recommend keeping it simple

---

7. Ibid., 9.

and using the Orphic Hymns. I thoroughly recommend investigating the magickal qualities of the hymns by reading them aloud, and then feeling the energies being evoked. Personal experiences should be journaled daily, including the time and date; writing out the steps you followed; the hymns or prayers used; any UPG received; and how you felt throughout. Also take note of any unusual occurrences (wind phenomena, animals making a ruckus, cloud formations, etc.).

Summary for Venerating Deities

- Purify the body of miasma if necessary.
- Wash hands in pure water.
- Set up altar with statue or picture of deity being worked with. Throw some barley grains on the altar.
- Place votive offering or first fruits on altar.
- Face east if possible.
- Fumigate (burn incense—frankincense, or one specific to the deity—alternatively use an oil burner).
- Choose pre-existing prayer, such as Orphic or Homeric Hymn.
- Alternatively construct your own prayer (using the guidelines in the Greek Religion—Public, Household, Countryside chapter).
- A tiny morsel of food or a libation can be offered, although the incense should be sufficient for the trial.
- Extend arms forward with hand bent back so that palms face up while praying.

The Athenian lunar month starts at the new moon and ends at the dark moon. A perusal will show that the first eight days and the last day of the month are the ones we will be focusing on. It is important to remember that superimposed onto the remaining days of the lunar month are the annual festival days, so the months are not quite as lopsided as they initially appear.

To get the most out of the trial, and to even out the workload, I propose that we limit ourselves to prayers on the festival days and save the daily meal-based offerings for the remaining days. However, I fully expect keen practitioners to perform the daily meal-based offerings throughout.

EXPERIENCING THE LUNAR CYCLE

Greek religion is based around the lunar month, and enables practitioners of Hellenismos to impart structure into their lives by harmonizing with it. The month starts with Noumenia and its honoring of all the deities. However, the success of this day is dependent upon the preparation undertaken on the previous day—the last day of the month, the day of Hekate. Thus, we will start with the last day of the month.

Day 30: Hekate

My understanding of this day comes from contemplating the nature of Hekate.

Hekate is the goddess of the crossroads, which to the ancient Greeks were Y-shaped. Statues of Hekate were left at the crossroads with each of her three faces looking along each of the three directions. To a traveler, the crossroads were a bifurcation, a division into two parts or a fork, a place where they would have to make a decision as to which of the two roads they would take. So it is for those living their lives by the lunar calendar. The last day is a day of reflection and introspection, a day of deciding what course to take during the following month, a day of seeing goals and challenges. Those for whom intuition isn't enough can turn to divination. Journal your goals and challenges, what your intuition tells you, and any messages received during divination. Plans should be made, but no action taken, as this should be saved for the Noumenia.

It was traditional to leave offerings of food at the crossroads, which were quickly appropriated by the poor (see Countryside Religion section of Greek Religion—Public, Household, Countryside chapter). This was probably surplus food in danger of spoilage, and so this day marked a time of cleaning out the larder in order for it to be restocked. There is a sense of "out with the old and in with the new." These suppers of Hekate consisted of breadstuffs, eggs, cheese, and perhaps red mullet. (I would be very disappointed if anyone used the traditional dog meat.)

I imagine that poor people would congregate at various crossroads locations, possibly competing against others for the choicest morsels. Food left at a crossroads in modern times, however, would either spoil or be taken by an animal. The object was to assist the poor, so either a small donation of money or non-perishables for a food bank, or perhaps assisting in a soup kitchen would be appropriate. In keeping with the "out with the old," refrigerators enable us to keep leftovers for long periods of time, but even then they are sometimes forgotten and become science experiments, so this day should be used to also clean out the refrigerators along with all the other cleaning tasks. I suspect that by giving charity we endear ourselves to Hekate and she assists us with planning the following month.

As a time of "out with the old and in with the new," there is a wonderful opportunity for cleaning the altar, the objects on it, and hopefully the whole home. Everything should be freshened up, and any perishable items that cannot be donated to charity should be thrown out and replaced.

An optional activity is to visit a crossroads in a wild area (such as a forest or even a graveyard) on this night to induce a feeling of closeness to Hekate. Also useful is an appreciation of the weird and uncanny, while a study of magick (over which she presides) is discretionary. Keep an eye open for dogs, as they normally accompany her.

Frankincense should be burned and the Orphic Hymn to Hekate recited.

Orphic Hymn to Hekate

(Ending of To Musaius)

No Fumigation given.

And to my holy sacrifice invite,

the pow'r who reigns in deepest hell and night;

I call Einodian [of the path] Hekate, lovely dame,

of earthly, wat'ry, and celestial frame,

Sepulchral, in a saffron veil array'd, leas'd

with dark ghosts that wander thro' the shade;

Persian, unconquerable huntress hail!

The world's key-bearer never doom'd to fail

On the rough rock to wander thee delights,

leader and nurse be present to our rites

Propitious grant our just desires success,

accept our homage, and the incense bless.

Note that the bracketed terms are explanations and are not to be read out aloud. This hymn is taken from the last few lines of the Orphic Hymn to Musaius, which is recited for Noumenia. Don't forget to journal your experiences.

Day 1: Noumenia

The first day of the lunar month is Noumenia, which begins the evening when the young lunar crescent first becomes visible, which will be either the day after the dark moon or the day after that. Many Hellenic reconstructionists celebrate Noumenia the day after the day of Hekate, which may or may not be correct, depending on whether the lunar crescent is visible at their latitude. However, on some occasions cloud cover may obscure the crescent, necessitating a guess. The other thing is that sometimes it's appropriate to compromise what you feel is right in order to better participate in group rituals, whether physically or in cyberspace. Consider, for instance, the ancient Greek philosophers who ignored their differences of opinion and participated in public rituals together, all in the name of building community.

Noumenia is a time of new beginnings, and hence presents a wonderful opportunity to adorn any statues or sacred images you may have. It is also a time to put into action whatever plans were decided on the last day of the month, the day of Hekate. As stated previously, the success of

Noumenia is dependent upon the preparation undertaken on the day of Hekate.

In its broadest context, Noumenia honors all the deities. This is very important, so that none are omitted. Offerings of frankincense, cakes, and first fruits should be made. Flowers are also appropriate.

Those who shop at grocery stores for their fruits and vegetables may well be challenged by the concept of first fruits, as most produce is available year round because much is shipped in from other climates. Eating locally grown produce by either growing it at home or shopping at a farmers' market automatically ensures familiarity with, and access to, seasonal produce. Cakes should ideally be baked at home, but this may not be possible for all practitioners.

Some practitioners will refill their offering jar for Zeus Ktesios with water, olive oil, and various seeds, grains, and fruits, as the old contents are often spoiled by this stage.

The Orphic Hymn for this day is quite daunting as so many deities are called upon that it becomes difficult to give each the respect they deserve. However, perseverance with the hymn is quite rewarding.

The Orphic Hymn to Musaios is recited. Note that no fumigation is given, so frankincense is used by default.

Orphic Hymn 0. To Musaios

Attend Musaius to my sacred song,
and learn what rites to sacrifice belong.
Zeus I invoke, Gaia [Earth], and Helios [Solar Light],
Mene's [the Moon] pure splendor, and the Stars of night;
Thee Poseidon, ruler of the sea profound,
dark-hair'd, whose waves begirt the solid ground;
Demeter abundant, and of lovely mien,
and Persephone infernal Hades' queen
The huntress Artemis, and bright Phoebus rays,
far-darting God, the theme of Delphic praise;
And Dionysos, honor'd by the heav'nly choir,
and raging Ares, and Hephaistos, god of fire;

The mighty pow'r who rose from foam to light,

and Pluto potent in the realms of night;

With Hebe young, and Herakles the strong,

and Eileithyia [you to whom the cares of births belong]:

Dikaisune [Justice] and Eusebia [Piety] august I call,

and much-fam'd nymphs, and Pan the god of all.

To Hera sacred, and to Mnemosyne [Memory] fair,

and the chaste Muses I address my pray'r;

The various year, the Charites [Graces], and the Horai [Hours],

fair-hair'd Leto, and Dione's pow'rs;

Armed Kouretes [rearers of Zeus] I call,

with those Soteroi [salvations spirits] who spring from Zeus the king
of all:

Th' Idaian Gods [Kouretes], the angel of the skies,

and righteous Themis [goddess of divine law], with sagacious eyes;

With ancient Nyx [Night], and Hemara [Day-light] I implore,

and Pistis [Faith], and Dike [Justice] dealing right adore;

Kronos and Rhea, and great Thetis too,

hid in a veil of bright celestial blue:

I call great Okeanos [Ocean],

and the beauteous train of nymphs,

who dwell in chambers of the main;

Atlas the strong, and ever in its prime, vig'rous Aion [Eternity],

and Chronos [endless Time];

The Styx [goddess of the underworld river], and Meilikhoi [placid
Gods] beside,

and various Daimones, that o'er men preside;

Illustrious Pronoia [Providence],

the noble train of daimon forms, who fill th' ætherial plain;

Or live in air, in water, earth, or fire,

or deep beneath the solid ground retire.

Dionysos and Semele the friends of all,

and white Leucothea [goddess who protects sailors] of the sea I call;

Palæmon [sea god] bounteous, and Adrasteia [nymph] great,

and sweet-tongu'd Nike [Victory], with success elate;
Great Asklepios, skill'd to cure disease,
and dread Athene, whom fierce battles please;
Brontoi [Thunders] and Anemoi [Winds] in mighty columns pent,
with dreadful roaring struggling hard for vent;
Attis [consort of Kybele], the mother of the pow'rs on high,
and fair Adonis [mortal lover of Aphrodite], never doom'd to die,
End and beginning he is all to all,
these with propitious aid I gently call;

(Note that the last few verses are an invocation to Hekate and have been separated.) Don't forget to journalize your experiences.

Day 2: Agathos Daimon

The second day of the lunar month is sacred to Agathos Daimon [Agathodaimon] ("Good Spirit"), a household spirit who appears as a snake, responsible for the protection of the household, bringing good luck, protection, and divine assistance.

On a daily basis, a few drops of unmixed wine (or more appropriately in this day and age, whatever beverage was being drunk) were poured on the ground (or a planter pot) as a libation to Agathos Daimon at the end of the meal. On this day, however, no compromise should be made, and unmixed wine should be poured out as a libation to Agathos Daimon.

Orphic Hymn LXXII. To the Daimon, or Genius

The Fumigation from Frankincense.
Thee, mighty-ruling, Daimon dread,
I call, mild Zeus, life-giving, and the source of all:
Great Zeus, much-wand'ring, terrible and strong,
to whom revenge and tortures dire belong.
Mankind from thee, in plenteous wealth abound,
when in their dwellings joyful thou art found;
Or pass thro' life afflicted and distress'd,

the needful means of bliss by thee supprest.

'Tis thine alone endu'd with boundless might,

to keep the keys of sorrow and delight.

O holy, blessed father, hear my pray'r,

disperse the seeds of life-consuming care;

With fav'ring mind the sacred rites attend,

and grant my days a glorious, blessed end.

Don't forget to journalize your experiences.

Day 3: Athene

On the third day of the lunar month, the Tritogeneia is celebrated, which is sacred to the goddess Athene. Athene presides over wise counsel and heroic endeavor, war and defense of the city, as well as crafts such as weaving and pottery.

While Agathos Daimon was responsible for the protection of the household, Athene was the patron and protector of Athens, and thus all Athenian households that made up the community. The third day thus builds on the protection obtained on the second, but has more of a community focus. This is a day to become involved in the community. Investigate whether there are any urgent needs that the community has and address those. This could mean assisting neighbors or even strangers. But it could also mean involvement in various community projects, particularly involving those who are less fortunate, like the elderly, the homeless, or veterans.

Orphic Hymn XXXI. To Athene

No Fumigation given.

Only-Begotten, noble race of Zeus,

blessed and fierce, who joy'st in caves to rove:

O, warlike Pallas,

whose illustrious kind, ineffable and effable we find:

Magnanimous and fam'd, the rocky height,

and groves, and shady mountains thee delight:

In arms rejoicing, who with Furies dire and wild,

the souls of mortals dost inspire.

Gymnastic virgin of terrific mind,

dire Gorgons bane, unmarried, blessed, kind:

Mother of arts, imperious; understood,

rage to the wicked, wisdom to the good:

Female and male, the arts of war are thine,

fanatic, Drakaina [female serpent or dragon], divine:

O'er the Phlegrean giants [Zeus transformed two forest creatures
    into monkeys] rous'd to ire,

thy coursers driving, with destruction dire.

Tritogeneia [sprung from the head of Zeus], of splendid mien,

purger of evils, all-victorious queen.

Hear me, O Goddess, when to thee I pray,

with supplicating voice both night and day,

And in my latest hour, peace and health,

propitious times, and necessary wealth,

And, ever present, be thy vot'ries aid,

O, much implor'd, art's parent, blue-eyed maid.

If you want more prayers, add Homeric Hymns 11 and 28. Don't forget to journalize your experiences.

Day 4: Herakles, Hermes, Aphrodite, and Eros

The fourth day of the lunar month is quite busy as one hero who became a god and three deities are celebrated.

Herakles

Herakes was a hero worshipped as the divine protector of mankind, and was known for his sporting prowess as well as his strength and determination.

Herakes can be honored by engaging in Olympic style sporting events, particularly those that involve strength or fighting ability. It is also a day to tap into the drive of Herakles and not give up on any projects undertaken, regardless how difficult they may seem.

Orphic Hymn XI. To Herakles

The Fumigation from Frankincense.
Hear, pow'rful, Herakles untam'd and strong,
to whom vast hands, and mighty works belong,
Almighty Titan, prudent and benign,
of various forms, eternal and divine,
Chronos [Father of Time], the theme of gen'ral praise,
ineffable, ador'd in various ways.
Magnanimous, in divination skill'd
and in the athletic labors of the field.
'Tis thine strong archer, all things to devour,
supreme, all-helping, all-producing pow'r;
To thee mankind as their deliv'rer pray,
whose arm can chase the savage tribes away:
Uweary'd, earth's best blossom, offspring fair,
to whom calm peace, and peaceful works are dear.
Self-born, with primogenial fires you shine,
and various names and strength of heart are thine.
Thy mighty head supports the morning light,
and bears untam'd, the silent gloomy night;
From east to west endu'd with strength divine,
twelve glorious labors to absolve is thine;
Supremely skill'd, thou reign'st in heav'n's abodes,
thyself a God amid'st th' immortal Gods.
With arms unshaken, infinite, divine, come,
blessed pow'r, and to our rites incline;
The mitigations of disease convey,
and drive disasterous maladies away.
Come, shake the branch with thy almighty arm,
dismiss thy darts and noxious fate disarm.

If you want more prayers, add Homeric Hymn 15.

Hermes

Hermes presides over travel, trade, communication, athleticism, diplomacy, cunning, thievery, functioning as a psychopomp, and animal husbandry.

Hermes can be honored by engaging in any of the activities in his domain. This includes gambling and public speaking. It can also include visiting the dying in hospital and helping them cross over.

Orphic Hymn XXVII. To Hermes

The Fumigation from Frankincense.
Hermes, draw near, and to my pray'r incline,
angel of Zeus, and Maia's son divine;
Studious of contests, ruler of mankind,
with heart almighty, and a prudent mind.
Celestial messenger, of various skill,
whose pow'rful arts could watchful Argus [hundred-eyed giant] kill:
With winged feet, 'Tis thine thro' air to course,
O friend of man, and prophet of discourse:
Great life-supporter, to rejoice is thine,
in arts gymnastic, and in fraud divine:
With pow'r endu'd all language to explain,
of care the loos'ner, and the source of gain.
Whose hand contains of blameless peace the rod,
Corucian, blessed, profitable God;
Of various speech, whose aid in works we find,
and in necessities to mortals kind:
Dire weapon of the tongue, which men revere, be present,
Hermes, and thy suppliant hear;
Assist my works, conclude my life with peace,
give graceful speech, and me memory's increase.

If you want more prayers, add Homeric Hymns 4 and 18 (4 is extremely long).

Aphrodite

Aphrodite presides over beauty, love, pleasure and procreation.

The primary way to honor Aphrodite is through love. Appreciate your existing relationships or start new ones. Be more loving toward those you interact with and cultivate compassion. Appreciate beauty through music, painting, sculpture, and even through nature. Beautify your immediate environment with perfume, flowers, and works of art.

Orphic Hymn LIV. To Aphrodite

Ourania [Heavenly], illustrious, laughter-loving queen,
sea-born, night-loving, of an awful mien;
Crafty, from whom Ananke [necessity] first came,
producing, nightly, all-connecting dame:
'Tis thine the world with harmony to join,
for all things spring from thee,
O pow'r divine.
The Moirai [triple Fates] are rul'd by thy decree,
and all productions yield alike to thee:
Whate'er the heav'ns, encircling all contain,
earth fruit-producing, and the stormy main,
Thy sway confesses, and obeys thy nod,
awful attendant of the brumal God [Dionysos or Bakkhos]:
Goddess of marriage, charming to the sight,
mother of Eortes [mother of Loves], whom banquetings delight;
Peitho [source of persuasion], secret, fav'ring queen,
illustrious born, apparent and unseen:
Spousal, lupercal, and to men inclin'd, prolific,
most-desir'd, life-giving, kind:
Great scepter-bearer of the Gods,
'Tis thine, mortals in necessary bands to join;

And ev'ry tribe of savage monsters

dire in magic chains to bind, thro' mad desire.

Come, Cyprus-born, and to my pray'r incline,

whether exalted in the heav'ns you shine,

Or pleas'd in Syria's temple to preside,

or o'er th' Egyptian plains thy car to guide,

Fashion'd of gold; and near its sacred flood,

fertile and fam'd to fix thy blest abode;

Or if rejoicing in the azure shores,

near where the sea with foaming billows roars,

The circling choirs of mortals, thy delight,

or beauteous nymphs, with eyes cerulean bright,

Pleas'd by the dusty banks renown'd of old,

to drive thy rapid, two-yok'd car of gold;

Or if in Cyprus with thy mother fair,

where married females praise thee ev'ry year,

And beauteous virgins in the chorus join,

Adonis [mortal lover of Aphrodite] pure to sing and thee divine;

Come, all-attractive to my pray'r inclin'd, for thee,

I call, with holy, reverent mind.

If you want more prayers, add Homeric Hymns 5, 6 and 10 (5 is extremely long).

Eros

Eros presides over love, instilling love in the hearts of the gods and men, and is a companion of Aphrodite. Eros can also be seen as the ideal side of Greek pedophilia, who "brings to boys sometimes a flower, a lyre, or a hoop, who addresses them with lively gesture or impetuously hurls himself down upon them: an ideal representation of the wooing of men in love." [8]

---

8. Hans Licht, *Sexual Life in Ancient Greece* (London: George Routledge & Sons Ltd., 1942), 441.

Some have differentiated the domain of Eros from that of Aphrodite by saying that hers was to rule over the love of men for women while associating Eros with the love of men for young men.

Some modern practitioners maintain the male-male associations of Eros, and employ depictions of him as a young man. Alternatively, Eros may be honored through love, alongside Aphrodite. Becoming a match-maker in this case would be very appropriate. A respect of the LGBT community is mandatory. Personally, I honor love in all its expressions so long as it is between two consenting adults, so my preference is for an inclusive approach toward Eros.

Orphic Hymn LVII. To Eros [Love]

The Fumigation from Aromatics.
I Call great Eros, source of sweet delight,
holy and pure, and lovely to the sight;
Darting, and wing'd, impetuous fierce desire,
with Gods and mortals playing, wand'ring fire:
Cautious, and two-fold,
keeper of the keys of heav'n and earth, the air, and spreading seas;
Of all that Deo's [an epithet of Demeter] fertile realms contains,
by which th' all-parent Goddess life sustains,
Or dismal Tartarus [the great pit beneath the earth] is doom'd to keep,
widely extended, or the sounding, deep;
For thee, all Nature's various realms obey,
who rul'st alone, with universal sway.
Come, blessed pow'r, regard these mystic fires,
and far avert, unlawful mad desires.

Don't forget to journalize your experiences for each of the deities worked with.

Day 5: Rest

There are no deities scheduled for this day. If you are not already doing so, you should try the daily meal-based offerings in the Personal Practice—Daily Observances chapter.

Just because this is a "rest" day doesn't mean you shouldn't journal your meal-based offerings—what you used and what you experienced.

Day 6: Artemis

Artemis presides over hunting, wilderness and wild animals, childbirth, protecting girls until marriage, as well as bringing sudden death and disease.

Artemis can be honored by caring for, and interacting with, the environment. Hiking, cleaning pollution, and engaging in wildlife protection are all very appropriate. When out in the wild, be very aware of your surroundings and engage your senses. Those who routinely hunt should consider going on this day, but be respectful of the animal that is killed. I personally do not think that inflicting sudden death and disease is an appropriate way of honoring Artemis.

Orphic Hymn XXXV. To Artemis

The Fumigation from Manna.
Hear me, Zeus' daughter, celebrated queen,
Bromia [Mount Nysa Nymph] and Titan, of a noble mien:
In darts rejoicing and on all to shine,
torch-bearing Goddess, Dictynna [Britomartis—virgin goddess of
    hunting and netting] divine;
O'er births presiding, and thyself a maid,
to labor-pangs imparting ready aid:
Dissolver of the zone and wrinkl'd care,
fierce huntress, glorying in the Sylvan [pastoral] war:
Swift in the course, in dreadful arrows skill'd,
wandering by night, rejoicing in the field:
Of manly form, erect, of bounteous mind,
illustrious daimon, nurse of human kind:

Immortal, earthly, bane of monsters fell, 'Tis thine;

blest maid, on woody hills to dwell:

Foe of the stag, whom woods and dogs delight,

in endless youth who flourish fair and bright.

O, universal queen, august, divine, a various form,

Cydonian [city in Crete] pow'r, is thine:

Dread guardian Goddess, with benignant mind auspicious,

come to mystic rites inclin'd

Give earth a store of beauteous fruits to bear,

send gentle Peace, and Health with lovely hair,

And to the mountains drive Disease and Care.

If you want more prayers, add Homeric Hymns 9 and 27. Note that a different translation of this Orphic Hymn lists powdered frankincense rather than manna as the fumigation. Don't forget to journalize your experiences.

Day 7: Apollon

Apollon presides over prophecy and oracles, healing, music and song, poetry, archery, protection of boys, as well as bringing plague and disease.

Apollon can be honored by practicing a form of divination; tending to, or visiting, the sick; playing an instrument or listening to music; reading or writing poetry; practicing archery; or assisting the boy scouts or some other organization that works with boys.

Orphic Hymn XXXIII. To Apollon

The Fumigation from Manna.

Blest Paian [title of Apollon], come, propitious to my pray'r,

illustrious pow'r, whom Memphian tribes revere,

Slayer of Tityus [giant who assaulted Leto], and the God of health,

Lycorian [sanctuary of Zeus] Phœbus [= bright, forename of Apollon],

    fruitful source of wealth.

Spermatic, golden-lyr'd,

the field from thee receives its constant, rich fertility.

Titanic, Grunian [temple of Apollon], Smynthian [town with many
     mice which are one of his symbols], thee I sing,
Python-destroying, hallow'd, Delphian king:
Rural, light-bearer, and the Muse's head,
noble and lovely, arm'd with arrows dread:
Far-darting, Bacchian, two-fold, and divine,
pow'r far diffused, and course oblique is thine.
O, Delian [Apollon was born on Delos] king,
whose light-producing eye views all within,
and all beneath the sky:
Whose locks are gold, whose oracles are sure,
who, omens good reveal'st, and precepts pure:
Hear me entreating for the human kind,
hear, and be present with benignant mind;
For thou survey'st this boundless æther all,
and ev'ry part of this terrestrial ball
Abundant, blessed; and thy piercing sight,
extends beneath the gloomy, silent night;
Beyond the darkness, starry-ey'd, profound,
the stable roots, deep fix'd by thee are found.
The world's wide bounds, all-flourishing are thine,
thyself all the source and end divine:
'Tis thine all Nature's music to inspire,
with various-sounding, harmonising lyre;
Now the last string thou tun'st to sweet accord,
divinely warbling now the highest chord;
Th' immortal golden lyre, now touch'd by thee,
responsive yields a Dorian melody.
All Nature's tribes to thee their diff'rence owe,
and changing seasons from thy music flow
Hence, mix'd by thee in equal parts,
advance Summer and Winter in alternate dance;
This claims the highest, that the lowest string,
the Dorian measure tunes the lovely spring

Hence by mankind, Pan-royal, two-horn'd nam'd,

emitting whistling winds thro' Syrinx fam'd;

Since to thy care, the figur'd seal's consign'd,

which stamps the world with forms of ev'ry kind.

Hear me, blest pow'r, and in these rites rejoice,

and save thy mystics with a suppliant voice.

If you want more prayers, add Homeric Hymns 3 and 21 (3 is extremely long). Note that a different translation of this Orphic Hymn lists powdered frankincense rather than manna as the fumigation. Don't forget to journal your experiences.

Day 8: Poseidon and Theseus

The eighth day of the lunar month celebrates Poseidon and Theseus.

Poseidon

Poseidon presides over the sea, rivers, flood and drought, earthquakes, and horses.

Poseidon can be honored by visiting the seaside and perhaps going out in a vessel. It would be appropriate to support seafarers, campaign to preserve marine life and also against ocean pollution. Swimming, diving or engaging in a water sport are fun ideas. Finally, there is the option to ride a horse. Be mindful of Poseidon's power over the mighty ocean and over earthquakes.

Orphic Hymn XVI. to Poseidon

The Fumigation from Myrrh

Hear, Poseidon, ruler of the sea profound,

whose liquid grasp begirts the solid ground;

Who, at the bottom of the stormy main,

dark and deep-bosom'd, hold'st thy wat'ry reign;

Thy awful hand the brazen trident bears,

and ocean's utmost bound, thy will reveres:

Thee I invoke, whose steeds the foam divide,

from whose dark locks the briny waters glide;

Whose voice loud founding thro' the roaring deep,

drives all its billows, in a raging heap;

When fiercely riding thro' the boiling sea,

thy hoarse command the trembling waves obey.

Earth shaking, dark-hair'd God,

the liquid plains (the third division) Fate to thee ordains,

'Tis thine, cairulian [cerulean or caerulean, a blue hue] daimon,

to survey well pleas'd the monsters of the ocean play,

Confirm earth's basis, and with prosp'rous gales

waft ships along, and swell the spacious sails;

Add gentle Peace, and fair-hair'd Health beside,

and pour abundance in a blameless tide.

If you want more prayers, add Homeric Hymn 22.

Theseus

As promised, we have Orphic Hymns to all the deities in the lunar cycle. Theseus, however, was a hero, and unfortunately missed out.

Theseus was the founding hero of Athens, and was considered as their own great reformer.

There is an Ode to Theseus by Bacchylides, who was a fifth-century-BCE Greek lyric poet. It is titled Ode 17 (Dithyramb 3) "Youths, or Theseus" and is available online.

If you're not Greek, then reflect on the founder(s) of the nation you live in.

Don't forget to journalize your experiences and the steps you took to honor the god Poseidon and the hero Theseus.

Days 9–28 or 29 Daily Meal-based Offerings

If you are not already doing so, you should perform the daily meal-based offerings in the Personal Practice—Daily Observances chapter. The emphasis should be on integrating these as seamlessly as possible into your daily routine. When eating out it probably will not be possible to make offerings, so let common sense be your guide.

By this stage, it will come as no surprise that you should briefly journalize your meal-based offerings—what you used and what you experienced.

REVIEW

Now it is time to reflect on the experiences of the trial lunar month.

You have had at least three weeks of daily meal-based observances. Review your daily journal entries. How tangible were the presences of Hestia, the Good Daimon, Zeus, and Apollon? Does your home feel any different? Do you feel somewhat closer to the divine (in an emotional sense) and perhaps safer?

What about the deities experienced on a one-off basis? How tangible were their presences?

The more these rituals are repeated, the more tangible the results become. Those who regularly work with the deities establish a bonded relationship with them. The deities will come to those who earnestly seek them with open hearts.

Once a practitioner develops a relationship with a deity, they can then start channeling information apparently from that deity. That information may, or may not, be consistent with existing myths. UPGs should not be ignored by those that receive them, but rather recognized as being of a solely personal nature.

Would you like to experience more of the deities? Then perhaps you should work the annual festivals in the Athenian calendar (see Experiencing the Annual Cycle—Athenian Festival Calendar). This is the traditional approach to use. Once you've worked through at least part of it, you'll be in a better position to decide whether you wish to stay with it or improvise.

I realize that some people will not have the patience to work through the calendar for an entire year, but will want results much sooner, especially if there are specific deities that they wish to experience. I would much rather have people working with the deities in a nontraditional sense, by using nontraditional days and/or nontraditional methods, than not working with the deities at all.

Day 30	Hekate	Reflection and introspection
Day 1	Noumenia—All deities	New beginnings
Day 2	Agathos Daimon	Protection of the household, bringing good luck, protection, and divine assistance
Day 3	Athene	Tritogeneia celebration: builds on the protection obtained on the second day
Day 4	Herakles, Hermes, Aphrodite, and Eros	Strength, travel, communication, love
Day 5	Rest	Daily meal-based offerings to Hestia, the Good Daimon, Zeus, and Apollon
Day 6	Artemis	Nature
Day 7	Apollon	Divination and the arts
Day 8	Poseidon and Theseus	Seaside
Days 9–29		Daily meal-based offerings to Hestia, the Good Daimon, Zeus, and Apollon

10: CONTROVERSIAL ISSUES
IN ANCIENT GREEK SOCIETY

Religion both shapes a society and is at the same time a product of society.[1] As society changes, religion is forced to change. If it does not evolve and adapt for contemporary usage, it loses its relevance and dies out. The prevailing religions in our society have all changed, and none can honestly claim to be identical to what they were when first established hundreds or, in some cases, thousands of years ago.

Ancient religions were the products of societies that were vastly different to our own. Many ancient societies took things for granted which would strike us as morally reprehensible. It has been previously pointed out that there is no word in the ancient Greek language for religion, probably due to it being seamlessly integrated into everyday life. Consequently, it is extremely important to develop an understanding of ancient Greek society in order to understand the social context of its religion.

In the course of my research for this book, however, I found myself stunned by several striking parallels between Greek religion and other religions of the time, including Judaism. Just as Judaism has evolved,

---

1. Bowra, *The Greek Experience*, 54.

Hellenism would also have evolved had it not been suppressed by Christians from the late Roman empire.

I will briefly outline what I consider to be the main issues within ancient Greek society that would be controversial to us today, giving comparisons in each section to the Old Testament in order to further aid in understanding the era in which they lived. It should be noted that ancient Greek culture is normally presented in a sanitized form, with a number of these issues being glossed over or covered up.

SLAVERY

The Greeks saw themselves as a race apart. They were privileged and educated, had slaves and helots (serfs) to perform menial tasks, and were surrounded by nations peopled with foreigners referred to as "barbarians." Thousands of slaves toiling in mining, agricultural, and manufacturing industries enabled the Greeks to enjoy their leisurely lifestyle.[2]

It has been suggested that slaves were mostly female domestics and were often treated virtually like members of the family. In the Homeric writings, slavery was an expected fact of life. In a captured town men were killed or sold into slavery, attractive women were taken as concubines, and unattractive women were sold into slavery. It was acceptable for kings to engage in marauding expeditions, plundering and enslaving. Historian and Athenian general Thucydides (c. 460 BCE–c. 395 BCE) wrote that the main source of livelihood for the early Hellenes was such marauding expeditions. As an example, Odysseus sacked food from the city of Ismarus, and ascended the river Aegyptus to pillage the field, carry off women and children, and kill the men.

During the so-called Golden Age (480–399 BCE), Attica had a population of 315,000. Power was in the hands of 43,000 citizens who were males aged twenty-one and over, with two free Athenian parents, and who did not engage in manual labor and were not subject to anyone.

---

2. J. C. Stobart, *The Glory That Was Greece* (Cambridge, MA: Sidgwick & Jackson, 1951) 163, 192.

These were the only people who had the right to vote and enjoy the fruits of democracy. Thus, democracy was limited to about 14 percent of the population. The remainder of the population consisted of free Athenian women and children, 115,000 slaves, 28,500 metics (*metikoi*, or resident aliens), freedmen (those who were once slaves), those who had to labor for a living, and those who were subject to another. Very few slaves in Greece were Greeks—most were foreigners. Even the poorest citizens had one or two slaves, while the richest homes had fifty or more.[3]

By the fifth and fourth centuries BCE, slavery became quite common in Athens. Aristotle had thirteen slaves and Plato had six. While some slaves were treated like members of the household, others were subjected to violence and sexual abuse. Slaves were required to be tortured before giving evidence in Athenian courts. Slaves working in mines were typically beaten to maintain production. Slaves were property and were treated as such, so as to maintain the status quo of free citizens. In the more prosperous cities, slaves made up 30–40 percent of the population.

Aristotle justified slavery quite simply by arguing that there were natural hierarchies, and so slaves deserved to be slaves, women should stay in their homes, and free Greek citizens should rule over them all.[4] With the exception of a few philosophers, very few Greeks disagreed with this. While Aristotle looked upon the slave as an animate tool, he effectively prophesied the end of slavery by stating that it would continue until all menial work was done by self-operating machines.[5] It is interesting to note that while certainly not the only factor, the Industrial Revolution contributed to the ending of slavery in the nineteenth century.

It should be noted that slaves brought into an Athenian household would undergo an initiation ceremony similar to that experienced by brides (see below), where they would have protection conferred on

---

3. Durant, *Life of Greece*, 46, 48, 254–5, 278–280.

4. Freeman, *Greek Achievement*, 3–4, 121–124, 192, 282–283, 434–436.

5. Durant, *Life of Greece*, 280.

them by Hestia, goddess of the hearth, which was the focal point of the house.[6]

The Hebrew Bible clearly sanctions the ownership of male and female slaves, who are "heathens" from neighboring nations (Leviticus 25:44–46), and states that it is permissible for a man to sell his daughter into slavery (Exodus 21:7).

Historically, slavery has been a worldwide phenomenon, and is attested in the earliest written records, implying that it has been practiced since the dawn of time. It was not until the American Civil War (1861–1865) that slavery was finally ended in the United States. Its vestiges still continue in the despicable practices of human trafficking, child labor, illegal sweatshops, and so on.

Subjugation of Women

With the rise in slavery came the marginalization of women. Dark Age villages had an open plan, while after 700 BCE houses were enclosed and women were segregated.[7]

For women from wealthy families, marriages were arranged between the parents of a child bride in her early to mid-teens and the groom, who was typically of similar age to the bride's father. The criteria used were normally elevation of social status rather than any sort of emotional bond.[8] Children were only legitimate if they were born within a marriage where both parents were children of Athenian citizens—thus, equality of birth and property were the chief considerations.[9] Marriage was a fulfillment of duty to the deities, ensuring future worshippers and continuation of the state.[10]

Five days after the birth of a baby, its father carried it around the hearth, so as to bring it into the household. In similar fashion, a bride

---

6. Garland, *Daily Life of the Ancient Greeks*, 71.
7. Freeman, *Greek Achievement*, 51.
8. Garland, *Daily Life of the Ancient Greeks*, 48.
9. Seyffert, *Dictionary of Classical Antiquities*, 376.
10. Licht, *Sexual Life in Ancient Greece*, 34.

was brought from the hearth of her father to the hearth of her husband.[11] It should also be noted that the ceremony for bringing a bride into the household was paralleled by that for bringing in a slave.[12] In these cases, there was a shower of sweetmeats at the hearth consisting of dates, cakes, candied fruit, figs and nuts.[13]

A wife's primary duty was to give birth to offspring—preferably male—so that her husband had an heir. Miscarriages and deaths of the mothers during childbirth were common.[14]

While the poor had to cope with one-room houses, the wealthy would invariably have separate living quarters for the women [*gynaikeion*] positioned so that they would remain out of sight, either at the back of a one-story house or in the top story of a two-story house.[15]

Women were expected to remain in the home and be in charge of all domestic activities. They would send the slaves to work outside, and contribute to the household by spinning and weaving. On the rare occasions when "respectable" women would venture outdoors, they would be accompanied by their slaves or female friends. These rare occasions were invariably connected with religion. Women would prepare corpses for burial. There were a few festivals exclusively for women, most notably the Thesmophoria (to venerate Demeter).[16] Other festivals included the Skira (to venerate Athene) and the Adonia[17] (to venerate Adonis[18]).

Women had no political rights and were always under the control of a man—either their father, husband, or next of kin.[19]

---

11. Burkert, *Greek Religion*, 255.

12. Zaidman and Pantel, *Religion in the Ancient Greek City*, 70.

13. Rice and Stambaugh, *Sources for the Study of Greek Religion*, 144.

14. Garland, *Daily Life of the Ancient Greeks*, 51–2.

15. Ibid., 85.

16. Ibid., 53.

17. Burkert, *Greek Religion*, 230, 258.

18. Seyffert, *Dictionary of Classical Antiquities*, 6.

19. Garland, *Daily Life of the Ancient Greeks*, 54–5.

Women who were poor, spinsters, or widows normally resorted to working as either prostitutes or courtesans to support themselves. Rather than marry, such women would enter into a less binding arrangement similar to that of a common-law, or de facto, wife.[20]

In Greek society, generally women fell into one of three classes—prostitutes or courtesans for pleasure, concubines for daily personal service, and wives to bear children and manage households.[21]

While all public offices were held by men, a small number of women had another option that was connected with religion—they served as priestesses. In general, female deities were served by priestesses, while male deities were served by priests. The exception was Apollon at Delphi being served by the Pythia, who was always a woman. Also, on Mount Parnassos above Delphi, women acted as Maenads in a festival of Dionysos. Religious office presented the one area where Greek women assumed roles equal and comparable to those of men.[22]

In the Hebrew scriptures, most women were treated as property with the status being marginally better than that of slaves. Before marriage, they were virtually imprisoned in the homes of their fathers. After marriage, they were virtually imprisoned in the homes of their husbands. They were normally barred from having any sort of authority, could not appear in public or testify in court (Ecclesiasticus 25:13, Ecclesiasticus 25:18, Ecclesiasticus 25:24, Ecclesiastes 7:26).

ANIMAL SACRIFICE

This has been outlined in the Greek Religion chapter.

The Hebrew Bible insists on the need for animal sacrifices. The very first one was made by Abel (Cain's brother), after which animal sacrifices to God were made in numerous locations by many Jews. Burnt offerings resulted in an aroma pleasing to God (Leviticus 1:9, Deuteronomy 12:4–14, I Kings 8:46–50, Hosea 14:3).

---

20. Garland, *Daily Life of the Ancient Greeks*, 55–6.

21. Licht, *Sexual Life in Ancient Greece*, 32.

22. Price, *Religions of the Ancient Greeks*, 68, 115; Connelly, *Portrait of a Priestess*, 2.

Roughly until the nineteenth century, animals were slaughtered in the open in the Western world. At this time in response to public opinion, slaughterhouses or abattoirs became hidden from view. Had any animal sacrifices been practiced, they may well have been either suppressed or driven underground.

HUMAN SACRIFICE

I find the idea of human sacrifice abhorrent, however, it is a recurring theme in Greek mythology.[23] Probably the best-known example is connected with Minos, the mythical king of Crete, who conquered Athens and exacted a tribute of seven girls and seven youths to be offered to the Minotaur in the Labyrinth every ninth year. On the third occasion of the tribute, Theseus, the son of King Aegeus of Athens, had himself included as one of the seven youths. Theseus won the heart of Ariadne, who supplied him with a magick sword to kill the Minotaur and thread to escape from the Labyrinth.[24]

In Homer, Agamemnon sacrificed his daughter Iphigenia so as to have sufficient winds to sail to Troy; while later, Achilles sacrificed twelve Trojan youths on the funeral pyre of his friend Patroclus (*Iliad* xxi, 27; xxiii, 22, 175).[25] Idomeneus, leader of the Cretan troops returning from Troy, in return for safe passage, vowed to sacrifice to Poseidon the first living creature that he met onshore. This was unfortunately his son, but he kept his vow.[26]

The Messenian king Aristodemus was advised by the oracle at Delphi that in order to defeat the Spartans, who had attacked his kingdom, he should sacrifice a virgin of his own race. Despite sacrificing his own daughter, he still lost the war.[27]

---

23. Davies, *Human Sacrifice*, 53–7.
24. Durant, *The Life of Greece*, 23.
25. Ibid., 193.
26. Tierney, *The Highest Altar*, 383–4.
27. Durant, *The Life of Greece*, 73.

Greek myths repeatedly describe animal sacrifices taking the place of human sacrifices, or animal sacrifices transforming into human sacrifices. In one example, a ram was sacrificed to Zeus Laphystios in Thessaly instead of a man fully covered in woolen fillets. By way of comparison, in the Karneia, an annual festival of the Dorians, a runner covered in woolen fillets would be chased by naked runners, and would pronounce a good wish upon the city-state when captured. This would be interpreted as agreement, whereupon the runner would be sacrificed.[28]

Human sacrifice was not limited to myths, and occurred throughout Greek history.

In the Minoan-Mycenaean world, it is claimed that the Archanes temple in the Knossos region of Crete dated to about 1700 BCE has the remains of human sacrifices. Elsewhere in Knossos a deposit of children's bones bearing knife marks have been found.[29]

A clay tablet from the Mycenaean period shows offerings to a deity, including men and women. While these may have been people dedicated to the service of the deity, sadly they could have been sacrificial victims.[30]

The Greeks traced the spilling of human blood to the land of the barbaric Tauroi in the far north. This included sacrifices to the Taurean Artemis, which originated in Colchis (*Kolchis*) in modern Georgia. The sacrifice for Artemis Tauropolos at Halai Araphenides on the northeast coast of Attica involved drawing blood with a knife from a man's throat. The sacrifice for Artemis Ortheia in Sparta involved the *epheboi* (male adolescents) being horribly whipped at the altar. (Pausanias iii, 16) This practice stemmed from an ancient game where one group of boys tried to steal cheese from the altar of Artemis, while another group defended the altar with whips.[31]

---

28. Burkert, *Greek Religion*, 65, 234–5; Grene, *Herodotus*, 539–40.
29. Burkert, *Greek Religion*, 31, 37.
30. Mary Beard and John North, *Pagan Priests* (London: Duckworth) 160.
31. Burkert, *Greek Religion*, 59, 152.

To the west of Greece, on the island of Leukas, a condemned criminal was thrown off a cliff into the sea every year to appease Apollon. Apollon was similarly sacrificed to when human victims were hurled from cliffs in Cyprus. Human sacrifices were made to Dionysus in Chios and Tenedos. Themistocles sacrificed Persian captives to Dionysus at the battle of Salamis (Pausanias iv, 9, vii, 19).

Zeus was presented with human sacrifices in Arcadia until the second century CE. In Massalia a poor citizen would be fed, clothed, and cast over a cliff to rid the community of pestilence. There were also cases of ugly or poor men being given lavish meals, only to be ceremonially driven out of their communities as scapegoats in a purification ritual.[32]

One of the ethnic groups in Greece, the Boeotians gathered every sixty years to celebrate a festival called the Great Daidala. In addition to sacrificing cows to Hera and bulls to Zeus, fourteen carved wooden images would be ritually burned. Each wooden image was called a *daidalon*, which was the ancient name for a *xoanon* (wooden cult image). Earlier Great Daidala festivals would have just one daidalon, which would be adorned as a bride for Zeus before being taken to the top of Mount Kithairon and burned. At its time of origin in the pre-Classical period, this festival was centered on an actual human sacrifice.[33]

Pausanias visited the sanctuary of Zeus on Mount Lykaion in Arcadia and heard rumors of an annual ritual begun by an ancient people. The ritual, which he did not wish to delve into, involved the sacrifice, dismemberment, and consumption of a child. (Pausanias viii, 38, 7) Those who engaged in this cannibalistic rite were banished for nine years to live like wolves in the forest.[34] This werewolf transformation could

---

32. Burkert, *Greek Religion*, 82–3; Durant, *The Life of Greece*, 193–4.
33. Matthew Dillon, *Pilgrims and Pilgrimage in Ancient Greece* (New York: Routledge) 124, 135–8.
34. Patrick Tierney, *The Highest Altar* (London: Blomsbury, 1989) 10, 443.

only be reversed by abstaining from human flesh throughout those nine years[35] (Pausanias vi, 8, 2).

It has been suggested that as time went on, human sacrifice was made more palatable by restricting its scope to condemned criminals. (This is much like today's death sentences in which criminals are put to death by several methods including the electric chair and lethal injection.) It was then largely replaced by animal sacrifice.[36]

The Hebrew Bible has many references to human sacrifice, suggesting that this was a prevalent practice of the time (Deuteronomy 18:10–11, Leviticus 18:21, 2 Kings 3:26–7, 2 Kings 21:6, Ezekiel 21, 1 Kings 13:2, 2 Kings 23:20, 2 Chronicles 34:2–5, Deuteronomy 13:13–19, Genesis 22:1–18, Judges 11:29–40).

DRUGS

Throughout Europe, from the Stone Age to as late as the seventh century CE, shamanism was endemic (common in a particular area). Shamans were known for traveling to the spirit world within a trance state, which was sometimes induced by mind-altering substances, or entheogens, which would change the brain's chemistry. Entheogens used included opium, cannabis; hallucinogens such as various mushrooms, ergot, artemisia, mandrake, henbane, convolvulus (morning glory); as well as alcohol (mead, ale, and fermented berry juice).[37]

Very little is known about the Mysteries of Eleusis as initiates kept their silence, although tantalizing glimpses highly praise "ineffable visions" after drinking a potion. Given the similarity between these descriptions and those of the Mesoamerican mushroom rite, it has been credibly proposed that perhaps the ancient Greeks hit on a method to

---

35. G. S. Kirk, *The Nature of Greek Myths* (Harmondsworth: Penguin Books Lt., 1985) 239.

36. Durant, *The Life of Greece*, 194.

37. Miranda Aldhouse-Green, *The Quest for the Shaman: Shape-Shifters, Sorcerers, and Spirit Healers in Ancient Europe* (New York: Thames & Hudson, 2005) 9, 12, 85–6, 122–5.

isolate a hallucinogen from ergot (specifically ergot of rye, purple-brown protrusions from the ears of rye—*Secale cornutum*), which would have produced an experience comparable to LSD or psilocybin. Ergot of rye actually provides the raw material to produce lysergic acid diethylamide, better known as LSD–25. While no rye grew in Greece, wheat and barley did and the ergots growing on them both were found to contain basically the same alkaloids as ergot of rye. In addition, ergot grows on the wild grass *Paspalum distichum* (knotgrass) which is found commonly all around the Mediterranean basin. A hallucinogenic extract from suitable kinds of ergot could have been prepared with the techniques and equipment available in antiquity.[38]

At the Oracle of the Dead on the Acheron, Professor Sotiris Dakaris of Ioannina University has discovered large quantities of black lumps of hashish. In ancient times, seekers would descend through a corridor into a small dark room accompanied by priests where they would spend 29 days. They dined on beans, mussels, and pork, which were foods related to the dead. Seekers would experience temple sleep, or incubation, with its inherent revelations.[39] Needless to say, living in almost total darkness for almost a full lunar month in the presence of chanting priests would lead to an altered state of consciousness, but once hashish vapor was added to the equation, revelatory visions could be virtually guaranteed.

At the Oracle of Delphi, the priestess dedicated to Apollon, known as the Pythia, would bathe in the Castalian spring, and enter the temple following a goat sacrifice. The temple was fumigated with barley meal and laurel leaves (sacred to Apollon). She would sit on a tripod over a fissure in the ground below the Apollon temple inhaling volcanic fumes

---

38. Wasson, R. Gordon, Albert Hofmann, and Carl A. P. Ruck, *The Road to Eleusis*: Unveiling the Secret of the Mysteries (San Diego, Harcourt-Brace, 1978) 4–10.

39. Philipp Vandenberg, *The Mystery of the Oracles: World-Famous Achaeologists Reveal the Best-Kept Secrets of Antiquity* (New York: Macmillan Publishing Co., 1979) 1, 7–9.

while holding a freshly cut bay branch, and then fall into a trance. Preliminary geological surveys by French archaeologists at the turn of the nineteenth century suggested that there was no possibility of any volcanic fumes,[40] leading many modern classical scholars to propose various alternate theories as to how she actually fell into a trance. A study published in 2001, however, has shown that under the site there is an intersection of a fault zone with a swarm of fractures, which provides pathways for rising groundwater, including a spring below the temple. Light hydrocarbon gases capable of producing mild narcotic effects may have escaped during and after seismic activity. Thus the preconditions for the Pythia becoming intoxicated and going into prophetic states are all present.[41]

It is evident that the ancient Greeks resorted to mind-altering substances for spiritual reasons. What is less known is that they were cognizant of the use of plant products for both healing as well as recreational use. Accounts of sexual practices and drug use have actually been deliberately distorted or censored by classicists to fit expected standards of morality. Recreational drugs of choice fell into the categories of opiates, anticholinergics and psychotropic fungi. Widely used herbs included wormwood, marijuana, henbane, belladonna, mandrake, jimson weed, and hemlock. They were taken most commonly mixed with wine, or pushed into the nostrils, as anal and vaginal suppositories, or breathing in vapors of burning plants (fumigation). Many of these substances could be lethal when taken in sufficient quantities, but at low doses were pleasurable or euphoric. Anticholinergics, like nightshade, taken in high doses lead to an experience similar to LSD with disorientation,

40. Burkert, *Greek Religion*, 116.
41. J. Z. De Boer and J. R. Hale, *The Geological Origins of the Oracle at Delphi.* (The Archaeology of Geological Catastrophes, Geological Society, London, special publications) 171, 399–412.

confusion, hallucinations, and psychosis.[42] Excessive doses of the thistle (*Skolymus hispanicus*) cause mental derangement.[43] None of these substances were criminalized or deemed immoral, and their use was widespread.[44]

The followers of Dionysus experienced ritualistic ecstatic frenzy, ostensibly from drinking wine. Dionysus was associated with several plants, including ivy, grapevines, and bryony. Each of these plants produces altered states of consciousness, yet only alcohol is discussed in connection with bacchanalian ecstasy. It is far more likely that ivy and bryony were mixed with wine and ingested. The savior figure Prometheus was said to have dripped blood, which became a plant, a source of a potent, painkilling, euphoria-producing drug, most probably an opium poppy. Myths of many other deities abound with references to psychotropic botanicals.[45]

Polish anthropologist Dr. Sula Benet (1903–1982), also known as Sara Benetowa, convincingly proposed that the Hebrew holy oil composed of "myrrh, sweet cinnamon, kaneh bosm and kassia" (Exodus 30: 23-4) should be reconsidered. She asserted that the term "kaneh bosm" usually translated as "calamus" or "aromatic reed" was actually cannabis.

It would appear that the association of entheogens with at least some deities would justify their use in order to achieve altered states so as to commune with those deities. I would not recommend this approach for a couple of reasons. First, many entheogens are illegal in many parts of the world. Second, actual dosages of the active components vary from plant to plant, making the risk of an overdose a very real possibility. An overdose

---

42. D. C. A. Hillman, PhD. *The Chemical Muse: Drug Use and the Roots of Western Civilization*, (New York: Thomas Dunne Books, 2008) 57, 59, 73, 75, 76, 79, 80.

43. Michael A. Rinella, *Pharmakon: Plato, Drug Culture and Identity in Ancient Athens* (Lanham, MD: Lexington Books, 2010) 37.

44. Hillman, *The Chemical Muse*, 78.

45. Ibid., 83–6, 100–1, 109.

can lead to permanent mental derangement or even death. Experimentation without expert oversight (from a trained shaman) is very risky.

INSTITUTIONALIZED SEXUAL ORIENTATION

Identifying sexual orientation as homosexual or heterosexual is a modern phenomenon and is of limited usefulness when applied to the ancient Greeks. Homosexual unions between males were acceptable when they involved a younger man with an older man.[46]

The subject of homosexuality is ignored to such an extent that those readers unable to read original source texts would mistakenly conclude that "it was a merely subsidiary phenomenon, something which happened in isolated cases, rarely, and only here and there." [47] The reality was that a love of post-pubescent youths was perfectly acceptable. Sexual intercourse with sexually immature youths was a punishable offense, however.[48]

In fourth-century-BCE Crete, a coming of age initiation rite involved a man, having first made known his intention, abducting a beautiful youth, as Zeus had carried off Ganymede. The two lovers spent two months in the countryside feasting and hunting. At the conclusion of this period, the youth was considered independent and his lover presented him with a warrior's robe, an ox, and a wine cup. The youth then joined with other independent youths, and they engaged in hunting, sports, and ritual contests. The youth then broke away from his peers in order to marry.

Throughout Greece, male youths would spend three quarters of their days in palaestrae (wrestling arenas) and gymnasia (training facilities also used for socializing and intellectualizing), exercising their bodies and minds, in the company of older men. Training the body was done naked. There is a wealth of Greek literature and art attesting to the appreciation of the youthful male form.[49]

---

46. Garland, *Daily Life of the Ancient Greeks*, 113.
47. Licht, *Sexual Life in Ancient Greece*, 412.
48. Ibid., 416–7.
49. Ibid., 411–436.

By way of explanation, in Greek society adult males were expected to be active, with a propensity toward warfare. Passive behavior was attributed to women (whose married role was that of procreation) and youths. The tendency was for men to aspire to war, and women to aspire to marriage.[50] The alternative for married men to loving youths was of course sexual gratification with prostitutes and slaves.[51]

There were men who continued to desire other males as they grew older, but were forced to marry in order to comply with law and custom.[52] Athenians who practiced homosexuality exclusively became targets of abuse.[53]

The problem with the Greek system was that while certain youths would have been very happy in the company of older men, others would have felt uncomfortable. Similarly the fact that fines were imposed on those who refused to marry indicates that certain men felt more comfortable with male company. There was a small minority who would have been happiest on their own. Individual desires were clearly secondary to what was perceived as being most beneficial for the state. In my opinion, the ideal would be to allow everyone to be with the lover of their choice, regardless of gender.

CLASS (OR CASTE) SYSTEM

In Athens, it was only the offspring of a citizen and his legitimate wife who would become a citizen.[54] Naturalized citizens were not allowed to hold offices, including priesthoods, which tended state cults.[55]

---

50. Luc Brisson, *Sexual Ambivalence: Androgyny and Hermaphroditism in Graeco-Roman Antiquity* (Berkeley & Los Angeles, CA: University of California Press, 2002) 61.

51. Morton Smith, *The Ancient Greeks*, 27.

52. Freeman, *The Greek Achievement*, 299–300.

53. Garland, *Daily Life of the Ancient Greeks*, 113.

54. Warrior, *Greek Religion*, 42.

55. Mikalson, *Athenian Popular Religion*, 86.

There was virtually no scope for improvement for those not born citizens.

REVIEW

I believe that the practice of Greek religion, had it been allowed to continue unmolested, would have undergone similar changes to those of Judaism. Blood sacrifice, slavery, the subordination of women, and the practice of institutionalized sexual orientation would probably have been removed from Greek religion, and the result would have remained just as relevant to those practicing it in today's world. Certain entheogens are not legal to take, meaning that either their use would mostly fall to the wayside or legal substitutes would be used. The provision of core rights to people, such as equality, is of crucial importance in a society aspiring to greatness.

In summary, the work undertaken by reconstructionists involves taking an accurate image of an ancient religion and projecting it into the present and future so as to make it relevant for practitioners today. A need for interpretation and interpolation to compensate for knowledge gaps combined with the need to speculate as to how the religion might have appeared today results in rather subjective conclusions, which will vary between reconstructionists. Nevertheless, much work has already been done in bringing many ancient religions back by numerous reconstructionists, and would-be practitioners have a number of approaches at their disposal so as to begin their journey. Once their journey begins, perhaps they will also eventually contribute their own understanding for the benefit of those who will follow.

11: MAGICK IN ANCIENT GREECE

Many contemporary practitioners of Hellenismos tend to be very negative toward magick and would doubtless argue that the inclusion of a chapter dealing with this very subject is somewhat out of place. Their attitude may well originate from prejudices within the academic community. Interestingly, while academics have traditionally disliked magick, there is little consensus among them as to what magick actually is, how it works, and how it differs from religion. In their haste to sweep magick under the carpet and view Greek culture with rose-tinted glasses, a number of academics have clouded the actual beliefs and practices of the ancient Greeks, claiming that in Classical times the Greeks practiced religion exclusively, and that magick made an unwelcome appearance when foreign influences were admitted in Hellenistic times. The reality is that there was never a time when the Greeks did not practice magick.

HISTORY OF MAGICK IN GREECE

The roots of magick stretch back to prehistory. Knowledge of what was termed superstition, but is now termed folklore, has shown that magick and the occult were a part of everyday life in ancient Greece. Virtually everyone believed in magick and practiced it, and periods of discrimination against magicians (and philosophers) were mainly politically motivated. Literary evidence shows that magick was practiced from the time of Homer until the Hellenistic period, during which time it underwent a resurgence. Various academics have proposed different theories to distinguish between magick and religion, but currently a number of scholars are suggesting that there is no fundamental difference. While there is no universal consensus as to how magick should be defined, one plausible suggestion is to define it as the imposition of the human will on nature or on other humans, using powers within the soul and permeating the universe.[1]

While the writings of Homer provide the first literary evidence of the practice of magick, the earliest physical evidence can be found in the funerary imprecations (spoken curses) in the Greek epitaphs of Asia Minor. These were magickal curses written on gravestones warning potential desecrators of what will befall them. Various deities were usually called on to prevent any violation of the grave. The oldest attestations of this tradition are from the seventh century BCE onward.[2]

An inscription from the fourth century BCE recreated an earlier magickal oath sworn by Spartan settlers on the island of Thera around 630 BCE. All the settlers came together and modeled wax dolls. As the dolls were burned, the settlers invoked a curse that should their oaths be broken then they, their descendents, and their property would melt like the dolls.[3]

The so-called curse tablets, which will be discussed below, are normally thought of as having been written during the period from the

---

1. Georg Luck, *Arcana Mundi: Magic and the Occult in the Greek and Roman World* (Wellingborough, UK: Crucible), 3131. Professor Luck provided a treasure trove of translated magickal writings, starting from the very first ones in Homer's *Odyssey*.

2. J. H. M. Strubbe, "Cursed be he that moves my bones," in *Magika Hiera: Ancient Greek Magic & Religion,* ed. Faraone and Obbink, 33–59.

3. Warrior, *Greek Religion,* 233.

fifth century BCE to the fifth century CE in an area spanning northern Africa and Europe. The earliest curse tablets were very simple and were found in Sicily and Attica from the fifth to the fourth centuries BCE.[4] It has been argued that the earliest Sicilian binding spells could actually be dated from the late sixth century or early fifth century BCE.[5] While the earliest curse tablets appear to have been limited geographically to Sicily, Olbia, and Attica in the fifth century BCE, they were all over the Graeco-Roman world by the second century CE.[6]

In the period between Homer and the Hellenistic period there were miracle workers, each of whom are referred to by some academics by the rather neutral term *shaman*. The three most famous of these were Orpheus, Pythagoras, and Empedocles (a fifth-century-BCE Greek philosopher who taught that all matter is composed of particles of fire, water, air, and earth). These figures were reputed to have had magickal powers, and hence healed the sick, communicated with animals, gave oracles, gave religious teachings, had the power of bilocation, and wrote poetry. While some scholars discard magickal claims, there are others who see them as part of a genuine tradition. Notably, after Empedocles, there is less attestation of magickal ability, suggesting that it seemed to deteriorate.[7]

Refreshingly, at least one academic did not mince words, and referred to Orpheus, Pythagoras, Empedocles, and a number of lesser-known

---

4. John G. Gager, *Curse Tablets and Binding Spells from the Ancient World*, (Westport, CN: Greenwood Press, 1998) 3–5.

5. Warrior, *Greek Religion*, 230.

6. Christopher A. Faraone and Dirk Obbink (ed.), "The Agonistic Context of Early Greek Binding Spells," in *Magika Hiera: Ancient Greek Magic & Religion*, ed. Faraone and Obbink, (New York: Oxford University Press, 1997) 3.

7. Eric Robertson Dodds, *The Greeks and the Irrational* (Berkeley, CA: University of California Press) 135–178.

figures as sorcerers.[8] Another academic formulated a ten-step life progression for the myth of a magus, or legendary magician, and demonstrated that Pythagoras fitted the pattern, while Empedocles was a close fit.[9] Yet another academic pointed out that while Orpheus was primarily a musician, he was also a magician, and that his name was incorporated into conjurations for a thousand years, starting in the fifth century BCE.[10]

One of the terms for a magician, *magos* (a word of Persian origin), occurred for the first time in a Greek text in the sixth century BCE and then came into frequent usage in the Classical period. By the fifth century BCE, the term lost its idealized connotation and began to imply an association with an ecstatic cult, after which associations with malevolent magick began to form. Another ancient term for a magician, *goês* (deriving from *goos*, ritual lament), was attested in literature after *magos*. The earliest term, *pharmakon*, could imply a witch, but could also be someone who healed, or killed, with herbs. The term incantation, *epaoidê/epoidê*, was positive in Homer's time, but by Plato's time could be positive or negative. Plato referred to begging priests, *agurtês*, who performed magick for the rich. These terms were connected with private mystery rituals, divination and magick.[11]

The Greek term for magick (*mageia*) was first attested in the latter half of the fifth century BCE, while the word necromancy (*psychagôgia*)

---

8. Ogden, *Magic, Witchcraft, and Ghosts in the Greek and Roman Worlds: A Sourcebook*. Ogden's sourcebook on magick and witchcraft, lets the texts speak for themselves, thus bypassing the biased commentaries found in the writings of some authors. This sourcebook gives an excellent idea of just how prevalent the practices of magick and witchcraft were in ancient Greece.

9. E. M. Butler, *The Myth of the Magus*, (New York: the Macmillan Company, 1948) 2–11, 44–55.

10. W. K. C. Guthrie, *Orpheus and Greek Religion*, 17–19, 39.

11. Fritz Graf, "Excluding the Charming: The Development of the Greek Concept of Magic," in *Ancient Magic and Ritual Power*, ed. Meyer and Mirecki, (Boston, MA: Brill Academic Publishers, 2001) 29–42.

was first attested in the first quarter of the fifth century BCE. Even though these terms did not appear in Homer's writings, no fifth-century-BCE Greek would have doubted that evidence of their operation was obvious. In Book 10 of Homer's *Odyssey*, the god Hermes warned Odysseus about the goddess (also referred to as a witch) Circe (*Kirkê*), and her use of a drug or medicine (*pharmaka* plural, *pharmakon* singular) which transformed men into swine. Hermes [*Hermês*] helped Odysseus obtain a medicine called *môly* which would protect him from Circe's drug. By the fifth century BCE, drugs and medicines (*pharmaka*) were considered to be part and parcel of magickal practice, as well as used by physicians. A fifth-century Greek would probably not have considered there to be any difference between the use of the drug *môly* by Hermes than those used by magicians. Another relevant example comes from the *Homeric Hymn to Demeter* wherein one interpretation had Demeter (*Dêmêtêr*) magickally protecting the gums of a teething baby. The conclusion is that there was no substantive difference between the magick practiced by Greek deities and that practiced by mortals or heroes, although obviously the abilities of the deities were far greater than those of mere mortals. The Sicilian Greek historian, Diodorus Siculus (90–21 BCE) claimed that there was a frequently quoted ancient saying that when doctors failed, everyone resorted to sacrificers, seers, spells, and amulets.[12]

Not all contemporary scholars see the practice of magick beginning with the Homeric writings, as at least one argues that magick only became a distinctive category in the minds of the Greeks in the Athenian tragic poetry of the fifth century BCE—for earlier writers, it was not a category of thought that influenced their thinking. Distinctions between the various terms for magicians are arguably artificial, and seers often practiced magick as well.[13]

---

12. Collins, *Magic in the Ancient Greek World*, 27–30, 36.
13. Matthew W. Dickie, *Magic and Magicians in the Greco-Roman World* (New York: Routledge, 2006) 6, 12–15, 20–22, 46. Dickie focused on those who practiced magick. To define magick, Dickie turned to Professor Graf.

Magick was widely practiced, if not on an everyday basis, then at least on special occasions. There was a magickal device to compel love in common usage consisting of a four-spoked wheel to which a type of bird called a dappled wryneck may have been bound. This wheel was reputedly gifted to humanity by either Aphrodite or Hekate. A vase painting from the third quarter of the fifth century portrays a mother spinning such a wheel around a stick to ensure all went well with her daughter's forthcoming wedding.[14] Childbirth called for the use of folk magick, which employed, in part, a sympathetic element. The mother-to-be consumed wolf meat, a woman who had recently given birth sat next to her, the midwife used her left hand to deliver, and a ritual cry of joy was uttered at the moment of birth.[15] As the child grew it had to be protected against the possibility of malevolent witchcraft and the evil eye, and so often at least the nurse would be skilled in magickal protection techniques.[16]

While there are other accounts of magickal practice during the Classical priod, there are no extant spell books (grimoires), suggesting that traditions either remained within families to be passed on from generation to generation, or perhaps tradition occurred from master to student. There was, however, a mammoth collection of magickal spells, hymns and rituals written in Egypt from the second century BCE to the fifth century CE, known as the Greek Magical Papyri (PGM, *Papyri Graecae Magicae*). Although mostly written in Greek, the material covered blended influences from Greek, Egyptian, Sumerian, Babylonian and Jewish sources, with a small Christian influence. These writings provide a window on magickal practice from the early Hellenistic period to late antiquity. Without magickal literature, academics would be limited to "the literature of the cultural elite" and archaeological re-

---

14. Robert Flaceliere, *Daily Life in Greece at the Time of Pericles* (London, Weidenfeld & Nicolson, 1965) 224.

15. Garland, *Greek Way of Life*, 73.

16. Ibid., 117.

mains. When Greek deities occur in the PGM, they are not portrayed as in literature, but rather as in Greek folklore.[17]

GREEK VIEW OF MAGICK

Quite often, ancient sources claim that those who practiced magick were either foreigners or women, or both. This could be referred to as cultural distancing where unacceptable attributes were projected onto other races or onto the opposite gender. The reality was that many Greek males practiced magick.[18] The presence of large numbers of curse tablets and papyri are physical proof of just how widespread involvement in magick was for the Greeks.[19] Magick was a part of daily life for the Greeks and was consequently thought of as mundane and unremarkable.[20]

Magickal rites and incantations were used to treat epilepsy according to the text titled *On the Holy Disease*. The lack of public mention of these suggests that they were practiced privately and probably lacked public acceptability, or perhaps were so common that it was not thought necessary to comment upon. We know from Plato that soothsayers were often itinerant and anonymous, offering their services by going to the doors of the wealthy. There were exceptions to Plato's statements about soothsayers, as can be seen in the case of Thrasyllus of Aegina who retired a rich man to his homeland, and Sthotys of Thasus who was awarded Athenian citizenship and pay. At the other end of the

---

17. Hans Dieter Betz, *The Greek Magical Papyri in Translation*, xli–liii. Professor Betz edited the PGM. He agreed with Professor Nock, stating that magickal beliefs and practices were not distinguished from religious beliefs and practices, as they were by contemporary academics, except among a few philosophers.
18. Daniel Ogden, *Greek and Roman Necromancy*, 128.
19. Sulochana Asirvatham, et al (ed.) *Between Magic and Religion, Interdisciplinary Studies in Ancient Mediterranean Religion and Society* (New York: Rowman & Littlefield, Publishers, 2001), xiv–xv.
20. Christopher A. Faraone, *Ancient Greek Love Magic* (Caambridge, MA, 1999), 16.

spectrum, the practice of malevolent magick in Athens was quite prevalent, as indicated by philosophers' criticisms, parodies in other writings, and actual curse tablets (to be discussed below).[21]

Contrary to popular perception, there is very little evidence for legislation against magick in classic Greek law. There are only two explicit examples, both of which address the use of magick to harm.

First, there is an inscription of seven curses, which may well have coincided with laws, from Teos, an Ionian city on the coast of Asia Minor, dating to shortly after 479 BCE. In the first five curses (the third is unfortunately not preserved), those who sought to harm either the Teian state or its citizens were condemned to death along with their families. This included those who made harmful spells or poisons. In the final two curses, those who either refused to take part in the first five curses or damaged the inscription were condemned to death along with their families. Second, the sacred laws for a private cult from Philadelphia in Lydia, dating to the first century BCE, required members to avoid wicked spells, incantations, and love charms, along with adultery, murder, robbery, and rape.[22] Magick was so widely practiced that the only concern of the authorities was with malevolent magickal practices, not magick in general.

Returning to Plato, he distinguished between two types of magick: *pharmakeia* (poisoning) and *goeteia* (incantations and techniques for hurting others). Both these types can involve hurting or killing. Plato also suggested harsh penalties for those experts in magick who do not harm, which may possibly be due to the social disruption that a fear of magick causes.[23] He was so negative toward the practice of magick that he proposed ideal laws against it in the early fourth century BCE. In *Laws*, Plato recommended that those guilty of sorcery should be confined in an inland prison where they would be approached with their

---

21. Mikalson, *Athenian Popular Religion*, 23, 41, 89, 111.

22. Ogden, *Magic, Witchcraft, and Ghosts*, 275–299.

23. Dickie, *Magic and Magicians*, 44–5.

food rations by slaves rather than free men. Upon death they would be denied a proper burial. There is no evidence, however, that Plato's vendetta against magick was ever enforced. Hippocrates in *On the Sacred Disease* also attacked the practice of sorcery in the fifth to fourth centuries BCE, using similar arguments to those of Plato.[24] Hippocrates believed that magick coerced the divine, in a way far beyond what was achievable through normal worship, and was thus impious. Even though magicians enjoyed such a reputation because of its beneficial effect on business, an analysis of Athenian curse tablets from the fourth century BCE to the fourth century CE shows that their approach was actually prayerful and supplicatory.[25] Both Plato and Hippocrates never doubted the effectiveness of magick, but rather were ethically concerned with whether magick actually imbued its practitioners with power over deities.[26]

The omnipresent practice of magick in classical antiquity was sometimes used to harm enemies and rivals, sometimes used for good, and was also used to provide access to a higher spirituality. As early as the writings of Pindar (c. 522–443 BCE), magick was seen as a gift of the gods. The ancients saw a strong connection between magick and the various mystery schools, as is evidenced by the many examples of common terminology. Magicians considered themselves to be adepts within a mystery cult, having undergone an initiation similar to that of the well-known mystery cults. The primary difference was that the experience of the mystery cults was a communal one, while magick was more of a solitary activity, although there did appear to be a communal spirit among some magicians.[27]

Further to the connection between magick and mystery schools, Plutarch stated that two particular daimôns, Picus and Faunus, traveled

---

24. Ogden, *Magic, Witchcraft, and Ghosts*, 18–23.

25. Dickie, *Magic and Magicians*, 26.

26. Collins, *Magic in the Ancient Greek World*, 31.

27. Fritz Graf, *Magic in the Ancient World* (Cambridge, MA: Harvard University Press, 1999) 1–2, 20–35, 96–117.

through Italy practicing the same magickal arts as those Greeks known as the Idaean Daktyls (initiates of the Idaean Zeus in Crete). The Daktyls were compared to the Kouretes, who were initiated into medicine and magick. I'll be discussing the Kouretes below.[28]

Diodorus Siculus, a Greek historian who wrote works of history between 60 and 30 BCE, quoted the Greek historian Ephorus [*Ephoros*] (c 400–330 BCE) on the Idaean Daktyls, who discovered both the use of fire and the means of working copper and iron. The Daktyls were wizards who practiced charms, initiatory rites, and mysteries. Orpheus became a pupil of theirs, and was the first to introduce initiatory ritese and mysteries to the Greeks.[29] Thus, at least some mysteries, and at least some magick, had a common origin and remained inextricably linked.

Plato described the training of Persian princes as coming from four exemplary teachers, but the one who was reputed to be the wisest gave instruction in magick [*mageia*] as well as kingly duties. By way of explanation, Socrates added that the art of the magician was the "service of the gods." Thus, magick was clearly practiced even by the highly educated upper echelons of society.[30]

TYPES OF MAGICK IN GREECE

Ancient Greece was in no way an idyllic utopia. Life was at times uncertain, competitive, and dangerous. Individuals would frequently resort to the practice of magick so as to improve their circumstances. Virtually everyone practiced magick regardless of gender, financial status, and

---

28. Harrison, 75–117. In *Themis*, Dr. Harrison presented a fascinating outline of the extent of magick. Her connecting of magick with the mystery schools and showing that it was practiced by the upper echelons of society was very progressive for the time of writing, given the prejudices of other academics.

29. C. H. Oldfather, *Diodorus Siculus: The Library of History, Volume III, Books 4.59–8, 5.64* (Cambridge, MA, Loeb Classical Library, 1939), 4–5.

30. Harrison, *Themis*, 75–76.

social standing.[31] Magick was very probably applied to every conceivable facet of everyday life.

The magickal practice of necromancy involved the evocation (calling up) of the spirit of someone recently deceased for the purpose of obtaining information and prophecy. The earliest Greek necromancy is found in Homer's *Odyssey* (Book 11), a text that was probably the culmination of hundreds of years of oral transmission. The basic rites of necromancy closely resembled observances paid to the dead in their tombs. As with many other magickal practices, necromancy continued till the Hellenistic era, up until the coming of Christianity.[32]

Binding spells or curses bind or restrain a victim using underworld powers or the spirit of someone recently deceased. Binding curses were typically written on strips of lead, and are referred to as curse tablets. Over 1,500 curse tablets have been found to date, and Plato wrote of professionals in the fourth century BCE preparing them for a fee. Curse tablets were applied to a number of functions—circus and theater (athletes and actors), eroticism (to cause reciprocated lust), separation (to end relationships), legal and political disputes, economic competitors, justice and revenge.[33] Limited evidence suggests that a prayer formula, virtually identical to a religious prayer, was in use as early as the mid-fifth century BCE in Sicily.[34] The distinction between religion and magick is quite blurry in this case. (The blurring of religion and magick is discussed below.)

Erotic spells (often called love spells) were practiced throughout all of Greek history beginning with Homer. There were two categories of

---

31. Faraone and Obbink, *Magika Hiera*, v–vii.

32. Ogden, *Greek and Roman Necromancy.*

33. Gager, *Curse Tablets and Binding Spells*, 3–5, 24–25. Professor Gager translated a selection of curse tablets. He avoided the use of the term magick as he felt it was used as a scrapheap for that which was outside "sanctioned or official beliefs." In short, Gager did not accept an artificial separation between magick and religion.

34. Faraone, "The Agonistic Context of Early Greek Binding Spells," in *Magika Hiera,* ed. Faraone and Obbink, 3–32.

erotic spells. There were those that produced love or affection through incantations over amulets, knotted cords, rings, potions or ointments— these were typically used to enhance existing relationships. Then there were the ones that caused uncontrollable lust through incantations over bound images, tortured animals, burning materials, or apples—these were typically used as part of seduction and would often destroy existing relationships and ties.[35]

Magickal images (which can resemble voodoo dolls) were used as part of binding curses, erotic spells, or for laying restless ghosts. Their use predates that of curse tablets, going back to the early archaic period, a time during which Greeks were illiterate.

Amulets were used for protection or empowerment. They were worn on the body, and were either tied threads or material, silver lamellae (a lamella is a sheet of gold, silver, copper, and bronze inscribed with a magickal formula), papyrus strips, or rings.[36]

Homeric writings provide the earliest testimony of the practice of Greek magick. Continuing this tradition, Homeric incantations were used between the first and fourth centuries CE in Graeco-Roman Egypt for protection, healing, overcoming misfortune and cursing enemies.[37]

Lesser known aspects of magick included weather magick so as to make the earth more fruitful, and focusing on birds for the purpose of divination.[38]

WHAT DIFFERENTIATES MAGICK FROM RELIGION?

Magick to the ancient Greeks was often indistinguishable from their officially sanctioned cult practices, which in turn could be referred to as their religion.[39] Expressing this more fully, magickal beliefs and practices were a part of everyday life, religious beliefs and practices were for

35. Faraone, *Ancient Greek Love Magic*, 5, 28.

36. Ogden, *Magic, Witchcraft, and Ghosts*, 179, 210, 227, 245, 261.

37. Collins, *Magic in the Ancient Greek World*, xiii, 104–5.

38. Harrison, *Themis*, 75–117.

39. Collins, *Magic in the Ancient Greek World*, 25.

the most part identical with forms of magick, and the neat distinctions used by contemporary academics between approved and disapproved forms of religion did not exist in antiquity except among a few philosophers.[40]

All aspects of ancient Greek life were permeated by religion and it would be meaningless to attempt disentangling the sacred from the profane. Modern notions of magick and religion cannot be applied to ancient contexts. It was at times difficult to distinguish between magick and acceptable religious practice. As an example, consider the Oracle of Claros, which was the oracle of Apollon located near Colophon in the second century CE. This oracle came to prominence later than the other oracles of Apollon and was characterized by the diversity of its visitors. An inscription from Ephesus concerned exporting the city's cult of Artemis and is widely accepted to have originated at Claros. Apollon predicted that Artemis would dissolve a deadly plague and melt down the wax figurines which were the product of the "magos' art." There was a prescription to avoid the anger of chthonic (underworld) deities by offering holocaust sacrifices, incense, and libations. Another oracular response recommended fumigating with sulphur (which was already attested in the *Odyssey*) and preparing a pure drink with water from seven springs (clearly a magickal formula). Still another oracular response called on a number of deities, bestowing upon each very specific titles, and ended by requesting that these deities save the city. By way of comparison, magickal incantations featured lengthy lists of proper divine names that were called upon with authority. It is evident that while the benevolence of divine power was being called upon, there was a distinctly magickal attempt to influence the deities in question, thereby blurring the boundaries between religion and magick.[41]

It is pertinent to consider a ceremony conducted in Chaeronea [*Chairôneia*] where the Archon [*Archôn*] or civil officer expelled a slave

---

40. Betz, *The Greek Magical Papyri*, xli.

41. Asirvatham, *Between Magic and Religion*, xi–xxix, 13–31.

and announced the expulsion of famine and the coming of health and prosperity. There was no priest involved and no deities were called upon, and so the rite could be seen as a magickal ceremony. The Greek philosopher Plutarch (46–c. 122 CE) described this ceremony as a sacrifice [*thusia*], a word that came to refer to all religious acts. Thus, Plutarch, a pious man who spent his life studying religion, blurred the distinction between religion and magick. A somewhat arbitrary distinction could be defined by stating that religion was social and for groups, however small, while magick was for the individual, the single unit.[42]

The ancient Greeks understood that magicians prayed as well as uttered spells. After analyzing numerous PGM spells, it can be concluded that there was virtually no difference between prayer within magick and prayer within religion. While coercion of the gods occurred occasionally in the PGM spells, it was infrequent, and was typically used as a last resort. The primary difference between magick and religion lay in the ritual—magicians sacrificed on their own, while in religion, sacrifice was a communal event.[43]

It should be noted that the current trend among academics is to ignore any distinctions between religion, magick and science in pre-Christian Mediterranean cultures. The ancient Greeks appeared to share this disinterest in distinguishing between these categories.[44]

ACADEMICS' TREATMENT OF MAGICK

Up until the late nineteenth century, ancient Greek civilization and religion was thought of as rational. At this point, the murky fringes came into focus as a zone characterized by irrational beliefs in superstition

---

42. Harrison, *Epilogemena*, 8–10. Despite accepting some of the theories of her peers as axiomatic, Dr. Harrison came to a number of conclusions which have stood the test of time by allowing texts to speak for themselves.

43. Fritz Graf, "Prayer in Magic and Religious Ritual," in *Magika Hiera*, ed. Faraone and Obbink, 188–197.

44. Faraone, *Ancient Greek Love Magic*, 17–18.

and magick.[45] It was commonly believed that magick was the primitive forerunner of polytheistic religion, which in turn was the forerunner of monotheism. Prejudice against that which is perceived as irrationality persists to this day among many academics.

In 1890, a widely accepted model proposed that belief systems began with primitive magick, which progressed to religion, which in turn was replaced by science.[46] Relegated to a mere precursor to religion, academics argued over a definition for magick. One academic saw magick as something that was resorted to in a practical situation where a person felt powerless.[47] Another essentially agreed with this and stated that magick had a biological function that was to "relieve pent-up and frustrated feelings which can find no rational outlet."[48]

Some academics were prepared to obscure the truth that the Greeks and their deities engaged in "primitive" magick. One academic claimed that magick almost completely perished in the matured Greek spirit of the Homeric age, and possessed no importance for the deities or humanity. While the deities sometimes appeared to practice ancient magick, their power actually derived from nature. The academic later conceded that there were a few traces of magick in Homer, but most of these were associated with Hermes. Hermes, however, was excused for having primitive magickal elements on the grounds that his cult significantly predated the Homeric age.[49] Another academic, unable to deny the practice of magick, laid the blame on foreign influences, and wrote "Just as the Greek gods, unlike those of many other peoples, are not concerned with magic, so the Greek myth, unlike the folk tale, has no

45. Luck, *Ancient Pathways & Hidden Pursuits*, 1–7.

46. Frazer, *The Golden Bough* (Ware, Hertforshire, UK: Wordsworth Reference, 1995); Luck, *Ancient Pathways & Hidden Pursuits*, 203. In 1890, Sir James Frazer in *The Golden Bough* proposed an evolution of belief systems.

47. Malinowski, *Magic, Science and Religion*.

48. Dodds, *The Greeks and the Irrational*, 45. Professor Dodds essentially agreed with Dr. Malinowski.

49. Walter F. Otto, *The Homeric Gods: The Spiritual Significance of Greek Religion* (New York: Pantheon Books, 1954), 37, 106.

magical ingredients. Magic first returns when the genuine Greek spirit vanishes in the great transformation of philosophy and religion which began during the Hellenistic period." He then went on to cautiously admit the presence of the witches Medea and Circe in classical myths, "but significantly enough they are foreign women."[50] While it is true that the Hellenistic period saw great transformations due to the influx of foreign cultures, the Greeks, as has been shown above, extensively practiced magick throughout their history, including pre-Hellenistic times.

Another academic stated that Greek magick grew from original indigenous elements (which were curiously culled from mythology) including Telchines [*Telchinês*], Curetes [*Kourêtês*]; and Corybantes [*Korubante]*, along with the witches Medea and Circe. Added to the melting pot were various foreign elements including Persian, Egyptian, and Jewish influences.[51] The role of the Idaean Dactyls as an origin for Greek magick has already been discussed.

By way of clarification, Telchines [*Telchinês*] were a primeval people who reputedly sprang from the sea and lived on the Island of Rhodes. They were the earliest metallurgists, having made the sickle of Kronos and the trident of Poseidon. They were portrayed as envious sorcerers and daimones, which resulted in their demise. One account has them killed by Apollon; another has them killed in an inundation sent by Zeus; still another has them forced to leave Rhodes following Zeus' inundation.[52] Regarding their magickal abilities, they were said to have had the ability to draw down rain, hail, and snow, and could change their own shapes, while guarding their abilities jealously.[53]

The Curetes [*Kourêtês*] in Cretan mythology were demi-gods who protected the infant Zeus against his father Kronos by striking their

---

50. Nilsson, *A History of Greek Religion,* 52–53.

51. Jerome-Antoine Rony, *A History of Magic* (New York: Walker & Co.), 58–61.

52. Seyffert, *Dictionary of Classical Antiquities,* 614–5.

53. Harrison, *Epilogemena,* 107–8.

spears against their shields to drown out any crying. Priests of the Cretan goddess Rhea and of the Idaean Zeus subsequently referred to themselves as Curetes, and would perform noisy war dances at festivals.[54] As previously mentioned, they were initiated into medicine and religion, and were a specialized society of sorcerers.[55]

The Corybantes [*Korubantes*] were mythical attendants of the Phrygian goddess Rhea Cybele who accompanied her with wild dances and music. The eunuch priests of the goddess in Phrygia adopted the name.[56]

In one of his books, Professor Walter Burkett echoed the nineteenth-century view that "magic must be seen as the origin of religion," and added that magick was "for the few, and is developed into a highly complicated pseudo-science."[57] In another text he blamed foreign influences by pointing out that myths, seership, rites of purification, ritual appeasement of the dead, and various malevolent magickal practices, such as directing wrathful spirits of the dead against enemies, all had their precedents in the Near East.[58]

The prejudice against magick continues in some recent texts. As an example, the deliberate exclusion of magick in one relatively recent text is justified "precisely because magic is not a publicly sanctioned religious activity."[59]

Fortunately it has at last been recognized that the study of various magickal inscriptions found on papyri, amulets, and lead curse tablets provides insights into the folk beliefs and religious attitudes of the time.

---

54. Seyffert, *Dictionary of Classical Antiquities*, 168.

55. Harrison, *Epilogemena*, 107.

56. Seyffert, *Dictionary of Classical Antiquities*, 165.

57. Burkert, *Greek Religion*, 55. Professor Walter Burkert made a few short references to magick in his *Greek Religion* and echoed Frazer's definition.

58. Burkert, *The Orientalizing Revolution*, 41–87, 124–127. Burkert blamed foreign influences for the presence of magick in ancient Greece.

59. Zaidman and Pantel, *Religion in the Ancient Greek City*, xv. The quote is from Professor Cartledge's translator's introduction.

This has made the study of ancient magick acceptable in some sections of the academic community.[60] Since the publishing of the PGM texts in 1986, there has been an explosion of interest in Greek magick and numerous scholarly books and articles have been written studying the phenomenon from a multitude of angles.[61] The rose-tinted glasses have come off and the ancients are at last being seen as individuals who frequently turned to the practice of magick so as to improve their circumstances in an uncertain world.[62]

The Fate of Greek Magick After the Hellenistic Period

With the Christian suppression of pagan magickal practices, changes were forced. A tradition of magick practiced by Coptic Christians began in the first century CE and endured till the eleventh or twelfth century CE. A comparison of these Coptic spells with those in the PGM texts reveals many parallels, indicating a continuity of practice.[63]

The *Picatrix*, or *Ghayat Al-Hakim*, is an eleventh-century Arabic text compiling material from 224 sources, encompassing astrology, magick, and hermetic knowledge. Much of this wisdom comes from Aristotle, Plato, and Pythagoras, as well as Persian, Indian, and Arabian sources.[64] Had it not been for the thirst for knowledge of Arab scholars, very little wisdom from the ancient world would have survived.

---

60. Z. Steward, *Arthur Darby Nock: Essays on Religion in the Ancient World: Volume 1*, 34. It was Professor Arthur Darby Nock who wrote that the study of magickal inscriptions would provide insights into the folk beliefs and religious attitudes of the time.
61. Collins, *Magic in the Ancient Greek World*, xi.
62. Faraone and Obbink, *Magika Hiera*, v–vii.
63. Marvin Meyer and Richard Smith. *Ancient Christian Magic: Coptic Texts of Ritual Power* (New York: Harper San Francisco, 1994).
64. Hashem Atallah and William Kiesel, *Picatrix: Ghayat Al-Hakim: The Goal of the Wise*, Volume One (Seattle, WA: Ouroboros Press, 2002). Atallah and Kiesel, *Picatrix: Ghayat Al-Hakim: The Goal of the Wise*, Volume Two (Seattle, WA: Ouroboros Press, 2008).

The Key of Solomon is the most widely disseminated grimoire in Europe, and is the ancestor of most grimoire-based ceremonial magick. Its oldest manuscript dates to the sixteenth century. *The Key of Solomon* is written in Latin and is popularly believed to be translated from a Hebrew original. However, it is actually based on *The Magical Treatise of Solomon, or Hygromanteia*, which is written in Greek, and its earliest manuscript dates to the fifteenth century.[65] Hygromancy was not a reference to the ancient Greek practice of scrying in a bowl of water, but rather to evocation and its attendant "binding" of spirits using water vessels.[66]

A case can be made for claiming a continuity of magickal practice in the West from the pre-Olympian cults of Dionysus and Cybele, to the Greek Magical Papyri, and finally to the Byzantine and subsequent Solomonic grimoires. There was another path of transmission where the Greek Magical Papyri along with Hermetic, Gnostic, and Neoplatonist traditions continued in the Arab world, particularly among the Sabians of Harran. Islamic expansion, particularly into Spain, resulted in these texts being reintroduced into the West. Among these texts was the *Picatrix*, a compendium of magickal knowledge, which became a major source of information on conjuring planetary spirits within the Solomonic and other grimoires.[67]

Review

There has been a lot of prejudice against magick in the academic community, but the tide is slowly turning. There is no consensus as to what magick is and how it differs from religion, simply because such distinctions are

---

65. Ioannis Marathakis, *The Magical Treatise of Solomon, or Hygromanteia* (Singapore: Golden Hoard Press, 2011).

66. Stephen Skinner and David Rankine, *The Veritable Key of Solomon*, (Singapore: Golden Hoard Press, 2008), 56–7.

67. Jake Stratton-Kent, *Geosophia: The Argo of Magic Volume I;* Stratton-Kent, *Geosophia: The Argo of Magic Volume II* (Brighton: Scarlet Imprint, 2010), 156, 227–30.

artificial. While magick is often performed by solitary magicians, it can also be performed for the benefit of an entire community, as in the case of a magician asked to manifest rain in a drought-stricken area.

Magick has been practiced throughout recorded history by the gods and all human social classes, from the poor to the privileged. Magick in ancient Greece was used for worldly aims, just like popular religion, as well as for spiritual exploration, just like the mystery schools. Because it was so widely practiced, there was no legislation against magick unless it was used to harm.

For those practicing Hellenismos in contemporary society, there is a clear precedent for the incorporation of magick. However, there are some who are content to practice a religion that borders on the magickal without ever performing any spells. This is their prerogative and it comes down to a matter of choice. Only do what feels right and resonates well with you.

For those who choose to incorporate Greek magick the road is difficult. It has already been pointed out that there are no surviving spell books from the pre-Hellenistic era. There are, however, accounts of magickal practice during the Classical period, and there are ancient Greek curse tablets. The Greek Magical Papyri (PGM), produced in Hellenistic Egypt, are mostly written in Greek but blend influences from Greek, Egyptian, Sumerian, Babylonian, and Jewish sources, with a small Christian influence. These writings can be used to recreate the magickal practices described in Greek literature and have instructions on how to produce and empower curse tablets. Spells that are composed of primarily Greek influences should be chosen, and those so inclined could perform experiments wherein non-Greek influences are removed, so as to plausibly approximate Classical Greek magick. The other option is to leave the spells as written, with all of their non-Greek components.

The decision to practice or not to practice magick is a personal one, and is not a decision to be imposed upon others. Each person should be given the choice to do that which they feel is best for them.

The ancient Greeks clearly never doubted the power and effectiveness of magick as it was so widely practiced. With power comes responsibility. I strongly believe that those seeking to recreate ancient magick should do so ethically. Thus, spells that harm innocents or impose the will of the magician upon another should not be attempted.

12. EXPERIENCING THE ANNUAL CYCLE—ATHENIAN FESTIVAL CALENDAR

PREAMBLE TO EXPERIENCING THE ANNUAL CYCLE

As stated previously, there were a number of calendars in ancient Greece, but the best known was the Athenian state religious calendar. It consisted of lunar monthly festival days concentrated at the beginning of each month and annually recurring festivals, to give a combined total of about 120 festival days each year that are positively established. Added to this were the festivals whose dates are not firmly established, to give a total of slightly less than half the year. This was, however, less than the Tarentians, who had more festival days than nonfestival days at the height of their prosperity according to Strabo (6.280).

The monthly festivals have already been covered in the Experiencing the Lunar Cycle chapter. These festivals are to be repeated every lunar month, and will not be outlined in detail again.

The Athenian calendar was a lunisolar calendar,[1] as each date indicated the lunar phase as well as time within the solar year. As is the case in many lunisolar and lunar calendars, each lunar month began the evening

---

1. Zaidman and Pantel, *Religion in the Ancient Greek City*, 102–3.

when the young lunar crescent first became visible, which occurred a day or two after the dark moon.

As a point of interest, some Muslims have adopted mathematical models to define when to start lunar months. Others follow the Holy Quran's injunction to see the new crescent. At sea level, observing a very tiny new lunar crescent in the airglow just after the sunset is difficult, even with clear skies, due to dust, humidity, and pollution. Some Muslims climb up high mountains. A more modern solution for a cloudy day has been to send up a plane, known as a Moonplane, above the highest clouds. The two Imams on board look for the new crescent with naked eyes or with a refractor. If seen, it is photographed using a telescope equipped with a CCD camera. The images, along with a message, are sent to mosques and Muslim TV networks around the world.[2] I cite this to show the lengths that some cultures will go in order to be totally faithful to tradition regarding the start of the lunar month.

At the time of writing, there are a couple of modern websites that can help practitioners know when the moon has been spotted—www.moonsighting.com[3] and www.crescentwatch.org.[4] Both predict the visibility of the new crescent moon over the first three days of the lunation. One predicts whether the crescent will be visible, and provides a three-day map starting from the dark moon showing where it is visible on the earth. The former also stores archival maps.

The Athenian calendar normally consisted of twelve months, each being either 29 or 30 days long. This would correspond to a lunar year of 354 days that was 11¼ days short of the solar year. By way of compensation, the Athenians resorted to intercalation, which meant introducing

---

2. François René Querci and Patrick Martinez, "An Aircraft Equipment for New Lunar Crescent Observations," Project Islamic Crescent Observation, www.icoproject.org/pdf/querci_2001.pdf.

3. www.moonsighting.com.

4. www.crescentwatch.org.

an extra month every third, sixth, and eighth year. The intercalary month was a second Poseideon. The Athenian calendar started on the first Noumenia after the summer solstice according to three sources,[5] but on the Noumenia before the summer solstice according to another.[6] One of the three sources clarifies that the summer solstice approximately coincides with the Skira festival, which occurs in the middle of the last month of the year, Skirophorion. (This will be discussed below.) As an aside, most, if not all, Hellenic reconstructionists consider the Athenian calendar to begin after the summer solstice.

The Athenian months were as follows, and were named after various festivals:

Summer

Hekatombaion (from epithet of Apollon) June/July

Metageitnion (from neighborhood festival, and cult title of Apollo) July/August

Boedromion (from a festival for Apollon the Helper) August/September

Autumn

Pyanepsion (from the boiling of the beans) September/October

Maimakterion (from unknown festivals) October/November

Poseideon (from unknown festivals) November/December

Winter

Gamelion (from a marriage festival) December/January

Anthesterion (from Dionysus) January/February

Elaphebolion (from Artemis the Deershooter) February/March

---

5. Paul Harvey, *The Oxford Companion to Classical Literature* (Oxford, UK: Oxford University Press, 1986), 86; Seyffert, *Dictionary of Classical Antiquities*, 109; Burkert, *Greek Religion*, 230.

6. H. W. Parke, *Festivals of the Athenians* (Ithaca, Cornell University Press, 1986), 29.

Spring

Mounichion (from Artemis of Munichia) March/April

Thargelion (introduced the corn harvest) April/May

Skirophorion (ended the year) May/June[7]

The months as listed above appear to be the ones agreed upon in contemporary texts. In a couple of older texts, most notably Harrison's *Prolegomena to the Study of Greek Religion* (first published in 1903) and Durant's *The Life of Greece*, the Athenian months are shown starting a month later, hence Hekatombaion is July/August, with the others following sequentially. This is an example of the importance of checking multiple sources, so as to have the most accurate information available.

This calendar takes very little account of the agricultural year; there is no month for sowing or reaping. Other Greek calendars also seem to ignore the agricultural year.[8] (By comparison, modern Wicca is bound to the agricultural cycle.)

The climate in Greece is similar to southern California, with hot and dry summers, enabling people to live outdoors much of the time. Autumn sees westerly winds and frequent rain, with twice as much falling in the west as in the east. Snow is only to be found in mountainous areas in winter.[9]

There were a number of annual festivals, which covered a broad range of deities, including most of the Olympians, during every month except Maimakterion.[10]

Working out the Athenian Festival Calendar is quite easy. You need a calendar that spans at least a couple of years, and preferably has the lunar

---

7. Burkert, *Greek Religion*, 225–227. Durant, *The Life of Greece*, 199. Harrison, *Prolegomena to the Study of Greek Religion*, 29. Price, *Religions of the Ancient Greeks*, 28. Warrior, *Greek Religion*, 116–117.

8. Burkert, *Greek Religion*, 226.

9. Garland, *Daily Life of the Ancient Greeks*, 22.

10. Zaidman and Pantel, *Religion in the Ancient Greek City*, 103.

phases marked. Note that the last day of the lunar month, the dark moon, is often designated as "new moon" on commercially available calendars. Similarly, mark the date of the summer solstice in all the years being considered. If the dark moon dates or the summer solstice date aren't marked you will have to find them in an ephemeris or online. In the Gregorian calendar, which is currently used, the summer solstice dates vary between June 20 and June 22, depending on the year, with the June 22 date being fairly rare.[11]

Each lunar month begins the evening when the young lunar crescent first becomes visible, which occurs a day or two after the dark moon, which is the Noumenia. As already mentioned, many Hellenic reconstructionists will just assume that the Noumenia occurs the day after the dark moon.

Here is the process to be followed:

The first Noumenia after the summer solstice marks the first lunar month of the year, Hekatombaion.

Mark the next four Noumenia dates, which are for the months Metageitnion, Boedromion, Pyanepsion, and Maimakterion.

The following Noumenia is the sixth lunar month, Poseideon.

Now comes the slightly tricky bit. Count off six more lunar months. If this last lunar month ends after the following summer solstice, then there are no problems. If however, it ends before the following summer solstice, then add in another Poseideon month, right after the first, in which case you'll have Poseideon 1 and Poseideon 2, back to back.

Now mark off the next Noumenia dates, which signify the months Gamelion, Anthesterion, Elaphebolion, Mounichion, Thargelion, and Skirophorion. This way, you will always have the summer solstice occurring in Skirophorion.

Should the summer solstice coincide with the Noumenia you will have to work out the Athenian Festival Calendar two years before this point (or after, but it would be a little trickier). Remember that intercalation,

---

11. "The June Solstice."

meaning the introduction of a second Poseideon month, should only take place every third, sixth, and eighth year, and certainly not on consecutive years.

As in the Experiencing the Lunar Cycle chapter, the Orphic and Homeric Hymns make a wonderful starting point for all the deities that will be venerated. We also have the option of improvising a prayer following the formula given in the Public Religion subsection of the Greek Religion—Public, Household, and Countryside chapter. The monthly festival days and daily meal-based observances should now be a regular fixture. We should continue daily journaling, outlining everything we do for each festival day.

The Athenian state initially contained a hundred demes, which were administrative districts. Their number grew with time however. Although there were exceptions, people would normally live in the same demes as their ancestors.[12] The festivals for Athens and the demes Erkhia, Teithras, and Myrrhinos are as follows.[13]

HEKATOMBAION

The name Hekatombaion was derived from a cult title of Apollon, as the god to whom hecatombs, or hundreds of victims, were offered. No trace of a festival of the Hekatombaia remained in Classical times. There was no religious ceremony to mark the beginning of the year. Instead there was a sacrifice to Zeus Soter and Athene Soter on the previous day, namely the last day of the year, Skirophorion 30.[14] We should continue daily journaling, outlining everything we do for each festival day.

Hekatombaion 1:—Monthly festival day, Noumenia

Hekatombaion 2: —Monthly festival day for Agathos Daimon

Hekatombaion 3:—Monthly festival day for Athene

---

12. Seyffert, *Dictionary of Classical Antiquities*, 180.

13. Mikalson, *The Sacred and Civil Calendar of the Athenian Year*, 25–181.

14. Parke, *Festivals of the Athenians*, 29.

Hekatombaion 4:—Monthly festival day for Herakles, Hermes, Aphrodite and Eros

Hekatombaion 6:—Monthly festival day for Artemis

Hekatombaion 7:—Monthly festival day for Apollon

Hekatombaion 8:—Monthly festival day for Poseidon and Theseus

> *On this day, it was believed that Theseus returned to Athens.*

The usual Theseus celebration should be amplified, perhaps with an additional offering.

Hekatombaion 12:—Kronia

> *Kronia, the festival of Kronos, represented a suspension of hierarchy, with slaves joining their masters at a banquet. Slaves normally had no rights and were treated badly, but on this day they were permitted to rambunctiously race through the city. Kronos had been the ruler of the Golden Age, the mythological period prior to the ordered age inaugurated by Zeus. The Golden Age was a carefree time where no work had to be done. In homage to Kronos, all order was temporarily suspended.[15]*

This is a difficult festival to recreate within a nonhierarchical society. A suspension of order could be achieved through parents and children swapping roles, with the children tending to the needs of their parents. Dressing in drag is another possibility, or even a uniform or novelty costume. Unusual competitions such as sack races and three-legged races would be appropriate. A potluck feast would make for a perfect end to the day.

Make an offering to Kronos, recite Orphic Hymn 12.

Hekatombaion 15:—Unnamed biennial sacrifice associated with the following day

---

15. Burkert, *Greek Religion*, 231–2.

Hekatombaion 16:—Synoikia, associated with Theseus' legend

Synoikia represented the unification by Theseus of all the villages of Attica into a single state. Originally this involved sacrifice to Athene. In 374 BCE the recurring wars were brought to a temporary pause with the declaration of an armistice, whereupon the focus of the festival shifted to Eirênê, the goddess of peace,[16] to whom sacrifice was made on the Acropolis. The chaos of Kronia was over, and order was reestablished with slaves resuming their former roles.[17] Every second year the Synoikia was expanded to a larger extended form on the fifteenth and sixteenth, with a sacrifice being offered to Zeus Phratrios [the tribal brotherhoods].[18]

Make an offering to Athene, recite Orphic Hymn 31 and Homeric Hymns 11 and 28.

This is a wonderful day to engage in peace activism, an activity sometimes described as the highest calling. Honor the memory of activists such as Gandhi, Aldous Huxley, Martin Luther King, John Lennon, Bob Marley, and others.

Make an offering to Eirênê, the goddess of peace.

Make an offering to Zeus Phratrios (the tribal brotherhoods), recite Orphic Hymn 14 and Homeric Hymn 23.

Hekatombaion 28:—Panathenaia (could have included Hekatombaion 23–30)

The Panathenaia was the most important festival of Athens, marking its birthday festival, and featured the declaration of a legal amnesty. This was normally celebrated as the Little Panathenaia, but every fourth year was a Panhellenic festival called the Great Panathenaia. The Little Panathenaia featured the presentation of a new robe, called the peplos, to Athene Polias and sacrifices to Athene Hygieia [Health] and others. In the Great Panathenaia sacrifices were also made to Eros and Athene together. At the head of the procession a fig pastry was carried, as figs were the first cultivated food tasted by humani-

---

16. Parke, *Festivals of the Athenians*, 31–3.
17. Burkert, *Greek Religion*, 232.
18. Parke, *Festivals of the Athenians*, 31–2.

ty.[19] *Other offerings included cakes and honeycombs, jars containing water or wine, and oak-tree branches.*[20] *The peplos was woven from brightly colored wool, yellow and blue in particular. Initially the statue of Athene was of human scale, and so was the peplos. By the late fifth century BCE, the peplos was reputed to be as big as a ship's sail. It has been suggested that this was an exaggeration and that it only measured four by seven feet.*[21]

If you have a statue of Athene, obtain a length of colorful wool and wrap it around your statue like a peplos.

Make or buy a fig pastry, and buy honeycomb. Offer a little to Athene Polias and Athene Hygieia (Health) and consume the rest, recite Orphic Hymn 31 and Homeric Hymns 11 and 28.

If you have a group of people, various athletic contests such as running can be staged. Alternatively, a procession could be held, perhaps with people holding torches aloft.

Make an offering to Eros, recite Orphic Hymn 57.

METAGEITNION

Presumably there was a festival for Apollon Metageitnios at some time during this month, but no evidence remains. The name of this month has the connotation of changing neighbors, suggesting some sort of neighborhood festival. We should continue daily journaling, outlining everything we do for each festival day.

Metageitnion 1:—Monthly festival day, Noumenia

Metageitnion 2:—Monthly festival day for Agathos Daimon

Metageitnion 3:—Monthly festival day for Athene

Metageitnion 4:—Monthly festival day for Herakles, Hermes, Aphrodite and Eros

Metageitnion 6:—Monthly festival day for Artemis

---

19. Burkert, *Greek Religion*, 228, 231–3.
20. Parke, *Festivals of the Athenians*, 44.
21. Ibid., 38-42.

Metageitnion 7:—Monthly festival day for Apollon; also, the genos of the Salaminioi sacrificed to Apollon Patroos, Leto, Artemis and Athene.

Make an offering to Apollon Patroos and Apollon Metageitnios, recite Orphic Hymn 33 and Homeric Hymns 3 and 21.

Make an offering to Leto, recite Orphic Hymn 34.

Make an offering to Artemis, recite Orphic Hymn 35 and Homeric Hymns 9 and 27.

Make an offering to Athene, recite Orphic Hymn 31 and Homeric Hymns 11 and 28.

Metageitnion 8:—Monthly festival day for Poseidon and Theseus

Metageitnion 12:—The deme Erkhia sacrificed to Apollon Lykeios, Demeter, Zeus Polieus and Athene Polias

Consider honoring Apollon Lykeios through wolf conservation.

Make an offering to Apollon Lykeios, recite Orphic Hymn 33 and Homeric Hymns 3 and 21.

Some practitioners will honor Demeter by planting and caring for a garden. Others will scale this down to a small potted plant, which is cared for in order to foster a connection with her. Supporting local farmers by purchasing their produce is very appropriate. Another alternative is to lend support to a rape crisis center.

Make an offering to Demeter, recite Orphic Hymn 39 and Homeric Hymns 2 and 13.

Make an offering to Zeus Polieus, recite Orphic Hymn 14 and Homeric Hymn 23.

Make an offering to Athene Polias, recite Orphic Hymn 31 and Homeric Hymns 11 and 28.

Metageitnion 15:—The deme Erkhia sacrificed to Kourotrophos and Artemis Hekate

Make an offering to Kourotrophos (the boy-nursing goddess).[22]

---

22. Burkert, *Greek Religion*, 244.

Make an offering to Artemis Hekate, recite Orphic Hymn 35 and Homeric Hymns 9 and 27.

Hekate and Artemis both protect women and children, while Kourotrophos presides over child rearing. Giving assistance to women's and children's crisis shelters would be very appropriate on this day.

Metageitnion 19:—The deme Erkhia sacrificed to the Heroines
Make an offering to the Heroines.

Metageitnion 20:—The deme Erkhia sacrificed to Hera Thelkhinia

Some modern practitioners honor Hera by respecting marital vows, their own and those of others. They work hard on their relationships, keep romance alive—not taking anyone for granted. They engage in activities traditionally associated with mothers—unifying families, cooking, reviving family traditions, and dissipating stress during family conflicts.

Make an offering to Hera Thelkhinia, recite Orphic Hymn 15 and Homeric Hymn 12.

Metageitnion 25:—The deme Erkhia sacrificed to Zeus Epopetes

Make an offering to Zeus Epopetes, recite Orphic Hymn 14 and Homeric Hymn 23.

Some time during this month there was an annual celebration of Herakles, which took place either in Kynosarges gymnasium at Kynosarges[23] or in the city-deme of Diomeia. It should be noted that the Herakleion at Kynosarges is often identified with that at Diomeia.[24] Very little is known about this festival apart from it involving feats of strength among the participants.

If your health permits, have a workout, either in a gym or just with calisthenics and exert yourself. If your health is poor, opt for something low in intensity, perhaps Tai Chi or Chi Kung (Qi Gong). Always check with your doctor prior to starting an exercise program. Make an offering to Herakles, recite Orphic Hymn 11 and Homeric Hymn 15.

---

23. Parke, *Festivals of the Athenians*, 51–2.
24. Parker, *Athenian Religion*, 257, 306.

BOEDROMION

Boedromion takes its name from a festival of thanksgiving to Apollon as the god who rescued in war, held on Boedromion 7.[25] We should continue daily journaling, outlining everything we do for each festival day.

Boedromion 1:—Monthly festival day, Noumenia

Boedromion 2:—Monthly festival day for Agathos Daimon; Niketeria

In addition to honoring Agathos Daimon, make an offering to Nike, recite Orphic Hymn 32.

Boedromion 3:—Monthly festival day for Athene; Plataea

In addition to honoring Athene, read up on the Battle of Plataea (479 BCE), celebrating the victory won over the Persians.

Boedromion 4:—Monthly festival day for Herakles, Hermes, Aphrodite, and Eros

Boedromion 5:—Genesia; the deme Erkhia sacrificed to Epops

The Genesia was an ancient festival for the commemoration of the dead.[26] It appeared to have been a family festival, and there is no evidence for any other public festivals of the Athenian dead.[27] Also the deme Erkhia conducted a sacrifice to an anonymous Epops. The festival of Epops, also the name of the hoopoe [bird], was a holocaust sacrifice (the sacrificial victim was burned entirely rather than the meat being consumed by those who participated in the sacrifice) without wine.

For Genesia visit the graves of friends and relatives and offer libations of water, milk, oil, or honey.

This day was established as the feast of Artemis Agrotera [the Huntress], but also became associated with the Battle of Marathon. It should be noted that Artemis is not normally associated with war.[28]

---

25. Parke, *Festivals of the Athenians*, 53.
26. Zaidman and Pantel, *Religion in the Ancient Greek City*, 76.
27. Parke, *Festivals of the Athenians*, 53–4.
28. Ibid., 54–5.

I am inclined to ignore Epops, but otherwise you could make an effigy of a bird and burn it, dedicating it to Epops.

Boedromion 6:—Monthly festival day for Artemis; and Artemis Agrotera

Make an offering to Artemis Agrotera (the Huntress), recite Orphic Hymn 35 and Homeric Hymns 9 and 27.

Read up on the Battle of Marathon.

Boedromion 7:—Monthly festival day for Apollon; Boedromia

Make an offering to Apollon, being thankful for his ability to rescue those in war, recite Orphic Hymn 33 and Homeric Hymns 3 and 21.

Boedromion 8:—Monthly festival day for Poseidon and Theseus

Boedromion 12:—Democratia

On this day, the Athenians celebrated democracy, included sacrifices to Zeus Agoraios, Athene Agoraia and to the Goddess Themis. Images of Zeus and Athene were paraded in the agora below the Acropolis. Themis is the goddess of divine law.

Make an offering to Zeus Agoraios, recite Orphic Hymn 14 and Homeric Hymn 23.

Make an offering to Athene Agoraia, recite Orphic Hymn 31 and Homeric Hymns 11 and 28.

Contemplate the benefits of living in a democracy, and the importance of not taking it for granted.

Make an offering to Themis, recite Orphic Hymn 78.

Boedromion 15:—Eleusinian Mysteries

Boedromion 16:—Eleusinian Mysteries

Boedromion 17:—Unknown festival day

Boedromion 19:—Eleusinian Mysteries

Boedromion 20:—Eleusinian Mysteries

Boedromion 21:—Eleusinian Mysteries

Boedromion 22:—Eleusinian Mysteries

For those who had already experienced the first initiatory stage at the Mysteries at Agrai, or Lesser Mysteries, during Anthesterion, the next stage was the Great Mysteries of Eleusis.[29] *The procession from Athens to Eleusis took place on Boedromion 13, and another from Eleusis to Athens on Boedromion 14 in preparation for the Eleusinian Mysteries. Boedromion 15 was the first festival day of the Eleusinian Mysteries. Boedromion 16 was another festival day. Boedromion 19 was the day of the procession from Athens to Eleusis for the Eleusinian Mysteries. The procession may well have arrived after sunset, which was Boedromion 20, and which marked the first full day at Eleusis. Boedromion 23 probably marked the return to Athens.*

On 15–16, 19–22:—Make an offering to Demeter, recite Orphic Hymn 39 and Homeric Hymns 2 and 13.

Study the speculations as to what the Eleusinian Mysteries were. Homeric Hymn 2 is particularly important as it gives the account of the kidnapping of Persephone by Hades. The important lesson is that death is not the end.

Boedromion 27:—*The deme Erkhia sacrificed to the Nymphs, Akheloos, Hermes and Ge; the deme Teithras sacrificed to Athene*

Make an offering to Nymphs, recite Orphic Hymn 50.

Make an offering to Akheloos, the primary river god, by possibly pouring a libation into a river.

Make an offering to Hermes, recite Orphic Hymn 27 and Homeric Hymns 4 and 18.

Gaia (Ge) can be honored by caring for the environment. Assist in cleaning up pollution, recycle, conserve energy, protect wildlife, and become familiar with ecological issues. Support local organic farmers. Think globally but act locally.

Make an offering to Ge, then recite Orphic Hymn 25 and Homeric Hymn 30.

Make an offering to Athene, recite Orphic Hymn 31 and Homeric Hymns 11 and 28.

---

29. Parke, *Festivals of the Athenians*, 56.

PYANEPSION

Pyanepsion takes its name from the feast of *Pyanepsia*, which is derived from the words for beans and boiling. While the dish obviously contained beans, cereals were also included. This dish was usually called *panspermia* (all seeds), and the ingredients were all boiled together in one pot.[30] We should continue daily journaling, outlining everything we do for each festival day.

Pyanepsion 1:—Monthly festival day, Noumenia

Pyanepsion 2:—Monthly festival day for Agathos Daimon

Pyanepsion 3:—Monthly festival day for Athene

Pyanepsion 4:—Monthly festival day for Herakles, Hermes, Aphrodite, and Eros

Pyanepsion 6:—Monthly festival day for Artemis; Proerosia?; Oschophoria?

   The Proerosia (preliminary to the ploughing) was a festival to Demeter, where Apollon at the Delphic Oracle commanded that Athenians should offer portions of their barley and wheat crops to Demeter at Eleusis. Thus Demeter's blessing was sought prior to ploughing and sowing.[31] A festival which occurred on a day of the year not known with absolute certainly, but estimated by an academic to be Pyanepsion 6, was the Galaxia, which provides an example of a dish that was dedicated to Demeter, called galaxia (barley and milk porridge).[32]

   The Oschophoria was claimed to have been introduced by Theseus. Its name is derived from oschos or ôschos, meaning shoots of vine with bunches of grapes attached. Twenty youths of noble descent and living parents were chosen to compete in a race, while bearing the vine shoots, from the temple of Dionysos to the sanctuary of Athene Skiras. The victor was awarded a drink called the pentaploa ("having five ingredients"), representing the chief local products, made of wine, honey, cheese, barley, and olive oil, as well as an honorary place

---

30. Parke, *Festivals of the Athenians*, 75.

31. Ibid., 73.

32. Ibid., 173.

in the procession returning back to the temple of Dionysos. The procession was led by two youths disguised as women [the Oschophoroi], and concluded with a sacrifice and a banquet.[33] *At the conclusion of the ceremony during the libations, those present shouted "Eleleu, Iou, Iou." The first word signified triumph, while the second and third words signified amazement.*[34]

For the Proerosia make an offering of *galaxia* to Demeter, recite Orphic Hymn 39 and Homeric Hymns 2 and 13. (See Appendix 3: Diet for recipe.) Beseech Demeter's blessing for farmers and home gardeners.

For the Oschophoria (festival in honor of Dionysos, possibly on Pyanepsion 6), make an offering of a drink made from wine, cheese, meal, and honey, and pour a libation to Dionysos, recite Orphic Hymns 44, 45, 46 and Homeric Hymns 7 and 26. Read Plutarch's Life of Theseus. Chant "Eleleu, Iou, Iou." If your health allows it, consider either entering a race or just going for a run.

Pyanepsion 7:—Monthly festival day for Apollon; Pyanepsia in Eleusis; sacrifice to Konnidas (Theseus' tutor)

While Pyanepsion 7 in Athens Pyanepsia was celebrated with a mixed vegetarian stew, in Eleusis the Pythian Apollon was honored with the sacrifice of a he-goat, lamb and other offerings. Also associated with the festival was the eiresione, a symbol of fertility consisting of an olive bough entwined with wool yarn from which all sorts of objects were suspended such as models of figs, cakes, jars of honey. The bough was left at the front door for the whole year.[35]

For Pyanepsion make a mixed vegetarian stew called panspermia (all seeds), consisting of beans and cereals boiled together in one pot. (See Appendix 3: Diet for recipe.)

Make an eiresione to be left at the front door for the whole year.

Pyanepsion 8:—Monthly festival day for Poseidon and Theseus; Theseia; offering to the Amazons

33. Seyffert, *Dictionary of Classical Antiquities*, 189–90; Thomas F. Scanlon, *Eros and Greek Athletics* (New York: Oxford University Press, 2001) 90.

34. Parke, *Festivals of the Athenians*, 77.

35. Ibid., 75–7.

The Theseia was instituted in 475 BCE on Pyanepsion 8 as a chief state festival to celebrate the return of Theseus' bones from the island of Skyros where he had died. Apart from meat offerings, the festival called for athara, a milk porridge.[36]

Celebrate the return of Theseus' bones from the island of Skyros and make an offering to the Amazons with *athara*, a milk porridge, and meat. (Given that the ingredients of *athara* are unknown, I would substitute *galaxia*, a barley and milk porridge—see Appendix 3: Diet for recipe.) Read Plutarch's *Life of Theseus*.

Pyanepsion 9:—Stenia

The Stenia marked the ascent of a group of women to a temple of Demeter. The women celebrated by verbally abusing each other by night.[37]

I would be wary of reintroducing a ritual involving verbal abuse unless the women knew each other sufficiently to know that no malice was intended. In these modern-day politically correct times, some people seem to be less resilient to verbal abuse.

Pyanepsion 10:—Thesmophoria (later addition)

Pyanepsion 11:—Thesmophoria day of the Anodos (the way up)

Pyanepsion 12:—Thesmophoria day of the Nesteia (fasting)

Pyanepsion 13:—Thesmophoria day of the Kalligeneia

For Pyanepsion 10–13, make an offering of a votive in the form of a piglet, dough fashioned into snakes and phalluses, and pine branches to Demeter, recite Orphic Hymn 39 and Homeric Hymns 2 and 13. Fast on Pyanepsion 12 and feast on Pyanepsion 13. Beseech Demeter to ensure a bountiful harvest. Kalligeneia, the goddess of the beautiful birth, was called upon. Pomegranate pips, the red juice of which was associated with blood, should be eaten.

Pyanepsion 14:—The deme Erkhia sacrificed to the Heroines

---

36. Parke, *Festivals of the Athenians*, 81–2. Parker, *Athenian Religion*, 168.
37. Harrison, *Prolegomena to the Study of Greek Religion*, 136; Parke, *Festivals of the Athenians*, 88.

Perhaps focus on women you've known who are worthy of the title Heroine.

The Thesmophoria, the Proerosia and the Pyanepsia all had seed-time connections. The Thesmophoria was observed almost throughout the entire Greek world and honored Demeter.[38] It was the only festival that allowed participating women to leave their homes all day and all night. It was preceded by sexual abstinence and characterized by a pig sacrifice, for which it was apparently permissible to substitute a votary. The first day was known as the way up to the Thesmophorion on a hilltop. That evening piglets, dough fashioned into snakes and phalluses, and pine branches would be thrown into the chasms of Demeter and Kore. The decayed remains of these sacrifices, called thesmos, when mixed with seed would ensure a bountiful harvest. The second day, called fasting, involved the women laying on makeshift beds consisting of plants reputed to quell the libido strewn on the ground, during which they remained in the presence of Demeter. The fasting came to an end on the third day with a meat banquet. Kalligeneia, the goddess of the beautiful birth, was called upon. The women would also eat pomegranate pips, the red juice of which was associated with blood.[39]

This month also featured the Apatouria, a three-day festival, occurring either Pyanepsion 19–21 or Pyanepsion 26–28. At the Apatouria fathers would bring their legitimate children born since the previous Apatouria. For each child a sheep or goat would be sacrificed. On the third day the fathers would swear an oath that the children were legitimate and their names were inscribed on the roll of the phratry.[40] The deities sacrificed to were Zeus Phratrios and Athene Phratria.[41]

On the three-day Apatouria festival, make an offering to Zeus Phratrios, recite Orphic Hymn 14 and Homeric Hymn 23.

---

38. Parke, *Festivals of the Athenians*, 82.
39. Burkert, *Greek Religion*, 242–6.
40. Seyffert, *Dictionary of Classical Antiquities*, 88.
41. Zaidman and Pantel, *Religion in the Ancient Greek City*, 66.

Make an offering to Athene Phratria, recite Orphic Hymn 31 and Homeric Hymns 11 and 28.

Pyanepsion 30:—Chalkeia

The festival of the Chalkeia signified the setting of the warp on the loom to weave the peplos for the Panathenaia. It was woven by a team of maidens selected from aristocratic families. The festival appeared to have been originally one for metalworkers, as the name is derived from chalkos (copper) or chalkeis (smith). It was associated with Hephaestus and Athene Ergane ("work-woman," patron of craftsmen and artisans), where baskets full of corn were offered.[42]

The Chalkeia was primarily associated with artisans, especially metalworkers, and involved offerings of baskets full of corn. (Make sure that the corn is not genetically engineered.)

Make an offering to Hephaestus, recite Orphic Hymn 65 and Homeric Hymn 20.

Make an offering to Athene Ergane (Labor), recite Orphic Hymn 31 and Homeric Hymns 11 and 28.

MAIMAKTERION

Maimakterion was derived from an epithet of Zeus, meaning blustering. There were no major festivals, probably because the month had numerous storms, which would spoil any outdoor gatherings.[43] We should continue daily journaling, outlining everything we do for each festival day.

Maimakterion 1:—Monthly festival day, Noumenia

Maimakterion 2:—Monthly festival day for Agathos Daimon

Maimakterion 3:—Monthly festival day for Athene

Maimakterion 4:—Monthly festival day for Herakles, Hermes, Aphrodite and Eros

---

42. Parke, *Festivals of the Athenians*, 38, 92–3.

43. Ibid., 95.

Maimakterion 6:—Monthly festival day for Artemis

Maimakterion 7:—Monthly festival day for Apollon

Maimakterion 8:—Monthly festival day for Poseidon and Theseus

The Pompaia (procession) occurred during the last third of the month dedicated to Zeus Meilichios, kindly or open to propitiation. A sheep was sacrificed to Zeus and its fleece, the Sheepskin of Zeus [Dion Koidion] was used in magickal purificatory rites throughout Attic. Those seeking purification would stand on it with their left foot, and impurities would be absorbed. It is possible that those seeking purification prior to admission into the Mysteries of Eleusis went through a similar process. Also used in the procession was the caduceus of Hermes, which had the function of a magick wand, banishing evil. The Pompaia appears to have been limited to priestly officials, and its route may well have involved encircling the city so as to ensure its safety through magickal means.[44]

During the last third of the month, make an offering to Zeus Meilichios, recite Orphic Hymn 14 and Homeric Hymn 23. Obtain a sheepskin and seek purification by standing on it with your left foot, to absorb impurities. Consider also circling your dwelling, requesting that it be kept safe.

POSEIDEON

Poseideon implies the existence of a festival called *Poseidea*, but little evidence remains.[45]

Should the year have two Poseideon months, I would suggest repeating all the festivals. We should continue daily journaling, outlining everything we do for each festival day.

Poseideon 1:—Monthly festival day, Noumenia

Poseideon 2:—Monthly festival day for Agathos Daimon

Poseideon 3:—Monthly festival day for Athene

Poseideon 4:—Monthly festival day for Herakles, Hermes, Aphrodite, and Eros

---

44. Parke, *Festivals of the Athenians*, 38, 95–6.
45. Ibid., 97.

Poseideon 5:—The deme Myrrhinos celebrated the Plerosia

The deme Myrrhinos celebrated the Plerosia. Nothing is known about this, other than it being a festival of completion.

Poseideon 6:—Monthly festival day for Artemis

Poseideon 7:—Monthly festival day for Apollon

Poseideon 8:—Monthly festival day for Poseidon and Theseus

Poseideon 16:—The deme Erkhia sacrificed to Zeus (possibly Zeus Horios); rural Dionysia

The rural Dionysia was celebrated in the days prior to Poseideon 19, probably starting on Poseideon 16. It was celebrated on different days in different demes, and may have been at least four days long. It coincided with the first tasting of new wine. A procession progressed solemnly to the altar of Dionysos where a goat would be sacrificed. This was followed by feasting and revelry.[46]

Make an offering to Zeus, recite Orphic Hymn 14 and Homeric Hymn 23.

Pour a libation of new wine to Dionysos, recite Orphic Hymns 44, 45, 46, and Homeric Hymns 7 and 26. A votive offering in the form of a goat would be offered. Follow this by feasting and revelry.

Poseideon 26:—Haloa

The Haloa was a feast of Demeter, Kore, and Dionysos to celebrate the cutting of the vines and tasting the wine made from them. The festival, presided over by women, was a bloodless offering—no animal sacrifice was allowed. Sports would be engaged in at the threshing floors. The feast consisted of wine, cereals, fish, possibly fowl, but no flesh. There were in addition food taboos paralleling those of the mysteries.[47] Women would bring models of male and female genitals and engage in obscene conversation, suggesting that this was a fertility festival stimulating the growth of corn from seed.[48]

46. Seyffert, *Dictionary of Classical Antiquities*, 190.
47. Harrison, *Prolegomena to the Study of Greek Religion*, 145–150.
48. Parke, *Festivals of the Athenians*, 98–9.

This is a women's festival, which is inappropriate for young children because of the erotic practices. I would suggest that the offering be either a bunch of grapes or a libation of wine, or alternatively, seasonal locally grown fruits. Fish or fowl could be included for non-vegetarians. Those women capable of fashioning models of male and female genitals should do so, while others could procure sex toys, and engage in bawdy conversation. It's important to be mindful of this being a fertility rite.

Make an offering to Demeter, recite Orphic Hymn 39 and Homeric Hymns 2 and 13.

Make an offering to Kore, recite Orphic Hymn 28.

Make an offering to Dionysos, recite Orphic Hymns 44, 45, 46 and Homeric Hymns 7 and 26.

GAMELION

Gamelion (the month of marriage) was the most popular month for marriage and marked Gamelia, the sacred marriage of Zeus and Hera. No details of this festival remain.[49] We should continue daily journaling, outlining everything we do for each festival day.

Gamelion 1:—Monthly festival day, Noumenia

Gamelion 2:—Monthly festival day for Agathos Daimon

Gamelion 3:—Monthly festival day for Athene

Gamelion 4:—Monthly festival day for Herakles, Hermes, Aphrodite, and Eros

Gamelion 6:—Monthly festival day for Artemis

Gamelion 7:—Monthly festival day for Apollon; the deme Erkhia sacrificed to Kourotrophos, Apollon Delphinios and Apollon Lykeios.
Make an offering to Kourotrophos.

Make an offering to Apollon Delphinios and Apollon Lykeios, recite Orphic Hymn 33 and Homeric Hymns 3 and 21.

---

49. Parke, *Festivals of the Athenians*, 38, 104.

Gamelion 8:—Monthly festival day for Poseidon and Theseus; the
deme Erkhia sacrificed to Apollon Apotropaios, Apollon Nymphegetes and the Nymphs

Make an offering to Apollon Apotropaios and Apollon Nymphegetes, recite Orphic Hymn 33 and Homeric Hymns 3 and 21.

Make an offering to Nymphs, recite Orphic Hymn 50.

Gamelion 9:—The deme Erkhia sacrificed to Athene

*Occurring in this month was the Lenaia, or feast of vats, which cannot be
dated. Lenaia probably comes from lanai (Maenads—the female worshippers of
Dionysos). The Lenaia was at least four days long and included sacrificing to
Dionysos Leneus, and placing ivy on the statues of Dionysos. It began on
Gamelion 12, and continued at least until Gamelion 19, and possibly until
Gamelion 21. The festival was marked by revelrous processions to attend trag-
edies and comedies.*[50]

Make an offering to Athene, recite Orphic Hymn 31 and Homeric
Hymns 11 and 28.

If you have a statue of Dionysos, festoon it with ivy. The Lenaia
should be celebrated by going to the cinema, theater, or just staying in
and watching videos.

Make an offering to Dionysos Leneus, recite Orphic Hymns 44, 45,
46 and Homeric Hymns 7 and 26.

Gamelion 27:—Theogamia; Gamelia; the deme Erkhia sacrificed to
Kourotrophos, Hera, Zeus Teleios and Poseidon

*The Gamelia was the sacred marriage of Zeus and Hera, and was sacred to
Hera. Adult phratry members would hold a wedding sacrifice, or gamêlia, to
advertise his new status and his wife.*[51] *No details of this festival remain.*

If you are in a relationship, honor your partner. Think about the
mistakes you have made in your relationship and what you can do to
improve things. If you are single, honor the relationship of someone
close to you, or plan to attain your own healthy relationship, unless you

---

50. Seyffert, *Dictionary of Classical Antiquities*, 190.
51. Zaidman and Pantel, *Religion in the Ancient Greek City*, 66.

prefer being single. If you're planning on marrying, there is no better time than the month of Gamelion.

Make an offering to Zeus, recite Orphic Hymn 14 and Homeric Hymn 23.

Make an offering to Hera, recite Orphic Hymn 15 and Homeric Hymn 12.

Make an offering to Kourotrophos.

Make an offering to Poseidon, recite Orphic Hymn 16 and Homeric Hymn 22.

ANTHESTERION

Anthesterion takes its name from the Anthesteria, dedicated to Dionysos, and derived from the word for flowers.[52] We should continue daily journaling, outlining everything we do for each festival day.

Anthesterion 1:—Monthly festival day, Noumenia

Anthesterion 2:—Monthly festival day for Agathos Daimon; the deme Erkhia sacrificed to Dionysos.

Dionysos is honored by drinking wine, attending the theater, dancing, and singing. Learn to enjoy every moment of life, regardless of how pleasant or unpleasant.

Make an offering to Dionysos, recite Orphic Hymns 44, 45, 46 and Homeric Hymns 7 and 26.

Anthesterion 3:—Monthly festival day for Athene

Anthesterion 4:—Monthly festival day for Herakles, Hermes, Aphrodit, and Eros

Anthesterion 6:—Monthly festival day for Artemis

Anthesterion 7:—Monthly festival day for Apollon

Anthesterion 8:—Monthly festival day for Poseidon and Theseus

Anthesterion 11:—Anthesteria day of Pithoigia (jar opening)

---

52. Parke, *Festivals of the Athenians*, 107.

Anthesterion 12:—Anthesteria day of Choes (wine jugs)

Anthesterion 13:—Anthesteria day of Chytroi (pots)

Anthesterion was associated with the blossoming of spring, and was known as the Older Dionysia. The first day of jar opening involved carting clay vessels filled with wine to the sanctuary of Dionysos. After sunset Dionysos was honored with the first libations when the jars were broken open. The day of wine jugs involved drinking competitions for adults, slaves, and children older than three. Doors of houses were smeared with pitch and buckthorn leaves were chewed to banish the spirits of the dead, which on this day were free to wander. Those wishing to make offerings to the dead used wheaten flour mixed with honey and libations of water. At the end of the day the spirits were banished by shouting "Get out, Keres (goblins, or spirits that work harm), the Anthesteria is over." On the day of the pots a meal of pottage was consumed, which was a cereal dish of various boiled grains, sweetened with honey. This dish harks back to a time before grain milling and bread baking.[53] The pottage was offered to Hermes in his role as psychopomp, a guide to the souls of the dead.[54] During the Anthesteria, swinging was used to produce purification, presumably because of the rapid movement through air.[55]

Offer libations of wine to Dionysos, recite Orphic Hymns 44, 45, 46 and Homeric Hymns 7 and 26. I cannot imagine modern practitioners smearing doors of houses with pitch, but stranger things have happened.

If you have a group of people, you could try celebrating over a weekend, beginning Friday afternoon through Sunday. An option for U.S. residents is over the Presidents' Day weekend which falls near this time. Participants should bring food contributions for a pot luck, and either drink diluted wine as the ancient Greeks did, or alternate between wine and nonalcoholic beverages. There should either be a place

---

53. Burkert, *Greek Religion*, 237–41; Parke, *Festivals of the Athenians*, 116–7.

54. Seyffert, *Dictionary of Classical Antiquities*, 190.

55. Parke, *Festivals of the Athenians*, 119.

for participants to sleep, or designated drivers should be organized, so as to ensure the safety of participants. The ritual area should be decorated with flowers and images of Dionysos.

Offer some pottage to Hermes in his role as psychopomp, and recite Orphic Hymn 56 to Chthonic Hermes.

Anthesterion 23:—Diasia, the festival of Zeus Meilichios

The Diasi was the greatest festival of Zeus in Athens, and was dedicated to Zeus Meilichios (kindly or open to propitiation). According to one source, the event was celebrated by the whole population making bloodless offerings, including pastries in the shape of sheep and pigs. Some wealthy families, however, offered holocausts (whole burnt offerings of animals).[56]

Make an offering to Zeus Meilichios, recite Orphic Hymn 14 and Homeric Hymn 23.

This is a particularly appropriate festival to spend with family and friends. Prepare pastries or bread in the shapes of sacrificial animals. Those with a sweet tooth could use animal-shaped cookies (although commercially available ones are often prepared with GMO ingredients, so carefully read labels). Focus on the bond between yourself and your family and friends with offerings and libations.

The Mysteries at Agrai, otherwise referred to as the Lesser Mysteries, lasted at least three days including Anthesterion 23 in the period Anthesterion 20–26.

Make an offering to Demeter, recite Orphic Hymn 39 and Homeric Hymns 2 and 13, and study what is known about the Lesser Mysteries. (George E. Mylonas' *Eleusis and the Eleusinian Mysteries* is excellent.)

ELAPHEBOLION

Elaphebolion was named after Artemis Elaphebolios (Shooter of the Deer), which was presumably held on the sixth day, but no evidence remains. While originally stags had been sacrificed, in the classical period substitutes were offered. These *elaphoi* (stags) substitutes were actually

---

56. Parke, *Festivals of the Athenians*, 38, 120–2.

cakes made from dough, honey, and sesame seeds.[57] We should continue daily journaling, outlining everything we do for each festival day.

Elaphebolion 1:—Monthly festival day, Noumenia

Elaphebolion 2:—Monthly festival day for Agathos Daimon

Elaphebolion 3:—Monthly festival day for Athene

Elaphebolion 4:—Monthly festival day for Herakles, Hermes, Aphrodite, and Eros

Elaphebolion 6:—Monthly festival day for Artemis

Make an offering to Artemis Elaphebolios (Shooter of the Deer) of elaphoi (stags)—cakes made from dough, honey, and sesame seeds. Recite Orphic Hymn 35 and Homeric Hymns 9 and 27.

Elaphebolion 7:—Monthly festival day for Apollon

Elaphebolion 8:—Monthly festival day for Poseidon and Theseus; festival for Asklepios and Proagon for City Dionysia

The festival for Asklepios was introduced in 429 BCE.[58]

Honor Asklepios by being open to all healing modalities—mainstream and alternative.

Make an offering to Asklepios, recite Orphic Hymn 66 and Homeric Hymn 16.

This day also marked a Proagon (official theatrical presentation) for the City Dionysia.

This is another good excuse to go to the theater, a poetry reading, the cinema, or watch a video at home. Some practitioners will hold costume parties where wine is served and decorations include ivy and grape vines as well as flowers.

Elaphebolion 10:—City Dionysia; Marathonian Tetrapolis sacrificed to Ge

Make an offering to Ge, and recite Orphic Hymn 25 and Homeric Hymn 30.

---

57. Parke, *Festivals of the Athenians*, 38, 125.

58. Ibid., 125.

Elaphebolion 11:—City Dionysia

Elaphebolion 12:—City Dionysia

Elaphebolion 13:—City Dionysia

Elaphebolion 14:—City Dionysia

The City Dionysia was held over six days and involved a procession featuring choruses of singing boys and an old wooden statue of Dionysos, representing his liberation of the land from winter. The festival featured three days of tragedies, comedies, and dramas.[59] Myths of Dionysos being first rejected and then forcing the acceptance of his cult was universal throughout Greece. In this case, legend has it that Athenian males spurned Dionysos whereupon he caused their genitals to become diseased. Following the advice of an oracle they were cured once they introduced a procession with a phallus to honor Dionysos.[60]

This is another good excuse to go to the theater or the cinema.

Make an offering to Dionysos, recite Orphic Hymns 44, 45, 46, and Homeric Hymns 7 and 26.

Elaphebolion 16:—The deme Erkhia sacrificed to Dionysos and Semele

Make an offering to Dionysos, recite Orphic Hymns 44, 45, 46, and Homeric Hymns 7 and 26.

Make an offering to Semele, recite Orphic Hymn 43.

Elaphebolion 17:—Pandia

The Pandia was a festival of Zeus about which almost nothing is known.[61]

Make an offering to Zeus, recite Orphic Hymn 14 and Homeric Hymn 23.

---

59. Seyffert, *Dictionary of Classical Antiquities*, 190.
60. Parke, *Festivals of the Athenians*, 126.
61. Ibid., 136.

MOUNICHION

Mounichion was named after the Mounichia, a festival dedicated to Artemis as the goddess presiding over the hill of Mounichia, which in turn was named after the hero Mounichos.

Mounichion 1:—Monthly festival day, Noumenia

Mounichion 2:—Monthly festival day for Agathos Daimon

Mounichion 3:—Monthly festival day for Athene

Mounichion 4:—Monthly festival day for Herakles, Hermes, Aphrodite, and Eros; the deme Erkhia sacrificed to Herakleidai (children of Herakles)

At a sanctuary of Aphrodite, a mid-fifth-century-BCE inscription was found which mentioned an otherwise unattested festival to Eros on Mounichion 4.

Mounichion 6:—Monthly festival day for Artemis; Delphinia (procession of young girls in honor of Artemis)

The Delphinia was a procession of Athenian maidens carrying boughs of olive wood entwined with white wool. The procession was probably dedicated to Artemis.

Make an offering to Artemis, recite Orphic Hymn 35 and Homeric Hymns 9 and 27.

Mounichion 7:—Monthly festival day for Apollon

Mounichion 8:—Monthly festival day for Poseidon and Theseus

Mounichion 16:—Mounichia (in honor of Artemis)

Legend had it that a she-bear wandered into the sanctuary at Mounichia and was killed. Artemis was associated with she-bears, and as punishment, she afflicted the Athenians with plague. An oracle advised that someone would have to sacrifice his or her daughter. Artemis was deceived by a man who substituted a she-goat dressed up like his daughter. Also offered to Artemis on the Mounichia were amphiphontes (shining all round) which were cakes topped with a circle, in the middle of which was a lit candle, to symbolize the circle of the moon.

Make or purchase round cakes, perhaps cupcakes or muffins, topped with a circle and a small lit candle.

Recite Orphic Hymn 35 and Homeric Hymns 9 and 27.

Mounichion 17:—Salaminioi (men from Cyprian Salamis) sacrificed to Eurysakes (son of the Telemonian Ajax and the former-princess captive-slave girl Tecmessa).

Mounichion 19:—Olympieia (cavalry procession for Zeus)

The Olympieia (not to be confused with the Olympic Games) was held in honor of the Olympian Zeus and featured a procession of the Athenian cavalry. The festival probably would have included sacrifices of bulls.[62]

Either attend a horse-riding exhibition or ride a horse yourself. Make votive offerings in the form of a bull, such as a clay figurine of a bull or a cake shaped as a bull. A nonvegetarian option is to offer a large beef steak.

Make an offering to Zeus, recite Orphic Hymn 14 and Homeric Hymn 23.

Mounichion 20:—The deme Erkhia sacrificed to Leukaspis (a hero)

Mounichion 21:—The deme Erkhia sacrificed to the Tritopatores (three elder gods described as winds, the first-born, and gods of marriage and birth)

THARGELION

Thargelion took its name from the Thargelia, which featured the offering of *thargelos* (boiled first fruit offerings of corn and vegetables), and which in turn were associated with *thalusia* (first fruit offerings to the gods). This was a time when crops were almost, but not quite, ripe. The Thargelia was held over two days. The sixth was a day of purification and the seventh was a day of offerings.[63] We should continue daily journaling, outlining everything we do for each festival day.

Thargelion 1:—Monthly festival day, Noumenia

Thargelion 2:—Monthly festival day for Agathos Daimon

---

62. Parke, *Festivals of the Athenians*, 38, 137–45.

63. Ibid., 146–7.

Thargelion 3:—Monthly festival day for Athene

Thargelion 4:—Monthly festival day for Herakles, Hermes, Aphrodite, and Eros

Thargelion 6:—Monthly festival day for Artemis; purification of the city

On the sixth day, according to one source, a man and a woman who were condemned to death were chosen to represent the male and female population. The pair were led with garlands of figs to the seashore where they were sacrificed, their bodies burnedt, and their ashes cast into the sea, so as to ensure that Apollon would not burn up the harvest. In later times the pair were cast into the sea and then banished.[64] According to another source, two loathsome men were chosen to represent the male and female population. They were draped in figs and driven out with stones.[65]

It would hardly be appropriate to reintroduce human sacrifice or the banishing of undesirable members of society. Instead, make an offering of figs to Apollon, recite Orphic Hymn 33 and Homeric Hymns 3 and 21. Purify your home, carry out household trash and any stale food, much as you would on the day of Hekate.

Thargelion 7:—Monthly festival day for Apollon, Thargelia

The Thargelia was originally a harvest festival, the principal feast of Apollon, being held on his birthday. Thus, on the seventh day, first fruits were offered to Apollon, Artemis, and the Horae ("seasons"—goddesses of the seasons and the natural portions of time).[66]

For Thargelion, prepare an offering of *thargelos* (boiled first fruit offerings of corn and vegetables), which in turn were associated with *thalusia* (first fruit offerings to the gods). The Thargelia was held over two days.

---

64. Seyffert, *Dictionary of Classical Antiquities*, 622.
65. Burkert, *Greek Religion*, 82–3.
66. Ibid., 83.

The sixth is a day of purification, during which some practitioners undertake a ritual fast, after which they bathe and undergo whatever forms of purification they feel are appropriate. The seventh is a day of offerings.

Make an offering of *thargelos* to Apollon, recite Orphic Hymn 33 and Homeric Hymns 3 and 21.

Make an offering of *thargelos* to Artemis, recite Orphic Hymn 35 and Homeric Hymns 9 and 27.

Make an offering of *thargelos* to the Horae, recite Orphic Hymn 42.

Thargelion 8:—Monthly festival day for Poseidon and Theseus

Thargelion 16:—The deme Erkhia sacrificed to Zeus Epakrios

Make an offering to Zeus Epakrios, recite Orphic Hymn 14 and Homeric Hymn 23.

Thargelion 19:—Bendideia; the deme Erkhia sacrificed to Menedeios (a local hero)

The Bendideia involved a solemn procession to venerate Bendis, a Thracian moon goddess.[67] The cult of Bendis was introduced in 429 BCE, and the Greeks identified her as approximately equivalent to Artemis, as she too was a huntress.[68] What function Bendis served is not described anywhere.

Make an offering to Bendis as best you can.

The Kallynteria occurred this month, probably on Thargelion 19, 24, 26, 27, or 28, and was the adorning of a statue of Athene. It is also possible that this was a day of sweeping out, rather than a day of adornment.

Make an offering to Athene, recite Orphic Hymn 31 and Homeric Hymns 11 and 28.

Thargelion 25:—Plynteria

The Plynteria is normally thought of as a washing festival where the statue of Athene was washed in the sea.[69]

This could be a day for a general cleanup of the home. If you have a statue of Athene that is waterproof, wash it in the sea or some other

---

67. Seyffert, *Dictionary of Classical Antiquities*, 96.

68. Parke, *Festivals of the Athenians*, 149–52.

69. Harrison, *Prolegomena to the Study of Greek Religion*, 114–6. Seyffert, *Dictionary of Classical Antiquities*, 112.

body of water. If the statue is not waterproof, then clean it, perhaps with tissues or a soft rag.

Make an offering to Athene, recite Orphic Hymn 31 and Homeric Hymns 11 and 28.

Skirophorion

Skirophorion was named after the Skiraphoria or Skira. While it appeared to be a women's festival of Athene, some scholars believe it was actually for Demeter and Persephone.[70] We should continue daily journaling, outlining everything we do for each festival day.

Skirophorion 1:—Monthly festival day, Noumenia

Skirophorion 2:—Monthly festival day for Agathos Daimon

Skirophorion 3:—Monthly festival day for Athene; the deme Erkhia sacrificed to Kourotrophos, Athene Polias (one of the three daughters of the first king of Athens), Aglauros, Zeus Polieus, Poseidon and Pandrosos (one of the three daughters of the first king of Athens).

Make an offering to Kourotrophos.

Make an offering to Athene Polias, recite Orphic Hymn 31 and Homeric Hymns 11 and 28.

Make an offering to Aglauros.

Make an offering to Zeus Polieus, recite Orphic Hymn 14 and Homeric Hymn 23.

As part of honoring Zeus Polieus, some will ensure that commitments are being fulfilled and justice is being manifested in daily life. Fatherhood is contemplated. Thunderstorms are listened to, and Zeus is thanked for supplying life-bringing rain.

Make an offering to Poseidon, recite Orphic Hymn 16 and Homeric Hymn 22.

Make an offering to Pandrosos.

Skirophorion 4:—Monthly festival day for Herakles, Hermes, Aphrodite, and Eros

---

70. Parke, *Festivals of the Athenians*, 156–7.

Skirophorion 6:—Monthly festival day for Artemis

Skirophorion 7:—Monthly festival day for Apollon

Skirophorion 8:—Monthly festival day for Poseidon and Theseus

Skirophorion 12:—Skira

The Skira festival involved a procession of the priestess of Athene, the priest of Poseidon, and the priest of Helios from the Acropolis to Skira, near which there was a sanctuary of Demeter and Kore where Athene and Poseidon were also venerated. This was one of the few days during the year when women could leave their chambers and assemble. The Skira festival roughly coincided with the summer solstice.

Make an offering to Athene Skiras, recite Orphic Hymn 31 and Homeric Hymns 11 and 28.

Given that this festival roughly coincides with the summer solstice, it would also be appropriate to make offerings to Helios by reciting Orphic Hymn 8 and Homeric Hymn 31, as well as to Apollon by reciting Orphic Hymn 34 and Homeric Hymns 3 and 21.

Skirophorion 14:—Dipolieia

The Dipolieia involved a bull sacrifice to honor Zeus of the City, Dii Poliei.[71]

Make a votive offering of a bull with either clay or pastry to present to Zeus Polieus as the primary deity of your city or country. Recite Orphic Hymn 14 and Homeric Hymn 23.

Skirophorion 30:—Diisoteria

The Diisoteria was a sacrifice to Zeus Soter and Athene Soter on the last day of the year.[72]

---

71. Burkert, *Greek Religion*, 230–1.
72. Parke, *Festivals of the Athenians*, 29.

Make an offering to Zeus Soter, recite Orphic Hymn 14 and Homeric Hymn 23.

Make an offering to Athene Soter, recite Orphic Hymn 31 and Homeric Hymns 11 and 28.

Metageitnion	Monthly Festival Day	Hymns
Metageitnion 1	Noumenia	Orphic 0. to Musaius
Metageitnion 2	Agathos Daimon	Orphic 72. To the Daimon, or Genius
Metageitnion 3	Athene	Orphic 31. To Athene
Metageitnion 4	Herakles, Hermes Aphrodite, Eros	Orphic 11. To Herakles, Orphic 27. To Hermes, Orphic 54. To Aphrodite, Orphic 57. To Eros
Metageitnion 6	Artemis	Orphic 35. To Artemis
Metageitnion 7	Apollon	Orphic 33. To Apollon
Salaminioi Genos	Apollon Patroos Leto Artemis Athene	Homeric 3 and 21. To Apollon Orphic 34. To Leto Orphic 35. To Artemis, Homeric 9 and 27. To Artemis Orphic 31. To Athene, Homeric 11 and 28. To Athene
Metageitnion 8	Poseidon and Theseus	Orphic 16. Hymn to Poseidon
Metageitnion 12 Deme Erkhia	Apollon Lykeios Demeter Zeus Polieus Athene Polias	Orphic 33. To Apollon, Homeric 3 and 21. To Apollon Orphic 39. To Demeter, Homeric 2 and 13. To Demeter Orphic 14. To Zeus, Homeric 23. To Zeus Orphic 31. To Athene, Homeric 11 and 28. To Athene
Metageitnion 15 Deme Erkhia	Kourotrophos Artemis Hekate	Pray from the heart to Kourotrophos Orphic 35. To Artemis, Homeric 9 and 27. To Artemis
Metageitnion 19 Deme Erkhia	Heroines	Pray from the heart to Heroines
Metageitnion 20 Deme Erkhia	Hera Thelkhinia	Orphic 15. To Hera, Homeric 12. To Hera
Metageitnion 25 Deme Erkhia	Zeus Epopetes	Orphic 14. To Zeus, Homeric 23. To Zeus
Metageitnion ?	Herakles	Orphic 11. To Herakles, Homeric 15. To Herakles

Hekatombaion	Monthly Festival Day	Hymns
Hekatombaion 1	Noumenia	Orphic 0. to Musaius
Hekatombaion 2	Agathos Daimon	Orphic 72. To the Daimon, or Genius
Hekatombaion 3	Athene	Orphic 31. To Athene
Hekatombaion 4	Herakles, Hermes Aphrodite, Eros	Orphic 11. To Herakles, Orphic Hymn 27. To Hermes, Orphic 54. To Aphrodite,Orphic Hymn 57. To Eros
Hekatombaion 6	Artemis	Orphic 35. To Artemis
Hekatombaion 7	Apollon	Orphic 33. To Apollon
Hekatombaion 8	Poseidon and Theseus	Orphic 16. Hymn to Poseidon
Hekatombaion 12	Kronia	Orphic 12. To Kronos
Hekatombaion 15	Unnamed	
Hekatombaion 16	Synoikia	Orphic 31. To Athene and, Homeric 11 and 28. To Athene Pray from the heart to Eirênê Orphic 14. To Zeus, Homeric 23. To Zeus
Hekatombaion 28	Panathenaia	Orphic 31. To Athene, Homeric 11 and 28. To Athene
Hekatombaion 28 (Possibly 23–30)		Orphic 57. To Eros

Boedromion 17	Unknown festival day	
Boedromion 19	Eleusinian Mysteries	Orphic 39. To Demeter; Homeric 2 and 13. To Demeter
Boedromion 20	Eleusinian Mysteries	Orphic 39. To Demeter; Homeric 2 and 13. To Demeter
Boedromion 21	Eleusinian Mysteries	Orphic 39. To Demeter; Homeric 2 and 13. To Demeter
Boedromion 22	Eleusinian Mysteries	Orphic 39. To Demeter; Homeric 2 and 13. To Demeter
Boedromion 27 Deme Erkhia Deme Teithras	Nymphs Akheloos Hermes Ge Athene	Orphic 50. To the Nymphs Libation into a river? Orphic 27. To Hermes, Homeric 4 and 18. To Hermes Orphic 25. To Gaia, Homeric 30. To Earth the Mother of All Orphic 31. To Athene, Homeric 11 and 28. To Athene

Boedromion	Monthly Festival Day	Hymns
Boedromion 1	Noumenia	Orphic 0. to Musaius
Boedromion 2	Agathos Daimon Niketeria	Orphic 72. To the Daimon, or Genius Orphic 32. To Nike
Boedromion 3	Athene	Orphic 31. To Athene
Boedromion 4	Herakles, Hermes Aphrodite, Eros	Orphic 11. To Herakles, Orphic 27. To Hermes, Orphic 54. To Aphrodite, Orphic 57. To Eros
Boedromion 5	Genesia	Visit graves
Deme Erkhia	Epops	Burn effigy of bird
Boedromion 6	Artemis Artemis Agrotera	Orphic 35. To Artemis, Homeric 9 and 27. To Artemis
Boedromion 7	Apollon Apollon; Boedromia	Orphic 33. To Apollon, Homeric 3 and 21. To Apollon
Boedromion 8	Poseidon and Theseus	Orphic 16. Hymn to Poseidon
Boedromion 12	Democratia Zeus Agoraios Athene Agoraia Themis	Orphic 14. To Zeus, Homeric 23. To Zeus Orphic 31. To Athene, Homeric 11 and 28 to Athene Orphic 78. To Themis
Boedromion 15	Eleusinian Mysteries;	Orphic 39. To Demeter, Homeric 2 and 13. To Demeter
Boedromion 16	Eleusinian Mysteries	Orphic 39. To Demeter, Homeric 2 and 13. To Demeter

Pyanepsion 12	Thesmophoria Nesteia	Orphic 39. To Demeter, Homeric 2 and 13. To Demeter
Pyanepsion 13	Thesmophoria Kalligeneia	Orphic 39. To Demeter, Homeric 2 and 13. To Demeter
Pyanepsion 14 Deme Erkhia	Heroines	Pray from the heart to the Heroines
Pyanepsion 19–21 or Pyanepsion 26–28	Apatouria Zeus Phratrios Athene Phratria	Orphic 14. To Zeus, Homeric 23. To Zeus Orphic 31. To Athene, Homeric 11 and 28. To Athene
Pyanepsion 30	Chalkeia Hephaestus Athene Ergane	Orphic 65. To Hephaestus, Homeric 20. To Hephaestus Orphic 31. To Athene, Homeric 11 and 28. To Athene

Pyanepsion	Monthly Festival Day	Hymns
Pyanepsion 1	Noumenia	Orphic 0. to Musaius
Pyanepsion 2	Agathos Daimon	Orphic 72. To the Daimon, or Genius
Pyanepsion 3	Athene	Orphic 31. To Athene
Pyanepsion 4	Herakles, Hermes Aphrodite, Eros	Orphic 11. To Herakles, Orphic 27. To Hermes, Orphic 54. To Aphrodite, Orphic 57. To Eros
Pyanepsion 6	Artemis Proerosia? Oschophoria?	Orphic 35. To Artemis Orphic 39. To Demeter, Homeric 2 and 13. To Demeter Orphic 44, 45, 46. To Dionysos, Homeric 7 and 26. To Dionysos
Pyanepsion 7	Apollon Pyanepsia	Orphic 33. To Apollon Panspermia (vegetable stew) and eiresione
Pyanepsion 8	Poseidon and Theseus Theseia; offering to the Amazons	Orphic 16. Hymn to Poseidon Milk porridge
Pyanepsion 9	Stenia	Orphic 39. To Demeter, Homeric 2 and 13. To Demeter
Pyanepsion 10	Thesmophoria (later addition)	Orphic 39. To Demeter, Homeric 2 and 13. To Demeter
Pyanepsion 11	Thesmophoria Anodos	Orphic 39. To Demeter, Homeric 2 and 13. To Demeter

Poseideon	Monthly Festival Day	Hymns
Poseideon 1	Noumenia	Orphic 0. to Musaius
Poseideon 2	Agathos Daimon	Orphic 72. To the Daimon, or Genius
Poseideon 3	Athene	Orphic 31. To Athene
Poseideon 4	Herakles, Hermes	Orphic 11. To Herakles, Orphic 27. To Hermes,
Poseideon 5	Aphrodite, Eros	Orphic 54. To Aphrodite,Orphic 57. To Eros
Deme Myrrhinos	Plerosia	Festival of completion - nothing else known
Poseideon 6	Artemis	Orphic 35. To Artemis
Poseideon 7	Apollon	Orphic 33. To Apollon
Boedromion 8	Poseidon and Theseus	Orphic 16. Hymn to Poseidon
Boedromion 16	Zeus Horios?	Orphic 14. To Zeus, Homeric 23. To Zeus
Poseideon 16–19?	Rural Dionysia	Orphic 44, 45, 46. To Dionysos, Homeric 7 and 26. To Dionysos
Poseideon 26	Haloa	Orphic 39. To Demeter; Homeric 2 and 13. To Demeter Kore: Orphic 28. To Persephone Orphic 44, 45, 46. To Dionysos, Homeric 7 and 26. To Dionysos

Maimakterion	Monthly Festival Day	Hymns
Maimakterion 1	Noumenia	Orphic 0. to Musaius
Maimakterion 2	Agathos Daimon	Orphic 72. To the Daimon, or Genius
Maimakterion 3	Athene	Orphic 31. To Athene
Maimakterion 4	Herakles, Hermes	Orphic 11. To Herakles, Orphic 27. To Hermes,
Maimakterion	Aphrodite, Eros	Orphic 54. To Aphrodite, Orphic 57. To Eros
Maimakterion 6	Artemis	Orphic 35. To Artemis
Maimakterion 7	Apollon	Orphic 33. To Apollon
Maimakterion 8	Poseidon and Theseus	Orphic 16. Hymn to Poseidon
Maimakterion	Pompaia	Obtain sheepskin
(last third of month)	Zeus Meilichios	Orphic 14. To Zeus, Homeric 23. To Zeus

Anthesterion	Monthly Festival Day	Hymns
Anthesterion 1	Noumenia	Orphic 0. to Musaius
Anthesterion 2	Agathos Daimon	Orphic 72. To the Daimon, or Genius
Deme Erkhia	Dionysos.	Orphic 44, 45, 46. To Dionysos, Homeric 7 and 26. To Dionysos
Anthesterion 3	Athene	Orphic 31. To Athene
Anthesterion 4	Herakles, Hermes	Orphic 11. To Herakles, Orphic 27. To Hermes,
	Aphrodite, Eros	Orphic 54. To Aphrodite, Orphic 57. To Eros
Anthesterion 6	Artemis	Orphic 35. To Artemis
Anthesterion 7	Apollon	Orphic 33. To Apollon
Anthesterion 8	Poseidon and Theseus	Orphic 16. Hymn to Poseidon
Anthesterion 11	Anthesteria Pithoigia	Orphic 44, 45, 46. To Dionysos, Homeric 7 and 26. To Dionysos Orphic 56. to Chthonic Hermes
Anthesterion 12	Anthesteria Choes	Orphic 44, 45, 46. To Dionysos, Homeric 7 and 26. To Dionysos Orphic 56. to Chthonic Hermes
Anthesterion 13	Anthesteria Chytroi	Orphic 44, 45, 46. To Dionysos, Homeric 7 and 26. To Dionysos Orphic 56. to Chthonic Hermes
Anthesterion 23	Diasia Zeus Meilichios	Orphic 14. To Zeus, Homeric 23. To Zeus
Anthesterion 20–26?	Mysteries at Agrai (Lesser Mysteries)	Orphic 39. To Demeter, Homeric 2 and 13. To Demeter

Gamelion	Monthly Festival Day	Hymns
Gamelion 1	Noumenia	Orphic 0. to Musaius
Gamelion 2	Agathos Daimon	Orphic 72. To the Daimon, or Genius
Gamelion 3	Athene	Orphic 31. To Athene
Gamelion 4	Herakles, Hermes	Orphic 11. To Herakles, Orphic 27. To Hermes,
	Aphrodite, Eros	Orphic 54. To Aphrodite, Orphic 57. To Eros
Gamelion 6	Artemis	Orphic 35. To Artemis
Gamelion 7	Apollo	Orphic 33. To Apollo
Deme Erkhia	Kourotrophos	Pray from the heart to Kourotrophos
	Apollon Delphinios	Orphic 33. To Apollon, Homeric 3 and 21. To Apollon
	Apollon Lykeios	
Gamelion 8	Poseidon and Theseus	Orphic 16. to Poseidon
Deme Erkhia	Apollon Apotropaios	Orphic 33. To Apollon, Homeric 3 and 21. To Apollon
	Apollon Nymphegetes	
	Nymphs	Orphic 50. To the Nympths
Gamelion 9	Athene	Orphic 31. To Athene, Homeric 11 and 28. To Athene
Deme Erkhia		
Gamelion 12–19?	Lenaia	Orphic 44, 45, 46. To Dionysos, Homeric 7 and 26. To Dionysos
Gamelion 27	Theogamia; Gamelia	Pray from the heart to Kourotrophos
Deme Erkhia	Kourotrophos	Orphic 15. To Hera, Homeric 12. To Hera
	Hera	Orphic 14. To Zeus, Homeric 23. To Zeus
	Zeus Teleios	Orphic 16. To Poseidon, Homeric 22. To Poseidon
	Poseidon	

Mounichion	Monthly Festival Day	Hymns
Mounichion 1	Noumenia	Orphic 0. to Musaius
Mounichion 2	Agathos Daimon	Orphic 72. To the Daimon, or Genius
Mounichion 3	Athene	Orphic 31. To Athene
Mounichion 4	Herakles, Hermes	Orphic 11. To Herakles, Orphic 27. To Hermes,
Mounichion 4	Aphrodite, Eros	Orphic 54. To Aphrodite, Orphic 57. To Eros
Deme Erkhia	Herakleidai	Pray from the heart to Herakleidai
Mounichion 6	Artemis	Orphic 35. To Artemis
Mounichion 6	Delphinia	Homeric 9 and 27. To Artemis
Mounichion 7	Apollon	Orphic 33. To Apollon
Mounichion 8	Poseidon and Theseus	Orphic 16. Hymn to Poseidon
Mounichion 16	Mounichia	Orphic 35. To Artemis, Homeric 9 and 27. To Artemis
Mounichion 17	Eurysakes	Pray from the heart to Eurysakes
Salaminioi		
Mounichion 19	Olympieia	Orphic 14. To Zeus, Homeric 23. To Zeus
Mounichion 20	Leukaspis	Pray from the heart to Leukaspis
Deme Erkhia		
Mounichion 21	Tritopatores	Pray from the heart to Tritopatores
Deme Erkhia		

Elaphebolion	Monthly Festival Day	Hymns
Elaphebolion 1	Noumenia	Orphic 0. to Musaius
Elaphebolion 2	Agathos Daimon	Orphic 72. To the Daimon, or Genius
Elaphebolion 3	Athene	Orphic 31. To Athene
Elaphebolion 4	Herakles, Hermes Aphrodite, Eros	Orphic 11. To Herakles, Orphic 27. To Hermes, Orphic 54. To Aphrodite, Orphic 57. To Eros
Elaphebolion 6	Artemis Artemis Elaphebolios	Orphic 35. To Artemis, Homeric 9 and 27. To Artemis
Elaphebolion 7	Apollon	Orphic 33. To Apollon
Elaphebolion 8	Poseidon and Theseus Asklepios festival and Proagon for City Dionysia	Orphic 16. to Poseidon Orphic 66. For Asklepios, Homeric 16, For Asklepios
Elaphebolion 10 Marathonian Tetrapolis	City Dionysia Ge	Orphic 44, 45, 46. To Dionysos, Homeric 7 and 26. To Dionysos Orphic 25. To Gaia, Homeric 30. To Earth the Mother of All
Elaphebolion 11–14	City Dionysia	Orphic 44, 45, 46. To Dionysos, Homeric 7 and 26. To Dionysos
Elaphebolion 16 Deme Erkhia	Dionysos Semele	Orphic 44, 45, 46. To Dionysos, Homeric 7 and 26. To Dionysos Orphic 43. To Semele
Elaphebolion 17	Pandia	Orphic 14. To Zeus, Homeric 23. To Zeus

Skirophorion	Monthly Festival Day	Hymns
Skirophorion 1	Noumenia	Orphic 0. to Musaius
Skirophorion 2	Agathos Daimon	Orphic 72. To the Daimon, or Genius
Skirophorion 3	Athene	Orphic 31. To Athene
Deme Erkhia	Kourotrophos	Pray from the heart to Kourotrophos
	Athene Polias	Orphic 31. To Athene, Homeric 11 and 28. To Athene
	Aglauros	Pray from the heart to Aglauros
	Zeus Polieus	Orphic 14. To Zeus, Homeric 23. To Zeus
	Poseidon	Orphic 16. To Poseidon, Homeric 22. To Poseidon
	Pandrosos	Pray from the heart to Pandrosos
Skirophorion 4	Herakles, Hermes	Orphic 11. To Herakles, Orphic 27. To Hermes,
	Aphrodite, Eros	Orphic 54. To Aphrodite, Orphic 57. To Eros
Skirophorion 6	Artemis	Orphic 35. To Artemis
Skirophorion 7	Apollon	Orphic 33. To Apollon
Skirophorion 8	Poseidon and Theseus	Orphic 16. Hymn to Poseidon
Skirophorion 12	Skira	Orphic 31. To Athene, Homeric 11 and 28. To Athene
		Orphic 33. To Apollon, Homeric 3 and 21. To Apollon
Skirophorion 14	Dipolieia	Orphic 14. To Zeus, Homeric 23. To Zeus
	Zeus Polieus	Orphic 14. To Zeus, Homeric 23. To Zeus
Skirophorion 30	Diisoteria	Orphic 14. To Zeus, Homeric 23. To Zeus
	Zeus Soter	
	Athene Soter	To Athene, Homeric 11 and 28. To Athene

Thargelion	Monthly Festival Day	Hymns
Thargelion 1	Noumenia	Orphic 0. to Musaius
Thargelion 2	Agathos Daimon	Orphic 72. To the Daimon, or Genius
Thargelion 3	Athene	Orphic 31. To Athene
Thargelion 4	Herakle, Hermes Aphrodite, Eros	Orphic 11. To Herakles, Orphic 27. To Hermes, Orphic 54. To Aphrodite, Orphic 57. To Eros
Thargelion 6	Artemis City Purification	Orphic 35. To Artemis, Homeric 9 and 27. To Artemis
Thargelion 7	Apollon Thargelia	Orphic 33. To Apollon Homeric 3 and 21. To Apollon, Orphic Hymn 35. To Artemis, Homeric 9 and 27. To Artemis, Orphic 42. To the Horae
Thargelion 8	Poseidon and Theseus	Orphic 16. Hymn to Poseidon
Thargelion 16	Zeus Epakrios	Orphic 14. To Zeus, Homeric 23. To Zeus
Thargelion 19 Deme Erkhia	Bendideia Sacrifice to Menedeios	Pray from the heart to Bendis
Thargelion 19, 24, 26 27, or 28,	Kallynteria	Orphic 31. To Athene, Homeric 11 and 28. To Athene
Thargelion 25	Plynteria	Orphic 31. To Athene; Homeric 11 and 28. To Athene

13: FUTURE DIRECTIONS: CHOICES

PURE HELLENISMOS

My aim in writing this book was to give those drawn to Hellenismos a solid foundation for future spiritual development. Recapping, the practice of Hellenismos must be based on diligent research drawn from primary and secondary source texts and then made relevant in today's world. We need to remember that there was no one way that the Greeks practiced their religion, as this varied geographically and throughout time. Because of this, there are numerous precedents to choose from in crafting a personal practice.

The number of people practicing Hellenismos is steadily growing, and from what I can tell most contact between them occurs on the Internet. There are numerous cyber groups practicing Hellenismos, or an equivalent term—there is a list of these in Appendix 4. If you choose to join any of these groups, make sure that their idea of Hellenismos is in keeping with your own. Do not allow yourself to be bullied into accepting something that does not feel right. However, you may feel it appropriate to compromise in order to have fellowship with like-minded individuals, saving what you believe is correct for private workings. If you do choose to compromise, make sure you hold true to yourself.

Determining which deities to venerate is a matter of choice. You can limit yourself to the deities worshipped in the home; those worshipped in rural areas; the twelve Olympians (even here you have to decide between Dionysos and Hestia); any of the other non-Olympic deities, spirits, and heroes available in the cities; or some combination of the above. As always, it's your choice as to how you wish to practice.

Determining how to venerate those deities is also a matter of choice. You can either venerate deities simply as was done in the home, or simulate the extravagance of public worship.

Determining whether to employ religious or magickal approaches with regard to venerating deities is also a matter of choice. While the majority of available information from archaic or classical times concerns religious veneration, there is ample literary evidence to prove that magick was practiced extensively throughout Greek history (see the Magick in Ancient Greece chapter).

For those who choose to engage in magickal practice, it is important to remember that while there are accounts, there are no surviving Greek grimoires (or how-to books) from archaic or classical times. There are, however, authentic Hellenistic Greek spells, which are not pure Greek, but have a very strong Greek influence. Unless an ancient magickal tome from ancient Greece is unearthed in the future, these Hellenistic spells are the next best thing.[1]

To grow in the practice of Hellenismos, as I have previously mentioned, requires further study of primary and secondary source texts, and then putting into practice what has been learned. Those who receive UPGs can implement those messages into their personal practices. Some people will feel motivated to learn the ancient Greek language, but this is not essential as there are many good translations available. Admittedly, however, subtle shades of meanings can be lost in translation.

---

1. For information on working with these, see Mierzwicki's *Graeco-Egyptian Magick*, Flowers' *Hermetic Magic*, and Skinner's *Techniques of Graeco-Egyptian Magic*.

Those who have become comfortable with performing the various practices may wish to consider performing a public ritual at a Pagan Pride Day, a local shop, or some other sort of gathering, for others to experience the beauty and wonder of Hellenismos. They may wish to create a Hellenic group in their area. This book will help teach and guide their group.

APPLIED HELLENISMOS

While it is my hope that many readers will be drawn to the elegant simplicity of Hellenismos in its pure form, I appreciate that those who are accustomed to complex rituals may wish to limit their involvement with Hellenismos to incorporating authentic Greek elements into their current practices. (Appendix 2: Greek Influence Within Contemporary Occultism provides a snapshot of some of the Greek-flavored occult literature available to date.)

Those readers whose practices involve setting up a sacred space by using a framework ritual consisting of an opening and a closing rite can readily sandwich a Hellenismos rite into the middle.

A generic Hellenismos rite has been detailed in the chapter "Experiencing the Lunar Cycle-Preamble to experiencing the lunar cycle."

Golden Dawn practitioners would insert the rite after Opening by Watchtower,[2] while Wiccans would insert it after casting the circle.[3, 4]

A number of traditions like to use an altar with a god and goddess. There are all sorts of options available depending on the purpose of the ritual. Apollon and Artemis can be used to symbolize the sun and moon. Zeus and Hera can be used for marriages. Zeus and Hestia can be used to symbolize everything and the center of everything—Pan and Hestia

---

2. Chic Cicero and Sandra Tabatha Cicero, *Self-Initiation into the Golden Dawn Tradition* (St. Paul, MN, Llewellyn Publications, 1995) 692–696.
3. Scott Cunningham, *Wicca: A Guide for the Solitary Practitioner* (St. Paul, MN: Llewellyn Publications, 1996) 115–120.
4. Janet and Stewart Farrar, *A Witches' Bible* (Berkeley and Los Angeles, University of California Press, 1960) 35–47, 55–57.

could be used the same way. Readers are limited only by their imaginations.

The Wiccan offerings of cakes and wine can be readily adapted to the offerings and libations within Hellenismos.

APPENDIX 1

PRONUNCIATION OF THE ANCIENT GREEK LANGUAGE

Transliteration from Greek into English is not universally agreed upon and varies between books. The convention adopted in this book and correct pronunciation is as set out below. The bolded capital letters are the English transliterations used. In brackets are the names of each of the letters, and the corresponding Greek capital and small letters.

Vowels

A (Alpha, A, α): Long as in f*a*ther, or short as in *a*ha.

E (Epsilon, Δ, ε): As in fr*e*t or p*e*t.

Ê (Eta, H, η): As in French p*e*re or within the third syllable of tête-à-tête

I (Iota, I, ι): Long as in f*ee*d, or short as in p*i*t.

O (Omicron, O, o): As in n*o*t.

U (Upsilon, Υ, υ): Long as in French r*u*e, short as in French d*u* pain.

Ô (Omega, Ω, ω): As in h*o*me or g*o*, but can be "aw" as in s*a*w.

The primary difference between Epsilon and Eta is that the former is short while the latter is long. Similarly, the primary difference between Omicron and Omega is that the former is short while the latter is long.

Diphthongs

Diphthongs are pairs of vowels that are slurred together when pronounced.

AI (AI, αι): As in "ai" in Is*ai*ah.

AU (AΥ, αυ): As in "ow" in g*ow*n.

EI (ΔI, ει): As in "ey" in gr*ey* or "ei" in *ei*ght.

EU (ΔΥ, ευ): As in "ew" in f*ew* or "eu" in f*eu*d.

ÊU (HΥ, ηυ): As in "ew" in f*ew* or "eu" in f*eu*d *(extending pronunciation)*.

OI (OI, οι): As in "oi" in b*oi*l or c*oi*n.

OU (OΥ, ου): As in "oo" in m*oo*n or p*oo*l.

UI (ΥI, υι): As in "ui" in French l*ui*.

Individual vowels that are repeated are pronounced twice, e.g. "di-isoteria."

Consonants

The pronunciation of **G** and **S** may vary depending on the consonant following it.

B (Beta, B, β): As in *b*ad.

G (Gamma, Γ, γ): As in *g*et.

GG (ΓΓ, γγ): As in "ng" in a*n*ger.

GK (ΓK, γκ): As in "ngk" in Chu*ng*king.

GCH (ΓK, γκ): As in "nkh" in mo*nkh*ood.

GX (ΓX, γχ): As in "nx" in ly*nx*.

D (Delta, Δ, δ): As in *d*oes.

Z (Zeta Z, ζ): As "zd" in Ma*zd*a or "sd" in wi*sd*om, in classical Attic pronunciation. Like "z" in do*z*e or "s" in ro*s*e after 350 BCE.

TH (Theta, Θ, θ): Aspirated T as "th" in po*th*ook, in classical Attic pronunciation. Like "th" in *th*in in late ancient pronunciation.

K (Kappa, K, κ): As in *k*ing.

L (Lambda, Λ, λ): As in *l*yre.

M (Mu, M, μ): As in *m*use.

N (Nu, N, ν): As in *n*ow or *n*et.

X (Xi, Ξ, ξ): As in wa*x* or fo*x*.

P (Pi, Π, π): As in *p*ush.

R (Rho, P, ρ): As in *r*ich (trilled).

S (Sigma, Σ, σ): As in mou*s*e.

SB (ΣB, σβ): As in ha*s b*een.

SG (ΣΓ, σγ): As in ha*s g*one.

SD (ΣΔ, σδ): As in ha*s d*one.

SM (ΣM, σμ): As in ha*s m*ade.

T (Tau, T, τ): As in *t*ap.

PH (Phi, Φ, φ): Aspirated P as "ph" in ha*ph*azard, in classical Attic pronunciation. Like "f" in *f*oot in late ancient pronunciation.

CH (Chi, X, χ): As in lo*ch*.

PS (Psi, Ψ, ψ): As in la*ps*e.

Pronunciation is very similar for classical Attic and late antiquity, except for the letters Zeta (Z), Theta (TH), and Phi (PH).[1]

Sigma is pronounced like the English S. But when Sigma occurs before Beta, Gamma, Delta, or Mu, it is pronounced like Z as in "zoo."

---

1. F. Kunchin Smith and T. W. Melluish, *Ancient Greek: A Foundation Course* (London: Hodder & Stoughton Educational, 1992); Donald J. Mastronarde, *Ancient Greek Tutorials Pronunciation Buide* (The Regents of the University of California, 2005) http://socrates.berkeley.edu/~andgreek/pronunc html/omegaU.html

APPENDIX 2

GREEK INFLUENCE WITHIN CONTEMPORARY OCCULTISM

As previously mentioned, since the 1990s the practice of Hellenismos has been resumed with its aim of as authentic a reconstruction as possible of ancient Greek religious practices. In the past, however, Greek elements have on occasion been incorporated within Ceremonial Magick and contemporary Paganism, imparting a pronounced Greek "flavor." A brief overview of these, listed in chronological order, will serve to demonstrate a persistant interest in Greek religious practices.

Agrippa's Three Books of Occult Philosophy

Henry Cornelius Agrippa (1468–1535) incorporated Greek as well as Egyptian, Latin, Hebrew, and Arabic esoteric lore into his *Three Books of Occult Philosophy*. The influence of this text cannot be overstated, as it is the primary reference for Western occultism.[1]

---

1. Henry Cornelius Agrippa, *Three Books of Occult Philosophy* (St. Paul, MN, Llewellyn Publications, 1995).

The Magical Treatise of Solomon, or Hygromanteia

The Key of Solomon is the most widely disseminated grimoire in Europe, and is the ancestor of most grimoire-based ceremonial magick. Its oldest manuscript dates to the sixth century. The Key of Solomon is written in Latin and is popularly believed to be translated from a Hebrew original. However, it is actually based on The Magical Treatise of Solomon, or Hygromanteia, which is written in Greek, and its earliest manuscript dates to the fifteenth century.[2]

Francis Barrett's The Magus

Francis Barrett wrote The Magus in 1801, spearheading the occult revival in England. The book ended with a series of biographies, a number of which were Greek philosophers.[3] Much of the material in Barrett's text was taken from Agrippa.

The Hermetic Order of the Golden Dawn

The Golden Dawn was founded in 1887 fusing Freemasonry, Rosicrucianism, Qabala, Hermeticism, Alchemy, Theosophy, Enochian magick, medieval grimoires, ancient Egyptian religion, and a few Greek elements. Many of the Golden Dawn systems were taken from Agrippa. The Golden Dawn was incredibly influential, having counted numerous luminaries among its ranks. It has been stated that the best books on magick and the Qabala have been written by people who were either members of or influenced by the Golden Dawn, including S. L. Mac-Gregor Mathers, A. E. Waite, Farrar, Israel Regardie, Aleister Crowley, Dion Fortune, Paul Foster Case, and H. P. Blavatsky.[4]

---

2. Marathakis, The Magical Treatise of Solomon.
3. Francis Barrett, The Magus: A Complete System of Occult Philosophy (New York, Citadel Press, 1995) 141–198.
4. Donald Michael Kraig, Modern Magick: Eleven Lessons in the High Magickal Arts (St. Paul, MN, Llewellyn Publications, 1998) xv.

A number of Golden Dawn rituals incorporate the call "*Hekas, Hekas, este Beboi*" as part of the process of banishing negative influences from the ritual area.[5]

It is claimed by Israel Regardie, Chic Cicero, and Sandra Tabatha Cicero that this magickal Greek phrase, which means "far, far away be the profane," was originally uttered at the Eleusinian Mysteries.[6]

Not surprisingly, the call has been subsequently incorporated into numerous rituals by ceremonial magicians drawing on Golden Dawn or Thelemic (see the following pages) influences. This is perfectly appropriate as ceremonial magicians, once they have achieved a certain level of competence, will compose their own rituals by cobbling together numerous influences and then adding their own flourishes. The magickal phrase in question certainly imparts an exotic Greek feel.

The call, however, has also been incorporated into rituals crafted by some practitioners of Hellenismos.[7] Given the aspiration toward authenticity inherent within Hellenismos, it is pertinent to ask whether the call is appropriate.

Because of the secrecy inherent within the Eleusinian Mysteries, little is known about them. But, having scrutinized what is available in academic texts, I have been unable to find evidence of any connection

---

5. Israel Regardie, *The Golden Dawn* (St. Paul, MN, Llewellyn Publications, 1998), 118, 131, 258, 303, 318, 323, 402, 435, 442.
6. Israel Regardie, et al. *The Tree of Life: An Illustrated Study in Magic* (St. Paul, MN, Llewellyn Publications, 2000), 417.
7. Drew Campbell, *Old Stones, New Temples* (Bloomington, IN, Xlibris Corp., 2000) 162, 195, 224, 227, 235, 242, 248, 252, 257, 261, 273, 277, 280, 284, 286, 291, and 296. Internet searches will readily show numerous other contemporary Hellenismos rites using this phrase.

whatsoever between the call *"Hekas, Hekas, este Bebeloi"* and the Eleusinian Mysteries.[8]

Unless a call such as *"Hekas, Hekas, este Bebeloi"* appears in a primary source text, including it in a Hellenismos ritual is of questionable appropriateness. (That being said, if someone's UPG warrants them to use it, then by all means they should do so, but this is something specific to them. As stated previously, people who have received UPGs shouldn't impose them on others, unless those others find that it resonates with them.)

The Golden Dawn's initiation ceremony for the Practicus grade claimed to incorporate elements from the ancient Greek mysteries of the Kabiri (Kabeiroi).[9] These mysteries originated on the island of Samothrace and little is known about them.[10] The Kabiri elements in the Golden Dawn initiation were mostly extracted from the Chaldean Oracles, which have no established connection with the Kabiri.[11]

A very widely used ritual coming from the Golden Dawn is "The Bornless Ritual for the Invocation of the Higher Genius," which is usually abbreviated to "The Bornless Ritual"[12] based on Charles Wycliffe

---

8. Burkert, *Ancient Mystery Cults* (Cambridge, MA, Harvard University Press, 1987); Burkert, *Greek Religion*, 285–290; Joseph Campbell, *The Mysteries: Papers from the Eranos Yearbooks* (Princeton, NJ, Princeton University Press, 1999) 1431; Michael B. Cosmopoulos, *Greek Mysteries: The Archaeology and Ritual of Ancient Creek Seccret Cults* (New York, Routledge, 2003); Foley. *Homeric Hymn to Demeter;* Jocelyn Godwin, *Mystery Religions in the Ancient World,* (London, Thames & Hudson Ltd, 1981) 32–35; Carl Kerenyi, *Eleusis: Archetypal Image of Mother and Daughter* (Princeton, NJ, Princeton University Press, 1991); Meyer, *The Ancient Mysteries,* 1745; Mylonas, *Eleusis;* Rice and Stambaugh, *Sources for the Study of Greek Religion,* 171–193; Charles Stein, *Persephone Unveiled: Seeing the Goddess and Freeing Your Soul* (Berkeley, CA: North Atlantic Books, 2006) 52–83; Wright, *The Eleusinian Mysteries & Rites.*

9. Regardie, *The Golden Dawn,* 169–171.

10. Burkert, *Greek Religion,* 281–285; Joseph Campbell, *The Mysteries,* 32–63.

11. Thomas Stanley, *The Chaldean Oracles* (New Jersey, Heptangle Books, 1989).

12. Regardie, *The Golden Dawn,* 442–446.

Goodwin's 1852 translation of a "Fragment of a Graeco-Egyptian work upon magic from a Papyrus in the British Museum."[13] Goodwin's translation of London Papyrus 46 is part of what is now known as the Greek Magical Papyri (written in Egypt from second century BCE to fifth century CE), and was an exorcism rite involving an invocation to a deity called the "Headless One."[14] The Golden Dawn version opted for invoking the "Bornless One," rather than the "Headless One," as a preliminary for Goetic evocations, which is a system for calling on seventy-two demonic entities taken from a medieval grimoire.

The Thelemic Magick of Aleister Crowley

Put simplistically, the system of magick advocated by Crowley was to live in accordance with one's True Will rather than one's free will. The term used by Crowley for Will was the Greek word *Thelêma* (will, wish, desire), and knowledge of one's True Will typically came about through accessing one's Holy Guardian Angel, which can be thought of as either a personal guardian spirit or the Higher Self. The Holy Guardian Angel acts as a conduit to divinity.

A number of Crowley's rituals incorporate Greek elements. A small selection follows.

Liber Samekh, which is a modified version of "The Bornless Ritual," was used by Crowley to access his Holy Guardian Angel. Crowley's version is characterized by his claimed corrections of the "barbarous names" (words of power) in the original ritual.

Crowley's *Liber XXV: The Star Ruby*, which is a reworking of the Golden Dawn's *Banishing Ritual of the Pentagram*, opens with the often quoted "*Apo Pantos Kakodaimonos*," which means "away, all evil spirits." *Kakodaimon* literally means evil spirit.[15] More Greek terms and phrases follow and no claims are made for the antiquity of any of them, other

---

13. Crowley et al., *The Goetia*, 53.
14. Betz, *The Greek Magical Papyri*, 103.
15. Crowley, *Magick in Theory and Practice*, 265–301, 327.

than for the names of a number of entities from the previously mentioned Chaldean Oracles.

In *777 and Other Qabalistic Writings of Aleister Crowley*, there are numerous attributions to the various parts of the Qabalistic Tree of Life, including a selection of Greek deities. This makes possible a magickal exploration through Qabalistic magick of the nature of the deities listed using the appropriate colors, fragrances, gemstones, plants, animals, and so on.[16]

Crowley presented his version of the Rites of Eleusis in Caxton Hall, Westminster, which were actually a series of planetary rites spread over seven consecutive Wednesday evenings from October to November, 1910. Being based primarily on Golden Dawn and Thelemic material, Crowley's rites had nothing in common with the original ancient Greek mysteries of the same name, other than seeking to induce an ecstatic state in those present.[17]

Israel Regardie's Ceremonial Magic

Israel Regardie looked at "The Bornless Ritual" at some length, discussing the original ritual, the Golden Dawn version, and Crowley's Liber Samekh.[18]

Robert Graves' The White Goddess *and Greek Myths*

In *The White Goddess*, poet Robert Graves introduced the idea of a "Triple Goddess" and tied her in with the three phases of the moon. The Triple Goddess has been embraced by Wiccans and other contemporary Pagans, where stages of the female lifecycle (Maiden, Mother, and Crone) are linked with lunar phases, and in turn linked with various goddesses,

---

16. Aleister Crowley, *777 and Other Qabalistic Writings of Aleister Crowley* (York Beach, ME: Samuel Weiser, 1989) 8 (Table 1, Column XXXIV).

17. Lon Milo DuQuette, *The Magick of Aleister Crowley: A Handbook of the Rituals of Thelema* (York Beach, ME: Samuel Weiser, 1989) 194–196; Sutin, *Do What Thou Wilt*, 209–210.

18. Regardie, *Ceremonial Magic*, 57–81, 109–120.

which vary depending on the tradition concerned.[19] In *Greek Myths*, Graves interpreted Greek mythology in accordance with his personal vision as outlined in *The White Goddess*.[20] Graves' writings tend to be ignored by scholars.[21]

Denning and Phillips' Aurum Solis

In the mid 1970s, Melita Denning and Osborne Phillips began publishing the teachings of their magickal order, Aurum Solis. These teachings are fairly similar to those of the Golden Dawn. A number of the Aurum Solis rituals give readers the option of performing key portions in either Hebrew or Greek.[22] There is far more Greek content in the Aurum Solis writings than in the Golden Dawn writings.

Murry Hope's Practical Greek Magic *and* The Greek Tradition

Prolific author Murry Hope, in the first part of *Practical Greek Magic*, outlined Greek creation myths, the Olympic and lesser deities, mystery schools, oracles and introduced her idea of a "Heroic Path." This Path, which occupies the more practical second part of her book, is a means of magickally experiencing the deities previously introduced.[23] *The Greek Tradition* is essentially a continuation of *Practical Greek Magic*, providing further information and a reconstructed incubation rite.[24] Hope did not, however, provide a step-by-step guide to constructing a Greek magickal ritual, leaving this up to the discretion of her readers.

---

19. Graves, *The White Goddess* (London, UK: Faber & Faber, 1948), 339.

20. Graves, *Greek Myths* (London, UK: Cassell, 1980), 339.

21. Donna R. White, *A Century of Welsh Myth in Children's Literature* (Santa Barbara, CA: Praeger, 1998), 75.

22. Melita Denning and Osborne Phillips, *Mysteria Magica: Volume 3 of the Magical Philosophy* (St. Paul, MN: Llewellyn Publications, 1986).

23. Murry Hope, *Practical Greek Magic* (Wellingborough, UK: The Aquarian Press, 1985).

24. Murry Hope, *The Greek Tradition* (Longmead, UK: Element Books, 1989).

Dolores Ashcroft-Nowicki's The Ritual Magic Workbook

Dolores Ashcroft-Nowicki, of the Servants of the Light School of Occult Sciences, presented a program of self-initiation into Golden Dawn influenced ceremonial magick drawing upon the Egyptian, Greek, Roman, and Celtic pantheons. The book takes the form of twelve lessons, each of which is allocated a month for completion. Included within a selection of season rituals are a Greek Ritual of Spring and a Greek Ritual of Summer.[25]

The Spring Ritual involves one person moving clockwise between the four cardinal directions and then between the four intermediate directions, pausing at each of the eight points to address various deities. Offerings of incense, wine, fruit, and seeds are then made. The Summer Ritual involves two people taking on the roles of Hermes and Flora, the goddess of flowers and performing joint blessings.

David Godwin's Light in Extension: Greek Magic from Homer to Modern Times

David Godwin provided a wonderfully accessible overview of the extent of Greek religious and philosophical influence from the time of Homer, to medieval, and then to modern times. Godwin pointed out that there are no surviving Greek grimoires from archaic or classical times, and then proceeded to use rituals taken from contemporary sources. The closest that he came to using an authentic ritual was when he compared "The Bornless Ritual" with the original text on which it was based.[26]

25. Dolores Ashcroft-Nowicki, *The Ritual Magic Workbook: A Practical Course of Self-Initiation* (London, The Aquarian Press 986) 121–125, 143–146.
26. David Godwin, *Light in Extension: Greek Magic from Homer to Modern Times* (St. Paul, MN: Llewellyn Publications, 1992).

Evangelos Rigakis' Threskia: The Greek Thelemic Tradition

Evangelos Rigakis has created a tradition, which he calls Threskia, from a blending of Crowley's Thelemic philosophy with the art of Orphism and the science of Pythagoras.[27]

Greek Numerology

Western occultism owes much to the practice of numerology, which can be seen as a magickal code connecting numbers with the letters of the alphabet, ascribing meanings, and providing rules for combinations.[28] Much Greek numerology can be traced back to the teachings of Pythagoras.[29] While Hebrew Qabala is popularly thought of as providing a logical framework for Western occultism, many of its numerical properties can be seen as based on earlier Greek writings, such as those of Pythagoras.[30]

Jennifer Reif's Mysteries of Demeter: Rebirth of the Pagan Way

Drawing inspiration from the Wiccan Wheel of the Year, Jennifer Reif produced a series of rituals to work a "Demetrian" Wheel of the Year. Little is known about the Mysteries of Eleusis, and so any attempted reconstructions are more creative rather than accurate.[31]

27. Mogg Morgan (ed.), *Thelemic Magick, II, Being the Proceedings of the Tenth International Symposium of Thelemic Magick* (Oxford, UK: Golden Dawn Publications, 1996) 33–43.

28. David Allen Hulse, *The Key of it All: Book Two* (St. Paul, MN: Llewellyn Publications, 1996) 3–46.

29. Kenneth Guthrie, *The Pythagorean Sourcebook and Library* (Grand Rapids, MI: Phanes Press, 1988).

30. Kieren Barry, *The Greek Qabalah* (York Beach, ME: Samuel Weiser, 1999).

31. Jennifer Reif, *Mysteries of Demeter: Rebirth of the Pagan Way* (York Beach, ME: Samuel Weiser, 1999).

Sorita D'Este's Hekate: Keys to the Crossroads

This text provides an overview of what the ancients believed about Hekate, along with a collection of accounts of contemporary experiences with her.[32]

REVIEW

It was never my intention to produce a comprehensive list of all of the occult texts that have incorporated Greek elements, as this would almost require a book in itself. Not mentioned here, but certainly deserving a mention, are the numerous texts on Wicca and Witchcraft, which encompass deities from a number of pantheons including the Greek one, as well as the writings of Manly P. Hall and the Theosophists. Texts range in authenticity from those that incorporate significant research to those that solely utilize the names of either deities or mystery schools and fit them to a modern paradigm.

While many people are lucky enough to find a pre-existing path or tradition that suits them perfectly, there are others who compromise. Knowledge of established paths is important for meaningful dialogue with other occultists, but those who are lacking deep spiritual satisfaction should, at the very least, look toward crafting their own practices for solitary workings. A number of the above texts are effectively new traditions crafted from pre-existing traditions that can be used as either inspiration or starting points for personal exploration.

While some people may feel the call of Hellenismos to such an extent that they will abandon all other spiritual practices, others will want to incorporate it into their existing workings. Rather than settling for a Greek flavor, perhaps authentic Greek elements could be incorporated instead.

---

32. D'Este, *Hekate*.

APPENDIX 3

DIET

As a result of the climate and thin semi-barren soil, the Athenian diet was frugal and monotonous. They ate twice daily—*ariston* (light lunch) and *deipnon* (dinner, the main meal). About 70 percent of their caloric intake came from cereal, primarily wheat and barley, which was largely imported. Barley was cheaper and formed the bulk of their diet, being normally baked into flat griddle-cakes, called *maza*. Wheat bread, called *artos*, was baked in round loaves and was consumed largely on feast days. Bread was often eaten with honey, cheese, and olive oil. All solid food that accompanied bread or cereal was known as *opson*—green vegetables, onions, garlic, olives, meat (the cheapest being suckling pig), fish, cheese (from sheep and goat milk), fruit or sweetmeats. The cheapest vegetables were beans and lentils, often served mashed, which was actually Herakles' favorite dish. Other popular vegetables included cabbages, asparagus, carrots, radishes, cucumbers, pumpkins, chicory, celery, and artichokes. Condiments included salt, sage, rosemary, thyme, mint, cinnamon, and silphium (a now extinct plant, possibly related to giant fennel).

The most common drink was water, which was sometimes sweetened with honey. The favorite drink was wine, mostly diluted and sweetened. Milk was used in cooking, but comparatively rarely drunk as a beverage. The milk was typically goat's milk.

Dessert was typically fresh or dried fruit, mostly figs, apples, pears, dates, almonds, walnuts, hazelnuts, chestnuts, raisins, or honey cakes. Honey and dried figs were used in place of sugar, which was unknown.[1] Black and white figs were thought of as male and female respectively.[2]

I am a firm believer in natural foods, especially for offerings to the divine, as this is what the ancients would have used. By natural, I mean preferably organic, or at least non-GMO (not genetically engineered). Once plants and animals are genetically engineered, they are no longer a gift from the divine, but rather a laboratory experiment unleashed onto the world which will ultimately negatively impact all life as we know it. It is the divine spark or divine essence that enables us to create change, and once lost through genetic engineering, the plant or animal material is without any value in a magickal sense. A full outline of the physical world dangers of GMOs is out of the scope of this book, but in my opinion, independent research has established that they are harmful for the health of those who consume them, and for the environment.

Modern wheat is very different to the wheat our ancestors enjoyed, and leads to numerous health complications. For the wheat bread mentioned above, I would recommend an ancient substitute such as einkorn or kamut. They are somewhat harder to chew, but are very flavorful.

Some of the festival observances require particular dishes. Here are ideas as to how these dishes could be prepared.

---

1. Robert Flaceliere, *Daily Life in Greece at the Time of Pericles* (London, UK:. Weidenfield & Nicolson, 1960) 168–73; Garland, *Daily Life of the Ancient Greeks*, 91–5.
2. Price and Kearns, *The Oxford Dictionary*, 218.

Galaxia (Barley and Milk Porridge)

- Whole barley, either pearled or hulled.

Pre-soak ½ cup whole barley in a saucepan with 1½ cups water for 1 hour. Then, optionally, add a cinnamon stick about 3-inch long.

Cover the saucepan and bring to a boil.

Reduce to medium heat until the barley is soft, roughly 30 minutes for pearled and 45 minutes for hulled.

At this point, sweeten to taste with honey and dried figs, and add a splash of goat's milk.

Goat's milk may not be to everyone's taste, so feel free to substitute cow's milk or non-dairy milk.

Remove the pot from the heat and sweeten with sugar and milk to taste, stirring until fully incorporated.

Panspermia (all seeds), Consisting of Beans and Cereals Boiled Together in One Pot

There are many possible variations to this dish, but I will base it on Greek fasolia gigandes (giant white beans), lentils, and barley. It would be easiest to cook up the components of this dish separately, but the recipe calls for them to be boiled together.

Start by soaking 1 cup fasolia gigandes in a pot. (Large lima beans make a suitable substitute.) Change the water frequently until the skins come off. Some people are happy to leave the skins on.

Add 1 cup of barley and let it soak for an hour, adding water.

Rinse 1 cup of lentils and toss them into the pot, adding water (or vegetable stock, which is nontraditional but really improves the flavor).

Add ¼ cup olive oil.

Chop up 2 onions, 2 large carrots, 2 sticks of celery, and add them.

Add pinches of salt, sage, rosemary.

Mince up a few cloves of garlic and add them.

When the beans have softened and all the liquid has been absorbed, the dish is complete.

APPENDIX 4

THE HELLENIC RECONSTRUCTIONIST AND/OR POLYTHEIST DIRECTORY

This listing is for primarily Hellenic reconstructionalists. If you contact any of them please understand their definition of "reconstruction" might not be the same as yours, and you may want to work to find a middle ground.

USA Hellenic Groups

Elaion: www.elaion.org
Hellenion: www.hellenion.org
Neokoroi: The Temple Keepers: www.neokoroi.org/
Thiasos Olympikos: http://home.pon.net/rhinoceroslodge/thiasos
    .htm

Northern Georgia and Surrounding Areas

Artemis Mounykhia Congregation: radiantbaby.tripod.com
    /artemis_mounykhia_pde

Facebook Groups:

A.H.R. Ancient Hellenic Religion—FORUM https://www.facebook.com/groups/A.H.R.FORUM/

Australian Hellenic Polytheists: https://www.facebook.com/groups/43223253129/

Greek Pagans: https://www.facebook.com/groups/209125449200700/

Hellenic Council YSEE of America: ´Ύπατο Συμβούλιο Ελλήνων Εθνικών Αμερικής https://www.facebook.com/groups/250460315154401/

Hellenic Mysticism and Magick https://www.facebook.com/groups/HellenicMysticismAndMagick/

Hellenic Pagan: https://www.facebook.com/groups/HellenicPagan/

Hellenic Pagans: https://www.facebook.com/groups/1781993542090349/about/

Hellenic Polytheism: https://www.facebook.com/groups/1633650223565115/

Hellenic Polytheistic Community - Ελληνική Πολυθεϊστική Κοινότητα: https://www.facebook.com/groups/596804250439931/

Hellenic Polytheistic Community (Ελληνική Πολυθεϊστική Κοινότητα): https://www.facebook.com/groups/4866586588/

Hellenic Underworld, Mystery Cults and Chthonic Deities: https://www.facebook.com/groups/1504039066506267/

Hellenion: https://www.facebook.com/HellenionOrg/

The LGBTQIA Hellenic Polytheistic Community: https://www.facebook.com/groups/139519342864460

GLOSSARY

Aegis: goat-skin cloak

Agathos Daimon: Good Spirit

Agaue: venerable

Agrotera: the Huntress

Agurtês: begging priests, who performed magick for the rich

Agyieus: of the street

Aidoneus: personification of the underworld

Aither: Upper Air

Amphiphontes: shining all round

Aphros: foam

Apotropaios: averter of evil

Athara: milk porridge

Aulos: shawm—a single- or double-reed pipe played in pairs

Caryatis: chestnut

Cedreatis: cedar

Chaos: chasm or gaping void

Charis: reciprocal favor

Choê: libation to the dead or the chthonic deities

Chlamys: short cloak worn by men in ancient Greece

Daidalon: wooden image (ancient name)

Delphinios: protector of the shrine at Delphi

Dêmos: Deme (political unit ranging in size from a town to a city)

Dryads: nymphs from trees, especially oak

Eiresione: olive bough entwined with wool, with models of figs, cakes, and jars of honey

Elaphebolios: Shooter of the Deer

Elaphoi: stags

Eleutherios: the liberator

Epaine: awesome

Epakrios: on the Heights

Epaoidê / epoidê: incantation

Epheboi: male adolescents

Epikourios: the Helper

Epoptes: the Overseer

Erebus: Nether Darkness

Ergane: Labor

Eros: love, desire, the principle of sexual reproduction

Eusebeia: piety

Fumigation: burn incense or aromatic substance for its fragrant odor

Gaia or Ge: Earth

Galaxia: barley and milk porridge

Genesia: day that the entire city honors its dead

Genos: particular kin group

Goês: magician (deriving from *goos*, ritual lament)

Gorgon: Homer wrote of a single Gorgon—a monster of the under-world. Later, Hesiod increased the number to three—Stheno (the Mighty), Euryale (the Far Springer), and Medusa (the Queen). They were portrayed as winged female creatures with snakes for hair, and with large teeth.

Gynaikeion: separate living quarters for women in a house

Hagna thymata: pure sacrifices

Hamadryads: nymphs who haunt trees and die when the tree dies

Kathiskos: offering jar for Zeus Ktesios (traditionally two-handled, but now more likely to be plain glass), topped with a strip of white wool, filled with water, olive oil, and various seeds, grains, and fruits

Hecatombs: sacrifices of one hundred beasts

Hekebolos: the afar, the distant one

Hekatebolos: strikes from afar

Hekatoncheires: Hundred-Handers

Hekatos: kills many

Helots: serfs

Hemera: day

Herkeios: household

Herm: square pillar with a bearded head and phallus

Herma: a heap of stones

Hieros gamos: holy marriage

Hoplite warriors: citizen-soldiers primarily armed with spears and shields

Horios: of the Boundaries

Hubris: excessive pride in abilities and good fortune

Hygieia: goddess of Health

Kerykeion (caduceus): herald's wand

Ktesios: of the house, or of property

Kyklopes: Cyclopes

Lanai: Maenads—the female worshippers of Dionysos

Leneus: of the Wine-Trough

Lygodesma: willow

Lykeios: wolf god

Mageia: Greek term for magick

Magos: magician (a word of Persian origin)

Mainades (Maenads): female devotees or nymphs of Dionysos

Meilichios: the Kindly

Metageitnios: from the month Metageitnion

Metikoi (metics): resident aliens

Miasma: pollution

Naiads: spring-nymphs

Nymphegetes: leader of the Nymphs

Nympholept: solitary male individual very devoted to the nymphs

Nyx: Night

Olympios: Olympian

Oreads: Nymphs of the hills

Ouranos: Sky

Ourea: Mountains

Pallas: female accidentally killed by Athene

Panspermia: all seeds—consisting of beans and cereals boiled together in one pot

Parthenogenesis: reproduction not requiring a male partner

Patroos: ancestral

Peplos: embroidered saffron-dyed robe worn by olive-wood cult statue of Athene

Pharmaka (plural): drugs or medicines

Pharmakon: witch, or someone who healed, or killed, with herbs

Phoibos: shining or radiant

Phratry: brotherhood or kinfolk—social division of the Greek tribe

Phratrios: tribal brotherhoods

Plouton: giver of wealth

Polias: protectress of the city

Polieus: protector of the city

Polis: city-state

Pompê: procession

Pontus [Pontos]: Sea

Potamiads: nymphs of rivers

Pottage: cereal dish of various boiled grains, sweetened with honey

Proagon: official theatrical presentation

Psychagôgia: necromancy

Psychopomp: guide bringing the dead to the underworld

Pythios: slayer of the python

Satyrs: originally forest men with pointed ears, who later took on goat
  attributes

Sileni: forest men with horse ears and sometimes also horse tails and
  legs

Skiras: Festival of the Skira or Skirophoria

Soter: Savior or deliverer

Spondê: libation to the deities to request their protection

Tartaros: a recess in the earth

Teleia: of the Rite (feminine guardian of marriage)

Teleios: of the Rite (masculine guardian of marriage)

Thalusia: first fruit offerings to the gods

Thambos: astonishment or amazement

Thargelos: boiled first fruit offerings of corn and vegetables

Thelkhinia: an epithet of Hera, its meaning has been lost

Thusia: blood sacrifice

Thyrsos: pine cone-tipped staff

Tritogeneia: epithet of Athena, possibly from her birthplace lake Tritonis in Libya, or the place where she was worshipped stream Triton in Boeotia, or from *tritô* (head) to signify she was born out of the head of her father

Xoanon: wooden cult image

BIBLIOGRAPHY

Agrippa, Henry Cornelius. *Three Books of Occult Philosophy*. St. Paul, MN: Llewellyn Publications, 1995.

Aldhouse-Green, Miranda. *The Quest for the Shaman: Shape-Shifters, Sorcerers, and Spirit Healers in Ancient Europe*. New York: Thames and Hudson, 2005.

Ashcroft-Nowicki, Dolores. *The Ritual Magic Workbook: A Practical Course of Self-Initiation*. London: The Aquarian Press, 1986.

Asirvatham, Sulochana, et al (ed.). *Between Magic and Religion: Interdisciplinary Studies in Ancient Mediterranean Religion and Society*. New York: Rowman & Littlefield Publishers, Inc., 2001.

Athanassakis, Apostolos N. (trans.). *The Homeric Hymns: Translation, Introduction, and Notes*. Baltimore: Johns Hopkins University Press, 1976.

———. *Orphic Hymns: Text, Translation, and Notes*. Baltimore: Johns Hopkins University Press, 2013.

Atallah, Hashem, and William Kiesel. *Picatrix: Ghayat Al-Hakim: The Goal of the Wise, Volume One*. Seattle, WA: Ouroboros Press, 2002.

———. *Picatrix: Ghayat Al-Hakim: The Goal of the Wise, Volume Two*. Seattle, WA: Ouroboros Press, 2008.

Barrabbas, Frater. *Mastering the Art of Ritual Magick: Volume Three: Greater Key*. Stafford, UK: Megalithica Books, 2010.

Barrett, Francis. *The Magus: A Complete System of Occult Philosophy*. New York: A Citadel Press Book, 1995.

Barry, Kieren. *The Greek Qabalah*. York Beach, ME: Samuel Weiser, 1999.

Beard, Mary, and John North (ed.). *Pagan Priests*. London: Duckworth, 1990.

Beckman, Gary. "Hittite Chronology." *Akkadica*, 119/120 (2000).

Betz, Hans Dieter (ed.). *The Greek Magical Papyri in Translation*. Chicago: The University of Chicago Press, 1986.

Boardman, John, et al. *The Oxford History of the Classical World*. New York: Oxford University Press, 1986.

Bodeus, Richard. *Aristotle and the Theology of the Living Immortals*. Albany, NY: State University of New York Press, 2000.

Bowman, John S. *Treasures of Ancient Greece*. New York: Gallery Books, 1986.

Bowra, C. M. *The Greek Experience*. New York: A Mentor Book, 1964.

Bremmer, Jan N. *Greek Religion*. New York: Cambridge University Press, 1999.

Brisson, Luc. *Sexual Ambivalence: Androgyny and Hermaphroditism in Graeco-Roman Antiquity*. Berkeley and Los Angeles, CA: University of California Press, 2002.

Burkert, Walter. *Ancient Mystery Cults*. Cambridge, MA: Harvard University Press, 1987.

———. *Greek Religion*. Oxford, UK: Blackwell Publishers Ltd., 2000.

———. *The Orientalizing Revolution: Near Eastern Influence on Greek Culture in the Early Archaic Age*. Cambridge, MA: Harvard University Press, 1992.

Butler, E. M. *The Myth of the Magus*. New York: The MacMillan Company, 1948.

Campbell, Drew. *Old Stones, New Temples: Ancient Greek Paganism Reborn*. Bloomington, IN: Xlibris Corporation, 2000.

Campbell, Joseph (ed.). *The Mysteries: Papers from the Eranos Yearbooks*. Princeton, NJ: Princeton University Press, 1990.

Chadwick, John. *The Decipherment of Linear B*. New York: Modern Library Paperbacks, 1958.

Chamoux, Francois. *The Civilization of Greece*. New York: Simon and Schuster, 1965.

Chuvin, Pierre. *A Chronicle of the Last Pagans*. Cambridge, MA: Harvard University Press, 1990.

Cicero, Chic, and Sandra Tabatha Cicero. *Self-Initiation into the Golden Dawn Tradition*. St. Paul, MN: Llewellyn Publications, 1995.

Cohen, Getzel M., and Martha Sharp Joukowsky (eds.). *Breaking Ground: Pioneering Women Archaeologists*. Ann Arbor, MI: University of Michigan Press, 2006.

Collins, Derek. *Magic in the Ancient Greek World*. Malden, MA: Wiley-Blackwell Publishing, 2008.

Connelly, Joan Breton. *Portrait of a Priestess: Women and Ritual in Ancient Greece*. Princeton, NJ: Princeton University Press, 2007.

Cooper, John M., and D. S. Hutchinson. *Plato: Complete Works*. Indianapolis, IN: Hackett Publishing Company, 1997.

Cosmopoulos, Michael B. *Greek Mysteries: The Archaeology and Ritual of Ancient Greek Secret Cults*. New York: Routledge, 2003.

Crowley, Aleister. *Magick in Theory and Practice*. Edison, NJ: Castle Books, 1991.

_____. *777 and Other Qabalistic Writings of Aleister Crowley*. York Beach, ME: Samuel Weiser, Inc., 1989.

Crowley, Aleister (ed.), Samuel Liddell, and MacGregor Mathers (trans). *The Goetia: The Lesser Key of Solomon the King.* York Beach, ME: Samuel Weiser, Inc., 1997.

Cumont, Franz. *Astrology and Religion Among the Greeks and Romans.* New York: Dover Publications, Inc., 1960.

Cunningham, Scott. *Wicca: A Guide for the Solitary Practitioner.* St. Paul, MN: Llewellyn Publications, 1996.

Cryer, Frederick H., and Marie-Louise Thomsen. *Witchcraft and Magic in Europe: Biblical and Pagan Societies.* London: The Athlone Press, 2001.

Dakyns, H. G. *Xenophon: Anabasis.* c. 1895. n.p.

———. *Xenophon: The Symposium.* c. 1895. n.p.

Davies, Nigel. *Human Sacrifice.* London: MacMillan London Limited, 1981.

De Boer, J. Z., and J. R. Hale. *The Geological Origins of the Oracle at Delphi, Greece.* From: W. G. McGuire, D. R. Griffiths, P. L. Hancock, and I. S. Stuart (eds.). The Archaeology of Geological Catastrophes, Geological Society, London, special publications, 171, 399–412.

Davies, Nigel. *Human Sacrifice.* London: MacMillan London Limited, 1981.

Denning, Melita, and Osborne Phillips. *The Foundations of High Magick: Volume 1 of the Magical Philosophy.* St. Paul, MN: Llewellyn Publications, 1991.

———. *Mysteria Magica: Volume 3 of the Magical Philosophy.* St. Paul: Llewellyn Publications, 1986.

———. *The Sword and The Serpent: Volume 2 of the Magical Philosophy.* St. Paul, MN: Llewellyn Publications, 1988.

D'Este, Sorita. *Hekate: Keys to the Crossroads.* London: Avalonia, 2006.

Dickie, Matthew W. *Magic and Magicians in the Greco-Roman World.* New York: Routledge, 2006.

Dillon, Matthew. *Pilgrims and Pilgrimage in Ancient Greece*. New York: Routledge, 1997.

Dodds, E. R. *The Greeks and the Irrational*. Berkeley, CA: University of California Press, 1951.

Doria, Charles, and Harris Lenowitz. *Origins: Creation Texts from the Ancient Mediterranean*. Garden City, NY: Anchor Books, 1976.

Drachmann, A. B. *Atheism in Pagan Antiquity*. Chicago: Ares Publishers Inc., 1977.

Dreyer, Ronnie Gale. *Venus: The Evolution of the Goddess and Her Planet*. Hammersmith, UK: Aquarian, 1994.

DuQuette, Lon Milo. *The Magick of Aleister Crowley: A Handbook of the Rituals of Thelema*. York Beach, ME: Red Wheel/Weiser, 2003.

Durant, Will. *The Life of Greece*. New York: Simon & Schuster, 1939.

Eliade, Mircea. *Rites and Symbols of Initiation: The Mysteries of Birth and Rebirth*. New York: Harper Torchbooks, 1975.

Evelyn-White, Hugh G. *Hesiod, Homeric Hymns, Epic Cycle, Homerica*. Cambridge, MA: Harvard University Press, 2000.

Evslin, Bernard. *Gods, Demigods and Demons. An Encyclopedia of Greek Mythology*. New York: Scholastic Book Services, 1975.

Faraone, Christopher A. *Ancient Greek Love Magic*. Cambridge, MA: Harvard University Press, 1999.

Faraone, Christopher A., and Dirk Obbink (ed.). *Magika Hiera: Ancient Greek Magic & Religion*. New York: Oxford University Press, 1997.

Farrar, Janet and Stewart. *A Witches' Bible: The Complete Witches' Handbook*. Custer, WA: Phoenix Publishing, 1996.

Festugiere, Andre-Jean. *Personal Religion Among the Greeks*. Berkeley and Los Angeles, CA: University of California Press, 1960.

Flaceliere, Robert. *Daily Life in Greece at the Time of Pericles*. London: Weidenfeld & Nicolson, 1965.

Flowers, Stephen Edred. *Hermetic Magic: The Postmodern Magical Papyrus of Abaris*. York Beach, ME: Samuel Weiser, 1995.

Foley, Helene P. (ed.). *The Homeric Hymn to Demeter*. Princeton, NJ: Princeton University Press, 1999.

Fowler, Harold North. *Plutarch: Moralia, Volume X*. Cambridge, MA: Loeb Classical Library, 1936.

Frazer, R. M. *The Poems of Hesiod*. Norman, OK: University of Oklahoma Press, 1983.

Frazer, Sir James. *The Golden Bough*. Ware, Hertfordshire, UK: Wordsworth Reference, 1995.

Fredrick, Daniel R. *The Voice Inside the Pen: What Rhetoric and Composition Can Learn from Orality and Literacy Studies*. 2007. www.speaking-writingconnection.com/swc.fredrick_voice.pdf

Freeman, Charles. *The Greek Achievement: The Foundation of the Western World*. New York: Penguin Books, 1999.

Fustel de Coulanges, Numa Denis. *The Ancient City: A Study of the Religion, Laws, and Institutions of Greece and Rome*. Baltimore, MD: Johns Hopkins University Press, 1980.

Gager, John G. *Curse Tablets and Binding Spells from the Ancient World*. New York: Oxford University Press, 1999.

Garland, Robert. *Daily Life of the Ancient Greeks*. Westport, CT: Greenwood Press, 1998.

———. *The Greek Way of Life*. Ithaca, NY: Cornell University Press, 1990.

———. *Religion and the Greeks*. London: Bristol Classical Press, 1998.

Gedalyahu, Tzvi Ben. "Rare Discovery of 3,500-Year-Old Objects." *Israel National News*, June 7, 2010.

Godwin, David. *Light in Extension: Greek Magic from Homer to Modern Times*. St. Paul, MN: Llewellyn Publications, 1992.

Godwin, Joscelyn. *Mystery Religions in the Ancient World*. London: Thames and Hudson Ltd, 1981.

Graf, Fritz. *Greek Mythology: An Introduction*. Baltimore, MD: The John Hopkins University Press, 1996.

———. *Magic in the Ancient World*. Cambridge, MA: Harvard University Press, 1999.

Grant, A. J. *Herodotus: The Text of Canon Rawlinson's translation, with the Notes Abridged*. New York: Charles Scribner's Sons, 1897.

Grant, Frederick C. (ed.). *Hellenistic Religions*. Indianapolis, IN: Bobbs-Merrill Company Inc., 1953.

Grant, Michael. *The Ancient Mediterranean*. New York: Charles Scribner's Sons, 1969.

Grant, Michael, and John Hazel. *Who's Who in Classical Mythology*. Oxford: Oxford University Press, 1993.

Graves, Robert. *Greek Myths*. London: Cassell, 1980.

———. *The White Goddess*. London: Faber and Faber, 1948.

Grene, David. *Herodotus: The History*. Chicago: The University of Chicago Press, 1988.

Grigson, Geoffrey. *The Goddess of Love: The Birth, Triumph, Death and Return of Aphrodite*. London: Quartet Books Limited, 1978.

Guirand, Felix. *New Larouse Encyclopedia of Mythology*. Twickenham, UK: Hamlyn Publishing, 1986.

Guthrie, Kenneth Sylvan (trans.). *The Pythagorean Sourcebook and Library*. Grand Rapids, MI: Phanes Press, 1988.

Guthrie, W. K .C. *The Greeks and their Gods*. Boston: Beacon Press, 1961.

———. *Orpheus and Greek Religion*. Princeton, NJ: Princeton University Press, 1993.

Hall, Manly P. *The Adepts in the Esoteric Classical Tradition*. Los Angeles: The Philosophical Research Society Inc, 1981.

Hard, Robin (trans.). *Apollodorus: The Library of Greek Mythology.* New York: Oxford University Press, 1998.

_____. *The Routledge Handbook of Greek Mythology: Based on H. J. Rose's Handbook of Greek Mythology.* New York: Routledge, 2004.

Harrison, Jane Ellen. *Epilegomena: A Brief Summary of the Origins of Greek Religion.* Edmonds, WA: The Alexandrian Press, 1992.

_____. *Prolegomena to the Study of Greek Religion.* Princeton, NJ: Princeton University Press, 1991.

_____. *Themis: A Study of the Social Origins of Greek Religion.* London: Merlin Press, 1963.

Harvey, Paul. *The Oxford Companion to Classical Literature.* Oxford, UK: Oxford University Press, 1986.

Hawkes, Jacquetta. *Dawn of the Gods: Minoan and Mycenaean Origins of Greece.* New York: Random House, 1968.

Herzberg, Max J. *Myths and Their Meaning.* Boston: Allyn & Bacon, Inc., n.d.

Hillman, D. C. A. PhD. *The Chemical Muse: Drug Use and the Roots of Western Civilization.* New York: Thomas Dunne Books, 2008.

Hooker, James. "Cult-Personnel in the Linear B Texts from Pylos." In *Pagan Priests*, edited by Mary Beard and John North, 159–174. London: Duckworth, 1990.

Hope, Murry. *The Greek Tradition.* Longmead, UK: Element Books, 1989.

_____. *Practical Greek Magic.* Wellingborough, UK: The Aquarian Press, 1985.

Hope, Richard (trans). *Aristotle—Metaphysics.* New York: Ann Arbor Paperbacks, 1990.

How, W. W., and J. Wells. *A Commentary on Herodotus: Volume I (Books I-IV).* London: Oxford at the Clarendon Press, 1964.

_____. *A Commentary on Herodotus: Volume II (Books V-IX)*. London: Oxford at the Clarendon Press, 1964.

Hrozny, Bedrich, PhD. *Ancient History of Western Asia, India and Crete*. Prague: Artia, 1953.

Hughes, Dennis D. *Human Sacrifice in Ancient Greece*. New York: Routledge, 1991.

Hulse, David Allen. *The Key of It All: Book Two*. St. Paul, MN: Llewellyn Publications, 1996.

Hyde, Walter Woodburn. *Greek Religion and Its Survivals*. London: George G. Harrap & Co., Ltd., 2012.

James, H. R. *Our Hellenic Heritage: Vol II*. London: Macmillan and Co., Ltd., 1924.

James, Peter. *Centuries of Darkness*. London: Pimlico, 1992.

Janowitz, Naomi. *Magic in the Roman World: Pagans, Jews and Christians*. London: Routledge, 2001.

Jarus, Owen. "Crete Fortifications Debunk Myth of Peaceful Minoan Society." *The Independent*, May 5, 2010.

Jayne, Walter Addison, M. D. *Healing Gods of Ancient Civilizations*. New Hyde Park, NY: University Books Inc., 1962.

Jones, Gladys V. *The Greek Love Mysteries*. La Cañada, CA: New Age Press, 1975.

Jones, Horace Leonard. *Strabo: The Geography: Vol. 4*. Cambridge, MA: Harvard University Press, 1960.

Jowett, Benjamin (trans). *Phaedrus by Plato*. Oxford, 1892.

Kenyon, Sir Frederic G. (trans.). *Aristotle: The Athenian Constitution* https://sourcebooks.fordham.edu/ancient/aristotle-athcon.txt.

Kerenyi, Carl. *Eleusis: Archetypal Image of Mother and Daughter*. Princeton, NJ: Princeton University Press, 1991.

Kerenyi, C., and Karl Kerenyi. *The Gods of the Greeks*. London: Thames and Hudson, 1979.

Kerenyi, Karl. *Hermes: Guide of Souls.* Putnam, CT: Spring Publications, 1976.

Kirk, G. S. *Myth: Its Meaning & Functions in Ancient & Other Cultures.* Berkeley and Los Angeles: Cambridge University Press, 1970.

_____. *The Nature of Greek Myths.* Harmondsworth, UK: Penguin Books Ltd., 1985.

Kitto, H. D. F. *The Greeks.* New York: Penguin Books, 1991.

Koester, Helmut. *Introduction to the New Testament: Volume One: History, Culture, and Religion of the Hellenistic Age.* Philadelphia: Fortress Press, 1982.

Kontorlis, Konstantinos P. *Mycenaean Civilization: Mycenae, Tiryns, Pylos.* Athens, GA: K. Kontorlis and Co, 1974.

Kraig, Donald Michael. *Modern Magick: Eleven Lessons in the High Magickal Arts.* St. Paul, MN: Llewellyn Publications, 1998.

Kramer, Samuel Noah. *History Begins at Sumer: Twenty-Seven "Firsts" in Man's Recorded History.* Garden City, NY: Doubleday Anchor Books, 1959.

Larson, Jennifer. *Ancient Greek Cults: A Guide.* New York: Routledge, 2007.

_____. *Greek Nymphs: Myth, Cult, Lore.* New York: Oxford University Press, 2001.

Levi, Peter (trans.). *Pausanias: Guide to Greece: Volume 1: Central Greece.* New York: Penguin Books, 1979.

_____ (trans.). *Pausanias: Guide to Greece: Volume 2: Southern Greece.* New York: Penguin Books, 1985.

Licht, Hans. *Sexual Life in Ancient Greece.* London: George Routledge & Sons, Ltd., 1942.

Liddell, H. G., and Robert Scott. *An Intermediate Greek—English Lexicon.* Oxford, UK: Oxford University Press, 2000.

Luce, J. V. *Homer and the Heroic Age*. London: Futura Publications Limited, 1979.

Luck, Georg. *Ancient Pathways & Hidden Pursuits: Religion, Morals, and Magic in the Ancient World*. Ann Arbor, MI, University of Michigan, 2000.

_____. *Arcana Mundi: Magic and the Occult in the Greek and Roman Worlds*. Wellingborough, UK: Crucible, 1987.

Malinowski, Bronislaw. *Magic, Science and Religion: and Other Essays*. London: A Condor Book, 1974.

Marathakis, Ioannis. *The Magical Treatise of Solomon, or Hygromanteia*. Singapore: Golden Hoard Press, 2011.

March, Jenny. *Cassell Dictionary of Classical Mythology*. London: Cassell, 1998.

Mastronarde, Donald J. *Ancient Greek Tutorials: Pronunciation Guide*. The Regents of the University of California, 2005.

Meyer, Marvin W. *The Ancient Mysteries: A Sourcebook*. San Francisco: Harper & Row, 1987.

Meyer, Marvin, and Paul Mirecki (ed). *Ancient Magic and Ritual Power*. Boston: Brill Academic Publishers, Inc., 2001.

Meyer, Marvin, and Richard Smith (ed.). *Ancient Christian Magic: Coptic Texts of Ritual Power*. New York: Harper San Francisco, 1994.

Mierzwicki, Tony. *Graeco-Egyptian Magick: Everyday Empowerment*. Stafford, UK: Megalithica Books, 2006.

Mikalson, Jon D. *Ancient Greek Religion: Second Edition*. Malden, MA: Wiley-Blackwell, 2010.

_____. *Athenian Popular Religion*. Chapel Hill, NC: The University of North Carolina Press, 1983.

_____. *Honor Thy Gods: Popular Religion in Greek Tragedy*. Chapel Hill, NC: The University of North Carolina Press, 1991.

_____. *The Noumenia and Epimenia in Athens*. Cambridge, MA: University Press and Harvard Divinity School, 1972.

_____. *The Sacred and Civil Calendar of the Athenian Year*. Princeton, NJ: Princeton University Press, 1975.

Morgan, Mogg (ed.). *Thelemic Magick, II, Being the Proceedings of the Tenth International Symposium of Thelemic Magick*. Oxford, UK: Golden Dawn Publications, 1996.

Mylonas, George E. *Eleusis: And the Eleusinian Mysteries*. Princeton, NJ: Princeton University Press, 1961.

Neugebauer, O. *The Exact Sciences in Antiquity*. New York: Dover Publications, Inc., 1969.

Nilsson, Martin P. *A History of Greek Religion*. New York: W. W. Norton & Company, Inc., 1964.

_____. *Greek Folk Religion*. New York: Harper Torchbooks, 1961.

Ogden, Daniel. *Greek and Roman Necromancy*. Princeton, NJ: Princeton University Press, 2001.

_____. *Magic, Witchcraft, and Ghosts in the Greek and Roman Worlds: A Sourcebook*. New York: Oxford University Press, 2002.

Olcott, William Tyler. *Sun Lore of all Ages: A Collection of Myths and Legends Concerning the Sun and Its Worship*. New York: G. P. Putnam's sons, 1914.

Oldfather, C. H. *Diodorus Siculus: The Library of History, Volume III, Books 4.59-8*. Cambridge, MA: Loeb Classical Library, 1939.

Ontario Consultants on Religious Tolerance. The Status of Women in the Hebrew Scriptures. www.religioustolerance.org/ofe_bibl.htm.

Otto, Walter F. *The Homeric Gods: The Spiritual Significance of Greek Religion*. New York: Pantheon Books, 1954.

Parisinou, Eva. *The Light of the Gods: The Role of Light in Archaic and Classical Greek Cult*. London: Duckworth, 2000.

Parke, H. W. *Festivals of the Athenians*. Ithaca, NY: Cornell University Press, 1986.

Parker, Robert. *Athenian Religion: A History*. Oxford, UK: Clarendon Press, 1997.

Peters, F. E. *The Harvest of Hellenism: A History of the Near East from Alexander the Great to the Triumph of Christianity*. London: George Allen & Unwin Ltd, 1972.

Price, Simon. *Religions of the Ancient Greeks*. New York: Cambridge University Press, 2004.

Price, Simon, and Emily Kearns (eds.). *The Oxford Dictionary of Classical Myth & Religion*. New York: Oxford University Press, 2003.

Pulleyn, Simon. *Prayer in Greek Religion*. New York: Oxford University Press, 1997.

Querci, François René, and Patrick Martinez. "An Aircraft Equipment for New Lunar Crescent Observations," Project Islamic Crescent Observation. http://www.icoproject.org/pdf/querci_2001.pdf

Rabinowitz, Jacob. *The Rotting Goddess: The Origin of the Witch in Classical Antiquity*. Brooklyn, NY: Autonomedia, 1998.

Rawlinson, George. *History of Herodotus*. London: John Murray, 1862.

_____. *The Religions of the Ancient World*. New York: John B. Alden, Publisher, 1885.

Regardie, Israel. *Ceremonial Magic*. Wellingborough, UK: The Aquarian Press, 1985.

_____. *The Golden Dawn*. St. Paul, MN: Llewellyn Publications, 2002.

Regardie, Israel, and Chic and Sandra Tabatha Cicero. *The Tree of Life: An Illustrated Study in Magic*. St. Paul, MN: Llewellyn Publications, 2000.

Reif, Jennifer. *Mysteries of Demeter: Rebirth of the Pagan Way*. York Beach, ME: Samuel Weiser, Inc., 1999.

Rice, David G., and John E. Stambaugh. *Sources for the Study of Greek Religion*. Atlanta, GA: The Society of Biblical Literature, 1979.

Rieu, E. V. (trans.). *Homer: The Iliad*. Baltimore, MD: Penguin Books, 1961.

_____. (trans.). *Homer: The Odyssey*. Baltimore, MD: Penguin Books, 1961.

Rinella, Michael A. *Pharmakon: Plato, Drug Culture, and Identity in Ancient Athens*. Lanham, MD: Lexington Books, 2010.

Robbins, F. E. (trans.). *Ptolemy: Tetrabiblos*. Cambridge, MA: Harvard University Press, 1980.

Robinson, Eric W. *The First Democracies: Early Popular Government Outside Athens*. Stuttgart: Franz Steiner Verlag, 1997.

Rohde, Erwin. *Psyche: The Cult of Souls & Belief in Immortality among the Greeks*. New York: Harper Torchbooks, 1966.

Rony, Jerome-Antoine. *A History of Magic*. New York: Walker and Company, 1962.

Rose, H. J. *Gods & Heroes of the Greeks: A Handbook of Greek Mythology*. London: Methuen, 1957.

Rubin, Vera (ed.). *Cannabis and Culture*. Berlin: Mouton de Gruyter, 1975. [Wikipedia: Benet, Sula. Early Diffusion and Folk Uses of Hemp. 1967]

Scanlon, Thomas F. *Eros and Greek Athletics*. New York: Oxford University Press, 2002.

Seltman, Charles. *The Twelve Olympians and their Guests*. London: Max Parrish, 1956.

Seyffert, Oskar. *Dictionary of Classical Antiquities*. New York: Meridian Books Inc., 1960.

Skinner, Stephen. *Techniques of Graeco-Egyptian Magic*. St. Paul, MN: Llewellyn Publications, 2014.

Skinner, Stephen, and David Rankine. *The Veritable Key of Solomon*. Singapore: Golden Hoard Press, 2008.

Smith, F. Kinchin, and T. W. Melluish. *Ancient Greek: A Foundation Course*. London: Hodder & Stoughton Educational, 1992.

Smith, Morton. *The Ancient Greeks*. Ithaca: Cornell University Press, 1960.

Stanley, Thomas (trans.). *The Chaldean Oracles: As Set Down by Julianus*. Gilette, NJ: Heptangle Books, 1989.

Stapleton, Michael. *A Dictionary of Greek and Roman Mythology*. New York: Bell Publishing Company, 1978.

Stein, Charles. *Persephone Unveiled: Seeing the Goddess & Freeing Your Soul*. Berkeley, CA: North Atlantic Books, 2006.

Steward, Z. (ed.). *Arthur Darby Nock: Essays on Religion in the Ancient World: Volume 1*. Oxford, UK: Clarendon, 1972.

Stewart, Charles. *Demons and the Devil: Moral Imagination in Modern Greek Culture*. Princeton, NJ: Princeton University Press, 1991.

Stobart, J. C. *The Glory that Was Greece*. Cambridge, MA: Sidgwick & Jackson, 1951.

Stratton-Kent, Jake. *Geosophia: The Argo of Magic Volume I*. Brighton, UK: Scarlet Imprint, 2010.

_____. *Geosophia: The Argo of Magic Volume II*. Brighton, UK: Scarlet Imprint, 2010.

Sutin, Lawrence. *Do What Thou Wilt: A Life of Aleister Crowley*. New York: St. Martin's Press, 2000.

Taunton, Gwendolyn. *Kratos: The Hellenic Tradition*. Colac Australia: Numen Books, 2013.

Taylor, Thomas (trans.). *On Abstinence from Animal Food* in *The Select Works of Porphyry*. London, 1823. http://www.ccel.org/ccel/pearse/morefathers/files/porphyry_abstinence_01_book1.htm

Taylor, Thomas. *The Hymns of Orpheus.* Los Angeles: The Philosophical Research Society Inc., 1981.

Tierney, Patrick. *The Highest Altar: The Story of Human Sacrifice.* London: Bloomsbury, 1989.

Vandenberg, Philipp. *The Mystery of the Oracles: World-Famous Archaeologists Reveal the Best-Kept Secrets of Antiquity.* New York: Macmillan Publishing Co., Inc., 1979.

Vermeule, Emily. *Greece in the Bronze Age.* Chicago: The University of Chicago Press, 1974.

Vernant, Jean-Pierre. *The Universe, the Gods, and Men: Ancient Greek Myths.* New York: Perennial, 2002.

Voight, Laura A. "Professor Alice Kober: 1907—May 16, 1950," in *Breaking Ground: Pioneering Women Archaeologists,* ed. Getzel M. Cohen and Martha Sharp Joukowsky. Ann Arbor, MI: University of Michigan Press, 2006.

Warrior, Valerie M. *Greek Religion: A Sourcebook.* Newburyport, MA: Focus Publishing, 2009.

Wasson, R. Gordon, Albert Hofmann, and Carl A. P. Ruck. *The Road to Eleusis: Unveiling the Secret of the Mysteries.* San Diego: Harcourt Brace Jovanovich, 1978.

White, Donna R. *A Century of Welsh Myth in Children's Literature.* Santa Barbara, CA: Praeger, 1998.

Winter, Sarah Kate Istra. *Kharis: Hellenic Polytheism Explored.* San Mateo, CA: CreateSpace, 2008.

Wright, Dudley. *The Eleusinian Mysteries & Rites.* Berwick, ME: Ibis Press, 2003.

Zaidman, Louise Bruit, and Pauline Schmitt Pantel. *Religion in the Ancient Greek City.* New York: Cambridge University Press, 1994.

INDEX

Aristotle, 15, 19, 68, 80, 89, 135, 166

Artemis, 33, 35, 41–43, 48, 49, 67, 72, 79, 95, 109, 116, 126, 132,
140, 161, 174, 177, 180, 181, 183, 185, 190, 191, 193, 195, 197,
199–202, 204, 206, 207, 209, 211–219, 223, 243

Asklepios, 50, 118, 197, 217

Athena, 250

Athenian, 8, 14, 16–19, 22, 23, 28, 29, 33, 35, 37–46, 49, 51, 53,
59, 68, 71, 77, 85, 89, 90, 97, 107, 109–112, 119, 131, 134–136,
147, 153, 155–157, 171–176, 181, 182, 187, 198–200, 239

Athens, 14, 16, 19, 29, 61, 68, 76, 85, 89, 90, 109, 110, 119, 130,
135, 139, 145, 147, 156, 176–178, 184, 186, 196

B

Bible, 96–98, 136, 138, 142, 223

Blood, 4, 12, 23, 26, 45, 69–72, 140, 145, 148, 188, 249

Boedromion, 173, 175, 182–184, 208, 209, 212

C

Crete, 34, 83–87, 139, 140, 146, 158

D

Daimon, 16, 23, 50, 61, 62, 65, 76, 109, 117–119, 127, 130–132,
177, 179, 182, 185, 190–192, 194, 197, 199, 201, 203, 206, 207,
209, 211–219, 245

Deity, 15, 17, 18, 24, 25, 31, 37, 45, 48, 55, 56, 60, 67, 69, 72–74,
77, 80, 102, 105, 112, 131, 140, 204, 206, 207, 209, 211–219,
233

Deities, 2–4, 6–8, 11, 12, 16–18, 22–24, 27, 28, 31–35, 39, 40, 45,
47, 48, 51, 53, 55, 58–65, 69, 71, 72, 74–77, 80, 81, 97, 98, 100,

To Write to the Author

If you wish to contact the author or would like more information about this book, please write to the author in care of Llewellyn Worldwide Ltd. and we will forward your request. Both the author and publisher appreciate hearing from you and learning of your enjoyment of this book and how it has helped you. Llewellyn Worldwide Ltd. cannot guarantee that every letter written to the author can be answered, but all will be forwarded. Please write to:

Tony Mierzwicki
℅ Llewellyn Worldwide
2143 Wooddale Drive
Woodbury, MN 55125-2989

Please enclose a self-addressed stamped envelope for reply,
or $1.00 to cover costs. If outside the U.S.A., enclose
an international postal reply coupon.

Many of Llewellyn's authors have websites with additional information and resources. For more information, please visit our website at http://www.llewellyn.com